THE HOLLYWOOD BOOK
OF SCANDALS

THE HOLLYWOOD BOOK
OF SCANDALS

The Shocking, Often Disgraceful Deeds and Affairs of More
than 100 American Movie and TV Idols

ENCORE FILM
BOOK CLASSICS

JAMES ROBERT PARISH

ISBN-13: 9781515264934

In memory of Doug McClelland (1934–2002)

*A superb writer, an enthusiastic supporter of movie history research,
and a good friend, who will be missed*

TABLE OF CONTENTS

ACKNOWLEDGEMENTS

With appreciation to the following for their kind assistance: Academy of Motion Picture Arts and Sciences: Margaret Herrick Library, Robert Bentley, Larry Billman (Academy of Dance on Film), Billy Rose Theater Collection of the New York Public Library at Lincoln Center, John Cocchi, Ernest Cunningham (research associate), Echo Book Shop, Allan Ellenberger, Film Magic/WireImage.com (Jenna Berkowitz), Alex Gildzen, Pierre Guinle, G. D. Hamann (Filming Today Press), JC Archives, Laurie Jacobson, Matthew Kennedy, Jane Klain (Museum of Television and Radio—New York), Lee Mattson, Alvin H. Marill, the late Doug McClelland, Jim Meyer, Eric Monder, Albert L. Ortega (Albert L. Ortega Photos), Photofest (Howard Mandelbaum and Rick Goeren), Michael R. Pitts, Charles Reilly, Barry Rivadue, Jonathan Rosenthal, Brenda Scott Royce, Brad Schreiber, Arleen Schwartz, Nat Segaloff, André Soares, Patrick Spreng, Sam Staggs, David Stenn, Allan Taylor (editorial consultant and copy editor), Vincent Terrace, Lou Valentino, Jane Ellen Wayne, Steven Whitney, Robert Young Jr., and Joseph Yranski.

Special thanks to my literary agent, Stuart Bernstein, and to my editor, Matthew Carnicelli.

INTRODUCTION

The word *scandal* comes from the Greek word *skándalon*, meaning a cause of moral stumbling. Webster's dictionary defines scandal as "a disgraceful or discreditable action or circumstance," with a secondary meaning as "an offence caused by a fault or a misdeed."

Scandalous behavior (whether of the improper, immoral, or illegal variety) seems to occur more often in Tinseltown than it does most anywhere else in the world. The public's fascination with such disgraceful—sometimes tragic—activity among Hollywood's famous is boundless. We crave to know *all* the intriguing details (and minutia) of such abnormal situations that seem so alien to our daily lives because they involve personalities—from the past or present—with whom we have a personal connection through watching their film/TV work and reading about their lives.

To put such scandals into their proper context, we really have to know the background of the colorful individuals involved and have a perspective on the particular Hollywood environment at the time the outrageous situation occurred. Providing such word pictures has been my goal in creating *The Hollywood Book of Scandals*.

Over the decades, as actors and directors in the film and TV arenas fought to be discovered, achieve fame, and then retain their hard-earned industry standing, they often endured exceedingly stressed lives. The weight of constantly competing in a mercenary, mercurial profession—while striving to be creative in their career endeavors—often built up pressure within the performers that needed to escape. Sometimes, in their efforts to find emotional release from such tensions, these personalities overindulged their whims. They pushed distracting and/or illegal activities to the limit and, in the process, often threw common sense and caution to the wind.

Because show business folk are generally more pampered, more affluent, and more ego-oriented than the typical person, they have tended to get into more scrapes than the law of averages would dictate. Sometimes, because of the individual's fame, these indulgences mushroomed out of proportion, fanned by the vigilant media and intrigued public into major events (e.g., the unrestrained affair of Elizabeth Taylor and Richard Burton—each wed to another at the time—during the Rome shoot of 1963's *Cleopatra*, or the breakup of Woody Allen and Mia Farrow's lengthy relationship and the resultant furor with which each party attacked the other).

Other times, the misdeeds of notables are claimed violations of the law and/or moral standards in one degree or another (e.g., Oscar-winning movie star Ingrid Bergman's leaving her husband and daughter in 1949 to have an affair—and baby—with already married Italian director Roberto Rossellini, filmmaker Roman Polanski's claimed statutory rape of a 13-year-old in 1977 Los Angeles, actor Robert Blake's alleged murder of his wife in 2001). These crises led to scandals of gigantic proportion that remained part of the celebrities' résumés long after they retired or died.

At yet other times, scandalous situations have verged on pathetic public tragedy (e.g., substance-abusing Judy Garland's debacle with her 1963 TV series that was supposed to have resurrected her once-fabulous career and provided her with great financial security, only to end in the embarrassment of a canceled show and her further self-destructive behavior). Then there have been those episodes in Tinseltown's long history that are as shocking and disgraceful today as when they first occurred: the American underworld's brazen stranglehold on the Hollywood film industry (especially in the 1930s and 1940s), the infamous entertainment industry blacklist and resultant shunning of suspected Communists and Communist sympathizers.

A different dimension of scandal surrounds the situation in which a famed member of the world of entertainment is murdered, especially when the notorious crime goes unsolved for decades, as in the 1922 killing of motion picture director William Desmond Taylor, the 1935 "suicide" of beautiful, fun-loving actress Thelma Todd, the controversial 1962 death of screen siren Marilyn Monroe, or the brutal drive-by assassination in 1996 Las Vegas of rap artist/film star Tupac Shakur.

Then there are those high-profile shocking situations that rip at our sense of stability of the world. Fairly recently, for instance, the world watched in mouth-gaping amazement as a young Los Angeles woman, the daughter of a noted physician, single-handedly threw Hollywood into a major panic. For a time in the early 1990s, after Heidi Fleiss was arrested on allegations of being Tinseltown's latest Madam to the Stars, the hottest topic of conversation everywhere was the spicy world of high-priced call girls who catered to the city's movers and shakers. The situation left everyone wondering which notables were listed in Fleiss's little black business book and what the repercussions would be if the VIPs' identities were ever revealed.

In *The Hollywood Book of Scandals*, I have selected 32 representative, intriguing episodes of different types of scandals from among the many that have dotted Hollywood's long history—covering the 20th century and the new millennium. (There are certainly sufficient scandalous stories in Tinseltown's past to fill several volumes on the topic.) Detailed in the brief introductions to each chronological part of this volume is a description of how some notable stars (and, in turn, their handlers and the studios/networks) dealt with the disgraceful—sometimes illegal—situations. The potential solutions depended greatly on the mores of the times, the power of the subjects' industry protectors, and how much the world was willing to ignore, discount, or forgive the famous person's claimed transgressions.

Reexamining these often-disreputable situations and the background of events and people involved in the high-profile episodes, we learn much about the behind-the-scenes workings of show business, a profession where fame is fleeting but infamy is extremely long lasting. For readers discovering in this book sensational incidents involving their entertainment favorites, learning the details surrounding such controversial situations may shed fresh light on their icons.

For better or worse, once we learn such revealing—sometimes appalling—facets of a favorite celebrity's private life, can we ever prevent that data from coloring our judgment of the person's talent? For example, since Christina Crawford's tell-all book *Mommie Dearest* (1978) revealed the highly abusive manner in which superstar Joan reared her adopted offspring, how can we ever watch *Mildred Pierce* (1945) without thinking about the star's disturbed real-life behavior toward her children?

In addition, from the many case studies presented herein, we can observe how the stars under discussion have handled highly charged, difficult situations. Then, we can see whether when they reached the other side of their unorthodox and/or unfortunate circumstances, they profited (or not) from their tumultuous experiences. Examining such human nature provides us with a fuller sense of these celebrities' real selves, the ones so often hidden behind makeup and costumes.

1

1900–1929

A s the American silent film industry gradually shifted its operation from the East Coast to the West Coast in the 1910s, Hollywood became the mecca of the movie business in the United States. In the process, the quiet suburb of the growing Los Angeles lost its sleepy little ways and became, in the 1920s, a burgeoning, sophisticated metropolis unto itself. Major studios in Tinseltown, such as Fox, Universal, Metro-Goldwyn-Mayer, and Warner Bros., corralled the biggest talents to work on their lots, often under exclusive long-term contracts.

Under the all-encompassing studio system, the moguls and their top executives became demigods, controlling the fate of their famous flocks. As part of this complex employer-employee situation, the bosses believed it was their paternalistic duty to manipulate—in any conceivable and expedient manner–the off-camera lives of their contractees. Their aim was to guarantee that nothing these workers did away from the movie lot would adversely affect their lucrative public image and, in turn, cut back on the company's profits at the box office.

With such a mind-set, it behooved the powerful and often ruthless studio heads to create strong ties to Los Angeles' crooked politicians and corrupt law enforcers. These civic groups were immediately called upon when a prominent luminary got into a bad scrape. Often, if everyone involved moved fast enough, the indiscretion could be covered over before the press and/or the public became any the wiser. Even in cases where a name talent was involved in manslaughter or homicide, it was not above the studios' hubris, ingenuity, and resources to tamper drastically with a crime scene in order to clear valuable contractees from possible taint and/or criminal arrest. With such huge accumulated investments in their stars (and their stars' reputations) as

the new talkie film era dawned in the late 1920s, seemingly there was noth-
ing a mighty movie studio would not do to keep its profits rolling in.

Rudolph Valentino: Hollywood's "Greatest" Lover

"Every American man was perfectly willing that his wife should be in love
with Gable, because Gable was what he'd have liked to have been. But they
were not willing that their wives should be in love with this foreigner, this
dago. He was a gigolo, and they didn't like that at all."
—JOURNALIST ADELA ROGERS ST. JOHN, IN 1979

In bygone decades—and even today—"dago," like "wop," was a derisive term used for a person of Italian (or sometimes Spanish) decent. Similarly, "gigolo" had negative connotations. It referred to a male professional dancing partner, and the word was often synonymous for a younger man who was supported financially by an older woman in exchange for sexual favors and companionship. Because Rudolph Valentino was Italian born and had been, in the 1910s, a dancer for hire at fancy Manhattan restaurants/cabarets, he already had a highly suspect reputation by the time he made his first movie in 1914 (*My Official Wife*). As such, he had great handicaps to overcome to becoming acceptable to American society, let alone to the snobbish world of 1920s' Tinseltown where image was everything.

Besides the challenges of his background, Rudolph's ascent to stardom in the silent cinema was filled with a controversial personal life full of intriguing ambiguities. On several occasions, these scandalous episodes nearly toppled his hard-won status as the screen's greatest lover. Then too, he suffered the problem that heterosexual American men found his innovative, glamorized movie image threatening, odd, and suspect as to its manliness. The majority of adult males became so tired of being compared unfavorably to this celluloid Romeo from abroad with his greased-down hairstyle that they jealously craved his downfall.

Fortunately for the actor, the bulk of his loyal fan base in the 1920s was females who generally rationalized and/or forgave his (alleged) moral transgressions and potentially scandalous behavior. More important, they adored his smoldering good looks, his natural grace (especially when dancing), his physical fitness (often emphasized on screen in scenes showing him partially unclothed), and his blazing sexuality. All of these qualities turned him into a box-office sensation. He became the first *and* greatest of a long line of what Hollywood termed "Latin lovers."

Valentino was at the height of his enormous movie fame when he died suddenly in 1926 at the age of 31. Mass hysteria resulted around the world as the public mourned the cherished star of *The Four Horsemen of the Apocalypse* (1921), *The Eagle* (1925), and *The Son of the Sheik* (1926).

Yet fame is fickle. In the ensuing decades, this great star was often on the verge of being forgotten by movie lovers or relegated to being merely an example of an outmoded screen type. After all, *all* his movie work was done in the silent picture era, and most of his movie vehicles were pure claptrap.

Over the years, specious book/screen biographies of Valentino raked up the notorious and unsavory aspects of his colorful history and distorted the facts of his intriguing life with spurious details and innuendoes about the scope and type of his sexual activity. (One account had him locked in a love affair with Ramon Novarro, another Latin lover of the silent screen.) Ironically, such titillating allegations helped to keep the star's name in the public eye and prompted later generations of movie enthusiasts to screen his surviving features. Such viewings demonstrated that although Rudolph's acting style was locked into the conventions of his time, he had tremendous screen presence.

Rodolfo Pietro Filiberto Raffaele Guglielmi was born on May 6, 1895, in Castellaneta, Italy, the second of three surviving children of an Italian veterinarian/biologist father and his French-descended schoolteacher spouse. In this middle-class household Rodolfo idolized his strong-willed mother. Before he was six, the boisterous boy was exhibiting a reckless streak such as when he played with his father's razor and was left with a slight scar on his right cheek. The blemish made the narcissistic youth self-conscious. (He also was quite nearsighted but too vain to wear eyeglasses.)

When Rodolfo was nine the family relocated to the (Ionian) seaside city of Taranto. In 1906, the father died. Hoping to give the youth much-needed discipline, the family sent him to a boarding school north of Rome. Young Guglielmi was easily distracted from his technical studies and often was punished by being locked in a cell.

By age 15 Guglielmi had relocated to Venice, hoping to gain admission to a naval technical school. Miraculously, he passed his entrance examinations, but he was rejected from the institution because his chest measurement did not quite meet the school's standards. This humiliation, which he interpreted as a slight on his manliness, haunted him for life.

Rodolfo was next enrolled in an agricultural institute in the mountain village of Nervi. There, he was distracted by his infatuation with the daughter of the school's cook. Because he was a dreamy romantic, the relationship never progressed beyond grand gestures.

Graduating from the institute and finding no suitable work at home, the young man traveled to Paris in 1912. There he led a Bohemian life. An aborted romance with a music-hall dancer left him depressed and broke. When his mother sent him more money, he headed to Monte Carlo, where he lost nearly everything at the gaming tables. He returned home in disgrace. His relatives, anxious to remove this embarrassment, paid for the young man's passage to New York in late 1913.

In contrast to most immigrants flocking to America, the 18-year-old Rodolfo could speak a few words of English, had relative financial security (thanks to his family), and looked upon the American sojourn in "the spirit of adventure." At nearly five feet, eight inches, the handsome, agreeable Guglielmi quickly built upon the contacts he had made aboard the S.S. *Cleveland*. He was promptly drawn to New York's glittering theater district and its fashionable restaurants. Taking advantage of his fluency in French and relying on his exaggeration of his background, he made friends with a trio of aristocratic European playboys. Tasting the high life, he used his good looks, his flair for dancing, and his knack for languages (he was quickly learning more English) to insinuate himself with the fast social crowd.

As in Paris, spendthrift Rodolfo quickly ran out of funds. Through a new connection, he was hired as a landscape gardener to an upper-crust Long Island gentleman. Some accounts suggest that a sexual relationship developed between the two, fueling the notion that the supposedly bisexual Guglielmi was not above using his charms and good looks on either sex to advance his cause. That post soon came to an end, although his benefactor provided him with a temporary stipend that kept the young man going for some weeks back in Manhattan.

Managing money was not one of the social climber's strong points, and he quickly found himself penniless and sometimes sleeping in Central Park. Too proud to ask his family for further assistance, he wrote his mother reassuring letters that he was doing well. Meanwhile, when his native Italy entered World War I, Rodolfo attempted to enlist in the Italian army, but its New York office rejected him because of his faulty vision. During this period he worked odd manual labor jobs and performed as an extra in a locally shot feature film.

Relying on his agility as a social dancer, he gained employment as a dance partner for hire at fashionable Maxim's in midtown Manhattan. As such, Signor Rodolfo (as he affectedly called himself) was available to unescorted women of all ages (and some means) on the dance floor of the chic establishment. Part of the job description included providing private dance lessons upstairs to wealthy female patrons. Frequently such arrangements led to paid sex, giving anyone who dallied in the profession a bad reputation. (Once Rodolfo became a famous actor, he would become highly sensitive about his past line of work as a "lounge lizard.")

Drawn by the exhibitionist aspects of show business, Rodolfo drifted into further film extra work in New York. He often appeared on screen as a ballroom dancer or in fancy party scenes. Meanwhile, with his grace on the dance floor he was a welcome addition at the fashionable dining establishments he visited after his Maxim's chores. In such surroundings he became friendly with beautiful Mae Murray, a Broadway personality who had been featured in a recent *Ziegfeld Follies*. (Later, when she was a rising movie star, Murray helped him gain a foothold in West Coast moviemaking.)

Through other helpful acquaintances, Rodolfo met entertainer Bonnie Glass, who hired him to partner her in exhibition dancing in vaudeville and cabarets. Later he teamed (at $240 weekly) with dancer Joan Sawyer, a more prominent performer.

With his prowess on the ballroom floor, his sleek looks, and his agreeable ways, Rodolfo became a well-liked member of the Manhattan social set. He developed a growing attachment with Blanca de Saulles, a Chilean who was among Manhattan's wealthiest socialites. She was then married to an American businessman (John de Saulles) and the mother of a young boy. With her older spouse preoccupied with a series of not-so-secret affairs, Blanca diverted herself by participating in the swank cabaret scene. When she divorced her philandering spouse in mid-1916, Rodolfo testified in court on her behalf. She won her suit and gained partial custody of her son.

Whether a coincidence or a situation engineered by Blanca's vengeful ex-spouse, several weeks later Rodolfo was arrested at the Manhattan apartment of Mrs. Georgia Thym, an alleged brothel keeper. The notorious incident was well reported by New York newspapers that referred to Guglielmi as a tango dancer who wore "corsets and a wristwatch" (two accoutrements *no* self-respecting virile man would ever use at this time). While no official charges were lodged against Rodolfo or Mrs. Thym, they were, nevertheless, held in jail as material witnesses in a pending case against a corrupt law enforcer supposedly tied to several brothels. Two days later, both detainees raised bail and were released. However, having spent time behind bars badly sullied the young man's reputation. (Later, when he had become famous as movie luminary Rudolph Valentino, his New York City police files would mysteriously disappear.)

He was unable to find work because of the widely publicized disgrace, and things turned worse in the summer of 1917 when Blanca de Saulles fatally shot her husband in a dispute over custody of their son. Fearful of being called as a court witness, which would only further sully his already precarious social standing, Rodolfo hastily left town. He joined a stage musical bound for the West Coast. Later, out of work in San Francisco, he toiled as a bond salesman and club dancer. In this period he encountered his New York actor friend Norman Kerry, who was in town making a film. Norman suggested Rodolfo come to Los Angeles and seriously try his luck in movies. (Some sources claim that a sexual relationship existed between the two men.)

Over the next few years Rodolfo paraded through several film roles, generally typecast as a screen villain because of his swarthy looks and his Italian background. In fall 1919 (now known as Rodolph Valentino, later Rudolph Valentino, and always Rudy to his American friends), the actor met Jean Acker, a 26-year-old actress. She was then the protégée of exotic stage/film star Alla Nazimova. The latter was well known in the film set as being bisexual and/or lesbian. Whatever Acker's own sexual orientation, ambitious Rudy was intrigued by Jean, as she had many acquaintances in the film business who, in turn, could help Valentino's career. (Then too, not long before, she had won a healthy cash settlement as the victim in a traffic accident and had money to spend on Valentino.) In addition, he missed the guiding influence of a strong woman in his life (especially after the 1918 death of his mother). For all these reasons, Valentino was drawn to the self-willed Acker.

After a mere two-month acquaintanceship, persistent Rudy convinced Jean to wed him in early November 1919. Following a modest celebration, the couple returned to the Hollywood Hotel where she resided. After dancing at the lobby salon Jean retired to her room. When Rudy came upstairs to the chambers, he found she had locked him out. The deeply humiliated actor went back to his own apartment. The short-lived marriage was soon the talk of the film colony. Some surmised that the bride had suddenly realized she would have to support her financially struggling actor husband. Others insisted her agreeing to wed Valentino was done on the spur of the moment to spite Nazimova.

Over the next months the young married couple engaged in a cat-and-mouse game of chasing/rejecting one another. The overly romantic, emotionally immature Valentino eventually tired of this draining, mortifying situation. The pair divorced in January 1922 in a court hearing that brought forth the extremely embarrassing details of the unconsummated wedding night. Meanwhile, Rudy became friendly with European-born Paul Ivano, a still photographer who would become a Hollywood cinematographer and good friend (and sometimes roommate) of Valentino.

In one of the great casting stories in Tinseltown's history, Metro Pictures scenarist June Mathis, a matronly type who had appreciated Valentino's past screen work and had seen him gliding gracefully on Los Angeles nightclub dance floors, promoted him for a starring role in her studio's big-budgeted entry *The Four Horsemen of the Apocalypse*. Thanks to her sponsorship, he was hired for the leading part as the wealthy South American gaucho who becomes a tango expert in 1914 Paris and then serves on the front lines in World War I. So charismatic was Rudy in the splashy lead assignment that the highly popular 1921 feature made him a major star "overnight."

Also in 1921, the fast-rising Valentino costarred with Nazimova in her expensive screen adaptation of *Camille*. On this production, he quickly came into the orbit of Natasha Rambova (born Winifred Shaughnessy in Utah in 1897), who designed the Art Deco sets for the costume drama. (Earlier, the striking young heiress had come under the spell of the Russian-born Nazimova; the full extent of their unique relationship remains unknown.) Rudy was immediately drawn to this dominating woman, an attraction that was enhanced when he realized the full wealth of her stepfather, cosmetic tycoon Richard Hudnut.

Soon Rudy and Natasha were sharing a bungalow with pal Paul Ivano (who slept in their living room). Later, for the sake of appearances as Valentino became increasingly known to the public and media, he and Ivano shared an apartment while Rambova officially resided at a nearby address but still spent most nights with Rudolph. Meanwhile, unhappy with the quality of his roles and pictures at Metro, Valentino signed with Famous Players-Lasky (Paramount Pictures) and starred in *The Sheik* (1921), which consolidated his great popularity with filmgoers.

After completing *Blood and Sand* (1922) in which Rudy played a Spanish matador, he and Natasha were impatient to legalize their camouflaged union by officially marrying. Rather than waiting until his divorce was final in March 1923, the impetuous couple wed in Mexico, thinking their foreign union would be acceptable under California law. However, a few days after the south-of-the-border nuptials, a Los Angeles superior court judge labeled Valentino a bigamist. The shameful situation was enough to fatally damage his career.

Upon advice of studio attorneys, Natasha fled to the East Coast, while a distraught Valentino turned himself in to the authorities, pleading ignorance of the law. For a man of such great pride, the new jail experience was a humiliating replay of his sad legal plight a few years earlier in New York City.

No help came from his studio, which did not want to be tainted by the spiraling scandal. It remained for friends to arrange Valentino's bail. Later, when Jean Acker refused to help the district attorney's case against Rudy, the proceedings were dropped. Eventually, Valentino and Rambova wed—lawfully—in March 1923 in Indiana. By then, urged on by his controlling mate who had an idealized career vision for her malleable spouse, Rudy had walked out on his lucrative studio contract and now was prevented from appearing in any other company's pictures. To support their indulgent lifestyle, the couple embarked on a national exhibition dance tour, and, thus, their marriage occurred in the Midwest.

Eventually Paramount and Valentino temporarily patched up their differences. However, such entries as 1924's *Monsieur Beaucaire* (on which pushy Natasha served as both an art and costume director, as well as general interferer) presented Rudolph as far too foppish and alienated the public who was used to their idol playing vigorous screen heroes. Illustrative of the great hold his wife held over him, Rudolph wore a slave bracelet and yielded to her whims that he pose for arty publicity pictures (e.g., as a near-naked Native American warrior). Such affections did nothing to endear him to male segments of the moviegoing public.

Once his Paramount tenure expired, United Artists signed Valentino to a film contract, convinced they could restore his box-office luster. However, a term of the rich deal provided that his wife was to have absolutely *no* part in his picturemaking. Bowing to such a condition signaled the end of his union to Natasha. She went East, later divorcing him in Paris in January 1926. Having two wives abandon him eroded Rudolph's aura of manliness with the public. To mask his loneliness and cover over his recent domestic embarrassment, the Great Lover found solace in a well-staged and highly publicized romance with Pola Negri, the Polish-born Tinseltown movie star (reputed to be lesbian or bisexual).

In mid-1926 Rudy headed to New York to promote the opening of *The Son of the Sheik*. During a Chicago stopover he read with horror an editorial (the article was headlined "Pink Powder Puffs") in the *Chicago Tribune*. It was a tirade against the pink powder vending machines recently installed in the men's restroom of the local Aragon Ballroom. The enraged anonymous author of the piece blamed this diminution of American manliness and the vogue for "masculine cosmetics, sheiks, floppy pants, and slave bracelets" on allegedly effete Rudy. The infuriated writer asked, "Why didn't someone quietly drown Rudolph . . . Valentino, years ago?"

Aghast at this virulent print attack, the star retaliated on this "slur [upon] my Italian ancestry" and for casting "doubt upon my manhood." In another Chicago newspaper he dared the unnamed writer to step into a boxing ring for a grudge match. The challenge went unanswered. Still steaming, Valentino had his pal, world heavyweight champion Jack Dempsey, arrange a demonstration bout between Rudy and a Manhattan sportswriter. The event, filmed by newsreel camera operators, showed the muscular picture star quickly subduing his taller, heavier opponent.

The explosive controversy surrounding the issue of Valentino's virility helped to sell a great many tickets to *The Son of the Sheik*. However, the mortification exacted a heavy toll on the sensitive star. Within days, the emotionally stressed Valentino was hospitalized in Manhattan and eventually operated on for a perforated ulcer and appendicitis. Unfortunately, infection set in and he died on August 23, 1926.

Thus was the untimely end of the screen's great lover who had stated less than a year earlier, "I would like to disappear at the height of my powers, in an accident. I find nothing more stupid than to die of a disease." He did not get his wish, but then he also did not live to experience the imminent changeover of Hollywood from silent to talkie films, a situation that might easily have robbed the accented actor of his screen stardom.

Roscoe "Fatty" Arbuckle: Tinseltown's Big Loser

"Virginia [Rappé] and I were in our room. Arbuckle came in and pulled Virginia into his room and locked the door. From the scuffle I could hear and from the screams of Virginia, I knew he must be abusing her. . . . Arbuckle had her in the room for over an hour, at the end of which time Virginia was badly beaten up. Virginia was a good girl. I know that she had led a clean life, and it is my duty to see this thing through."
—"WITNESS" BAMBINA MAUDE DELMONT, IN 1921

Few actors have been as badly abused by Hollywood as Roscoe Arbuckle has. The five-foot, ten-inch comedian, nicknamed "Fatty" by his appreciative audiences because of his girth (he often weighed nearly 300 pounds), had achieved great show business success during the 1910s. His screen popularity rivaled that of Charlie Chaplin. At the time of Roscoe's downfall in 1921, he was earning well over $1 million annually, a tremendous income in those times.

It is bad enough to fall from grace—let alone nearly go to prison—for one's own mistakes and the scandal surrounding them. It is quite another thing to be falsely accused by the legal system and made the pawn of an ambitious district attorney. (In the process, Arbuckle was the victim of opportunistic newspapers, especially the chain operated by William Randolph Hearst, who sensationalized Roscoe's plight and made a bundle in circulation sales.) Adding further insult to the grievous injury, Arbuckle's own studio, Famous Players-Lasky (Paramount Pictures), led the behind-the-scenes intrigue to sabotage his career. This was its twisted revenge on the star who the company felt had become a too-costly and uncontrollable commodity. Taking advantage of his ignominy, it sacrificed him to the wolves. The latter included the industry's newly formed self-censorship board headed by former U.S. postmaster general Will Hays.

Weighing 16 pounds at birth, Roscoe Conklin Arbuckle was born on a small farm in Smith County, Kansas, on March 24, 1887, the sixth and final child of William Goodrich Arbuckle and his wife Mary. The following year, William relocated his family to Santa Ana, California, where he opened a small hotel. William frequently traveled upstate seeking fresh business opportunities. When he returned, usually disappointed by failure and fueled by liquor, he took out his frustrations by whipping his boys.

In the summer of 1895 young Roscoe made his stage debut, playing in a blackface comedy routine with a visiting stock company. The shy youngster was immediately drawn to the stage, where he felt at home. Four years later, after his mother died, the boy was sent to live with his dad who was then residing in Watsonville, California. However, his father vanished and a local hotel owner took Roscoe in. When not working odd jobs, the youngster was tutored by a neighboring teacher. However, he preferred appearing on amateur night (often as a juggler) at the town's vaudeville theater. In 1902, 15-year-old Roscoe was reunited with his remarried dad, then operating a café in Santa Clara, California. When not attending high school (from which he did not graduate), the teenager was a waiter at his parent's establishment.

Returning to show business, Roscoe worked in San Jose, San Francisco, and then the Pacific Northwest as a vaudeville singer.

Later he performed in burlesque. During a 1908 summer stock engagement in Long Beach, California, he met 17-year-old singer/dancer Armanta "Minta" Durfee. They wed and toured the southern California vaudeville circuit. When he could find no stage work, he tried his luck in the burgeoning film industry.

In April 1913, Arbuckle became a member of Mack Sennett's Keystone Film Company, where his comic talents were effectively honed. Within two years, Arbuckle had gained great popularity as a screen actor and director.

In summer 1916, Arbuckle joined the East Coast–based Comique Film Corporation as star and director at an annual income of more than $1 million. Meanwhile, a painful thigh infection led to his becoming briefly drug-addicted. The next March, still wobbly from his leg ailment, he attended a banquet in Boston hosted by his studio for regional theater exhibitors. After the dinner, Arbuckle retired to his hotel room. However, company executives (included founder Adolph Zukor) and others continued their partying at a brothel in nearby Woburn.

Almost immediately news circulated in Boston about this orgy, and the gossip erroneously included Arbuckle as one of the celebrity participants. Because of the publicity, the city's mayor raided the whorehouse. After paying a fine, the madam was released. However, the goings-on at her establishment that particular night were far too titillating to fade away. Zukor was advised by Beantown authorities that unless major payoffs were made, the bawdy escapade would become national news. Zukor provided $100,000 to hush up the matter. In the process, however, Zukor did nothing to clarify that Roscoe had *not* been part of the night of dissipation.

By October 1917 Roscoe had transferred his filmmaking back to the West Coast. By now his marriage with Minta had crumbled. She remained in New York to pursue her acting career, and the marital union continued in name only. (The couple divorced finally in 1925.)

With 1920's *The Round Up*, Roscoe began making full-length movies. In January 1921, he finalized a new lucrative pact with

Paramount. Next, Zukor pushed him into a grueling schedule in which he filmed three pictures almost simultaneously in the summer of 1921. Exhausted by the schedule, Roscoe planned to relax in San Francisco over the Labor Day holiday. Zukor asked him to remain in town to participate in an exhibitors' convention on that weekend. When Roscoe refused, the top Paramount executive became apoplectic.

Actor friend Lowell Sherman agreed to join Roscoe on the trip up the Coast. Then director Fred Fischbach, whom the star had known for years, invited himself along. Before heading north, the actor had his mechanic inspect his new custom-made auto. While supervising the checkup, Roscoe accidentally sat on an acid-soaked rag, which burned through his trouser leg. The mishap discomforted him so much that he intended to cancel the trip. However, Fischbach was hysterically insistent that the holiday plans not be changed, and Roscoe yielded. Fischbach said that his San Francisco connections would provide bootleg liquor for the festivities.

Roscoe, Sherman, and Fischbach set out on early Saturday morning, September 3, for the nearly 500-mile excursion. The trio arrived in San Francisco that afternoon and checked into their accommodations (rooms 1219, 1220, and 1221) at the St. Francis Hotel. Soon thereafter, Fischbach's bootlegger arrived.

On Sunday the 4th the trio did sightseeing and visited friends. On Monday, Labor Day, the planned party got under way at the St. Francis. The first to show up was Ira Fortlois, a clothing/nightgown salesman who had been invited by Fischbach. Fortlois was staying at the nearby Palace House, which housed three other visitors who later came to Arbuckle's suite.

Among these newcomers was Fred's friend, film talent manager Al Semnacher. He was in San Francisco to concoct evidence for his pending divorce suit. He had brought along Bambina Maude Delmont to help him gather "facts." (It eventually came out that Maude had an extensive police record involving blackmail, prostitution, and swindling.) The third member of this disagreeable entourage was 25-year-old Virginia Rappé, a minor actress.

Rappé, born out of wedlock, had had several abortions by age 16 before having an illegitimate baby, which she gave away. By the late 1910s she was in L.A. and had wangled movie roles, including jobs on the Keystone lot where she first met Roscoe and his wife, Minta.

It was no secret in Hollywood that Virginia was a girl of loose morals—one who, when drunk, might yank off her clothes and launch into a screaming fit. Despite her negative reputation, she gained additional film roles and was sometimes interviewed by the fan magazines. In one such article, she disparaged Arbuckle. (Later it was learned that her protector, filmmaker Henry Lehrman, who was feuding with Roscoe, had put Rappé up to the bad-mouthing, a fact she subsequently regretted when Arbuckle acted gentlemanly toward her.)

In 1920 Rappé had begun dating movie director Jack White. When he left for New York, she was left to deal with an unwanted pregnancy. Her manager, Al Semnacher, suggested she should have an abortion in San Francisco away from Hollywood. Since she was going up north and Semnacher had plans in that city (with Delmont), he arranged for the trio to drive there on September 3.

Salesman Ira Fortlois arrived at Roscoe's suite on Monday at noon. When Roscoe learned that Fred had invited Semnacher, Delmont, and Rappé to the party, he strongly objected because he knew of the women's bad reputations. However, he did not force the issue.

At one point during the extended revelry, Fischbach suddenly left, claiming business elsewhere. Meanwhile, Maude, well liquored, disappeared into Sherman's suite with Lowell. As for Virginia, she had become roaring drunk and was tearing off her clothes and screaming hysterically. Because Delmont and Sherman were locked in the bathroom of room 1221 and 1220 had no such facility, Virginia rushed into room 1219 to use Roscoe's bathroom.

Soon, unaware of what was transpiring, Arbuckle tried to enter his bathroom, only to find Virginia vomiting in front of the toilet. He got her to rest on his bed. Next, he went in search of a bucket of ice. He hoped the ice would quiet down the woman as well as determine—by holding a piece of ice against her thigh to see if she reacted to the sudden chill—whether she was truly suffering from hysterics. By now Fischbach had returned. As Roscoe applied the ice to the screaming woman, Maude walked in. Rappé yelled that she was dying, words heard by two other female party guests. Next, the bathroom tub of Room 1219 was filled with cold water to cool off the distraught Virginia. The sick woman suddenly awoke and screamed at Roscoe: "Stay away from me!" She asked Delmont, "What did he do to me, Maudie?" Thereafter, the cold bath seemed to help Rappé, and she was removed to another room down the hall where Delmont could take care of her.

Later, a physician brought on the scene decided Virginia was merely suffering from inebriation. The party continued, with Arbuckle leaving the hotel for a time to arrange to have his car shipped back to Los Angeles (because he planned to return home by boat). By the time Roscoe reappeared, another doctor was administering morphine to the stricken woman. When the physician asked Delmont what had transpired, she calculatedly wove a fabricated tale.

On Tuesday, September 6, Roscoe checked out of the St. Francis, generously having paid for all the expenses involved. By now, Virginia, at Maude's direction, was being treated by yet another doctor, one associated with the private Wakefield Sanitarium. Assured that Rappé was in no danger, Arbuckle and his party returned by ferry to Los Angeles.

On September 8 the ailing Virginia was transferred from the St. Francis to the Wakefield Sanitarium, where she died the next afternoon. An illegal postmortem exam was conducted on the deceased, with her ruptured bladder and other organs placed in specimen jars, all of which would prevent a proper autopsy by police authorities. Convinced she could turn this situation to her own profit, Maude swore out a complaint against Arbuckle with the police. Back in Los Angeles, where Roscoe's new film (*Gasoline Gus*) had just opened successfully, the star learned of Virginia's death. Shocked, he volunteered to return to San Francisco. Meanwhile, Paramount, panicking at the potential repercussions for the nightmare turn of events, hired special counsel to represent their high-priced star.

From the start the tabloid newspapers were full of lurid headlines ("Fatty Arbuckle Sought in Orgy Death") and graphic—deceitful—details supplied by the crafty Delmont. In short order publications around the nation were revealing shocking "truths" about the supposed events in the death of virtuous Virginia at the hands of libertine, over-sized Roscoe. (Everything from Arbuckle's "past" was raked up, including the false information that he been part of the orgy in 1917 at the Massachusetts bawdy house and that he had a vendetta against Virginia because, supposedly, she had rebuffed his sexual advances.) Soon, churches and women's groups were crusading against "lustful" Arbuckle. Thanks to the snowballing effects of yellow journalism, Roscoe had been found guilty in the public's eyes, even before any legal proceedings began.

San Francisco district attorney Matthew Brady hoped this shocking case would be his ticket to the state's governorship. The coroner's inquest convened on September 12, with Brady demanding that Arbuckle be charged with murder. (By then, Brady had determined that most of what Delmont had stated to reporters were lies, but because his vow to prosecute the movie star to the fullest extent had already been published in the press, he proceeded with the case.) During the next days, with Arbuckle jailed without bail, the special grand jury voted twelve to two to indict the actor on a manslaughter charge. (It was their belief, given the "evidence," that Roscoe had used "some force" that led to Rappé's death. This led to the tabloids' speculation that Virginia had been mortally injured when Arbuckle put his great weight on her during copulation or that he had utilized a foreign object—e.g., a champagne or soda bottle or a piece of jagged ice—to penetrate her genitals.) On September 28, a police judge ruled that the defendant be tried for manslaughter but that the rape charge be dismissed. Roscoe was released on his own recognizance. He returned to Los Angeles, accompanied by his estranged wife, Minta, who had returned to give him moral support.

While the criminal case proceeded, theater owners in many cities banned the showing of Roscoe's movies. Soon Paramount announced that it had placed Arbuckle on suspension—invoking the morals clause in his contract.

The trial got under way on November 14, 1921. The defense introduced evidence of the deceased's past medical problems (including chronic cystitis) and her recurrent bouts of abdominal pain that often led to her yanking off her clothes. The defendant took the stand and calmly retold his account of the disastrous event. The key witness, Maude Delmont, *never* took the stand, which the defense repeatedly pointed out to the jury. After more than 40 hours of deliberation, the jury remained deadlocked and the judge had to dismiss them. (Later, it was learned that a woman on the jury was married to an attorney who had business dealings with the DA's office. She had insisted—from the start—that she considered Arbuckle guilty "until hell freezes over.")

Unwilling to give up, Brady pushed for a retrial. Before the new courtroom session began on January 11, 1922, film industry leaders hired U.S. postmaster general Will Hays to clean up the movies before federal and/or state censorship boards could further hamstring the industry. It was the start of the Motion Picture Producers and Distributors of America, structured to provide industry self-censorship and oversee the colony's morals.

One of the tactical errors of the second legal go-round was that the defense, overly confident that Arbuckle would be acquitted, did not have him testify anew because his prior testimony had been read into the record. Similarly, the defense lawyer made no closing statement, believing that the acquittal was a lock. To the defense's amazement, this time the jury was hung, but the vote was nine to three for conviction.

By the time the third trial got under way on March 13, 1922, Hays was already in his new Hollywood post and dealing with a new scandal, the murder of Paramount film director William Desmond

Taylor. At Arbuckle's retrial, the 35-year-old star took the stand and for three hours patiently answered questions about the fateful party. The defense team introduced into evidence further information about Rappé's checkered past, the prosecution's intimidation of witnesses, as well as the fact that the prosecution (understandably) still had not produced Maude Delmont to testify. This time the jury adjourned for only a brief five minutes. They returned with a vote of acquittal and a written apology: "We feel that a great injustice has been done him . . . for there was not the slightest proof adduced to connect him in any way with the commission of a crime. . . . We wish him success, and hope that the American people will take the judgment of fourteen men and women . . . that Roscoe Arbuckle is entirely innocent and free from all blame."

Unfortunately, Roscoe's suffering was far from over. Six days after being cleared of any wrongdoing in Virginia Rappé's death, Arbuckle was banned from the movies by Hays, who wanted to show that he meant business in his new industry position. Hays acted at the urging of Zukor and Paramount. (Years later, it was uncovered that Zukor had made a mysterious payment to DA Matthew Brady back on November 14, 1921. It was assumed to be a possible bribe to control the case's outcome. It has also been theorized by some sources that Zukor, eager to regain control over Arbuckle, had masterminded the St. Francis Hotel frivolity through Fred Fischbach, but that the situation had gotten wildly out of hand.) By that Christmas, Hays rescinded his ban on Roscoe, but civic groups and the press reacted in furor, and the onetime star was ostracized anew from performing on the screen. Arbuckle's treatment by Hollywood (and much of his fan base) illustrated once again how hard it is for a once-tainted star to regain his reputation with both Hollywood and the public.

While friends rallied around Roscoe during his emotional and financial ordeal, his next years were trying. He managed a few screen directing assignments using the name William Goodrich. He tried stage and vaudeville work and opened a club and a hotel, but they suffered in the onslaught of the Depression. He married and divorced a second time and then found happiness with a third wife, actress Addie McPhail (who died in 2003 at age 97). Reduced to being a scriptwriter/gag man for the studios, in 1931, Roscoe begged in a fan magazine article to be allowed to return to the screen. Filmmaker Hal Roach offered him a contract, but pressure from several women's groups caused the deal to be canceled.

After turning again to vaudeville, Roscoe starred in a 1932 film short comedy. That was so well received he made five more, all in preparation for a feature film. Before he could start that picture, he died of a heart attack in his Manhattan hotel room on June 29, 1934.

Even in death, however, Arbuckle received no peace. The slander still exists, despite evidence presented to the contrary in several histories of Hollywood, that allegedly rapacious Arbuckle was guilty of horrendous moral wrongdoings. The comedian's supposed gross misdeeds are still whispered about today by the public, most of whom have never seen graceful, antic Roscoe cavort on screen.

Such was the sad fate of good-natured Roscoe Arbuckle, Hollywood's tragic scapegoat.

William Desmond Taylor: The Man No One Really Knew

"He said would I go out and take dinner with him and I said no. I was tired; I had to go home and get up very early; he said he would call me up in about an hour. . . . That was the last time [that I saw him alive]."
—SCREEN STAR MABEL NORMAND AT THE CORONER'S INQUEST, ON FEBRUARY 4, 1922

During the early 1920s, in an era before radio, television, computers, VCRs, and DVD players, the public enjoyed frequent moviegoing. Then, silent cinema stars and major moviemakers commanded a lofty place in the public's estimation. At the time, media sources seldom revealed the truth behind celebrities' fabricated

guises, and the public mostly believed the contrived publicity fodder about their favorite celebrities and their glamorous lifestyles. In
many ways, it was a far more naive and trusting period, even though
the decade was known as the Roaring '20s.

Thus, when esteemed film director William Desmond Taylor
was murdered in Los Angeles in 1922, public curiosity was immediately aroused. Police/media investigations revealed that the elegant
Taylor had blatantly fabricated much of his background (even his
name!), and people became even more intrigued with this killing. As the homicide inquiry proceeded, two of Hollywood's most-
celebrated personalities—beloved comedian Mabel Normand and
beautiful Mary Miles Minter, who specialized in portraying virtuous
heroines—were labeled by the press as rival "lovers" of the deceased.
The much-headlined case had reached a sensational level, which
proved to be just the tip of the iceberg.

Representatives from Paramount Pictures (which employed
both Taylor and Minter) deliberately tampered with murder scene
evidence—even more than the law suspected or acknowledged.
Moreover, the Los Angeles police were under the thumb of Adolph
Zukor, the powerful head of Paramount, and thus the inquiry
(already bungled by careless police work) was further hamstrung.
Meanwhile, the newspapers fully exploited this latest extravagant
tragedy from Hollywood, and their circulations soared. As such, the
publications were in no hurry to have this latest three-ring circus
end, and they craftily increased readers' curiosity with a variety of
fantastic slants to the notorious case.

Paramount attempted large-scale damage control of the Taylor
case because the studio was then coping with the recent Roscoe
"Fatty" Arbuckle situation in which the famed comedian was on
trial for the rape and manslaughter of minor film actress Virginia
Rappé. To counter such a massive taint on the respectability of the
film colony and its movies, Hollywood—with Zukor spearheading
the movement—hired U.S. postmaster general Will Hays to direct
an industry self-regulatory board. Already, Hays was structuring the
Motion Picture Producers and Distributors of America to censor

Tinseltown product and to keep the morality of its workers in check (at least publicly). Now, with the salacious facts (including veiled references to alleged drug dealing) pouring forth about Taylor's murder, the world was stunned, horrified, and/or thrilled as each new lurid development unfolded in this most spectacular case.

The victim was born William Cunningham Deane-Tanner on April 26, 1872, in Carlow, Ireland, south of Dublin, the second of four children of a British army officer and his Irish society wife. Major Tanner ruled his household as if he were a despot. William was totally different from his martinet parent. The two constantly quarreled, and when William was 15, he left home.

By 1890, under the name Cunningham Deane, he was performing on stage in England. When the major learned of this dishonor to the family, he demanded that William enroll at Runnymede, an establishment in Kansas that turned disreputable wealthy young men into respectable farmers. William remained at the Midwest institution for 18 months. When Runnymede went bankrupt, the young man chose to remain in America.

After working as a manual laborer—as well as being a gambler, working as a magazine salesman, and operating a modest restaurant—William returned to stage work. In 1895 he worked on Broadway and on tour with actress Fanny Davenport and her company. That post ended when she died in 1898.

By then William had met Effie Hamilton, a pretty blond chorine from a well-to-do family. The couple wed in December 1901. The following year their daughter, Ethel Daisy, was born, and Effie never returned to the stage. To support his family, William Deane-Tanner began a new career. With a $25,000 loan from his wife's relatives, he acquired a stake in two eastside Manhattan antique shops. William was a great success in his new trade. He and his family lived well in suburban Larchmont.

By 1908 things fell apart. There was gossip that several vintage items sold in his shops were bogus. A projected inheritance from Effie's rich uncle evaporated when the relative wed and then died, leaving everything to his spouse. Deane-Tanner began drinking heavily. Later it was discovered that in the summer of that year he had vacationed in the Adirondacks with a woman who was *not* his wife. Unable to pay the sizable resort bill, he gave the hotel a diamond ring as security. (This episode came to light when Effie divorced William in 1912. She later married a well-heeled restaurateur.)

In September 1908 William vanished from New York, having taken $600 in cash from one of his antique shops. He sent $500 to his wife and used the balance for his new life. Now known as William Desmond Taylor, he acted with a stock troupe in New Jersey. Never more than an adequate performer, he soon turned to other employment, including factory worker and gold miner. His wanderlust took him to Colorado, the Yukon, Hawaii, and northern California. A great ladies' man and a frequent drinker, his years on the road were filled with wild adventures. While performing on the San Francisco stage, he was hired by pioneer filmmaker Thomas Ince to appear in silent pictures.

Relocating to southern California, Taylor began his career at the Inceville studio in Santa Monica. Within a short period he was working for Vitagraph and starring in *Captain Alvarez* (1914). Typically in this period, his screen credit read William D. Taylor. (It was a 1918 reissue of this feature that Taylor's daughter, Ethel Daisy, saw in New York and, thus, learned of his new profession. This led to a budding friendship between William and his offspring.)

Now in his mid-forties, William appreciated that his screen acting career would never be stellar, and he switched to directing. At the Balboa Amusement Producing Company in Long Beach, California, he fell in love with leading lady Neva Gerber. Unfortunately, Gerber, 20, was already married and had a child, and her much-older husband refused to divorce her. (Later, when she was single again, she hesitated to marry Taylor, fearing that this genteel but troubled man was not good marriage material. However, they remained good friends.) Meanwhile, Neva discovered that dignified William was subject to bouts of serious despondency. Sometimes, after completing a new picture, the moody moviemaker would head off for a trip to northern California, but he always remained vague about such sojourns.

William's directing career steadily progressed in the mid-1910s as he switched studios again. Taylor was brought to Pallas Pictures in 1915 by Julia Crawford Ivers, a twice-married screenwriter, producer, and director. When Pallas merged into Paramount, Julia and Taylor frequently worked together, maintaining a close friendship (that may have included romantic hopes on her part). At Paramount, Taylor was in his full element, directing a flow of major features.

In the fall of 1917, Taylor's new Paramount pact allowed him time off to join the Canadian army and serve in World War I. By August 1918, he was based in Nova Scotia for military training and then shipped out with fellow troops to England. Although the war was already over by the time he arrived, the filmmaker asked to be stationed in France until he was discharged. By spring 1919 he had risen to the rank of major.

Upon William's return to Paramount, he directed such films as *Anne of Green Gables* (1919), starring Mary Miles Minter. By then he was president of the Motion Picture Directors Association. Settling into his affluent life, he moved from the Los Angeles Athletic Club to one of the eight bungalows (each containing two apartments) that made up Alvarado Court in a pleasant section of Los Angeles then favored by film industry people. Among those living at the Court was comedy actor Douglas MacLean (and his wife), who was part of Taylor's social circle. To run his household, the director hired Edward F. Sands as a combination secretary and cook, with Earl Tiffany employed, for a time, as chauffeur.

During the spring of 1921 Taylor had surgery (possibly for a stomach ulcer) and went abroad in June to recuperate. During his absence, he loaned his bungalow to playwright Edward Knoblock in exchange for use of Knoblock's digs in London. To ensure his houseguest's comfort, William foolishly left a signed blank check for Sands to utilize in emergencies. While his employer was away, Sands not only cashed the check in the amount of $5,000 but forged other smaller checks. A week before Taylor returned, Sands disappeared.

When William arrived home, he discovered that, in addition to the pilfered funds, Sands had taken much of his wardrobe, some jewelry, a few personal objects, as well as a car (later found wrecked). Taylor filed a complaint with the police. At year's end, Taylor received a note from Sands half-heartedly apologizing for his many misdeeds. The letter also contained two pawn tickets that were for diamond cuff links that Mabel Normand had given the director. Sands's job at Taylor's residence was taken over by Henry Peavey.

Mabel Normand, then 27, had built her career as the Queen of Comedy as a member of the Keystone studio, run by Mack Sennett, who was her mentor and close friend. In 1918 she signed with producer Samuel Goldwyn (with whom she had an affair) to make features. It was during this period that the hard-partying performer developed a serious cocaine habit. Later, she became involved romantically with Taylor, who was sympathetic to her drug plight. He sought to wean her away from the dealers who were feeding her dangerous habit, as well as to be her mentor in cultural matters.

Another woman in the director's complex life was 19-year-old Mary Miles Minter, whom he directed in three 1920 features. Under the watchful eye of her mercenary stage mother (Charlotte Selby), fanciful Minter looked on Taylor as both a father figure and a dashing hero, fantasizing about marrying him despite his efforts to dissuade her. (Moreover, if she married before her current Paramount contract expired in 1923, she would violate terms of her studio pact.)

On Wednesday, February 1, 1922, Mabel visited Taylor at his bungalow to pick up two books that he had purchased for her. She left a few minutes before 8:00 P.M. He walked the actress to her car, leaving his front door open. She waved to him as her chauffeur-driven auto pulled away, and he returned to his white stucco bungalow apartment. At midnight, actress Edna Purviance, who also lived at the Alvarado Court, returned home and noticed the lights were still on at William's, but she thought it too late to stop by and chat with Taylor. The following morning around seven, there was a great ruckus in the courtyard of the U-shaped complex. Henry Peavey, arriving for his daily tasks as Taylor's cook and valet, discovered the director's dead body sprawled out faceup on the living room floor.

Soon several of the Court's residents traipsed in and out of Taylor's home, contaminating the death scene. When William's latest chauffeur, Howard Fellows, arrived, he phoned the news to his brother. The latter, Harry, was a prior driver for Taylor who had gone to work for the director at Paramount and was now an assistant director there. It was he who contacted Charles Eyton, Paramount's general manager, and told him of Taylor's death. Eyton ordered Harry, along with Julia Crawford Ivers and her son James (who was Taylor's cinematographer), to rush to Taylor's home. Their goal was to remove any possibly incriminating evidence that could taint the late filmmaker's memory (and, in turn, cause repercussions for the studio).

The trio had only a few minutes to accomplish their sweep of Taylor's place before the police arrived. Among the items whisked out of the bungalow were letters to William from Mabel Normand, Mary Miles Minter, and Neva Gerber, as well as notes from Ethel Daisy Deane-Tanner to her dad. The three coconspirators also removed bootleg liquor from the premises. While law officers were taking statements, Eyton arrived, and, because of his importance in Los Angeles, the police did not prevent him from going upstairs to look around or bother to question him when he came downstairs to learn whether he had moved anything or taken any items with him. (Eyton eventually returned a packet of Mabel's letters, some of which were published in newspapers, as were a few of Mary's coded communications to William overlooked by the Paramount people and found by reporters.)

Some minutes later, the deputy coroner and his helper arrived. It was only then that it was discovered that the victim had actually been shot in the back. This was a surprise to those on hand, and the homicide squad was called to handle the case. (Earlier, a doctor making a house call in the neighborhood had been attracted by the disturbance at Taylor's bungalow. Without fully turning over the body—because the coroner was not yet present—this stranger made a snap judgment that the man had died of a stomach hemorrhage. The police had made note of the diagnosis but failed to obtain the doctor's name. The physician left and was never heard from again.)

News reporters quickly converged on the scene, and so began a rash of wild accusations, innuendoes, hypotheses, and fabrications published around the world. Some newspapers insisted it must have been the vanished crook Edward F. Sands who committed the crime, a notion eventually dropped. For a time, some journalists suggested that houseman Henry Peavey was the culprit (suggesting that because he was African American and homosexual, he *must* be considered a prime suspect). Because Peavey was gay and the deceased had been scheduled to appear—the day after the murder—in court to testify on the man's behalf in a sexual misconduct allegation, it was hinted by the media that Taylor may have been gay and that, perhaps, had something to do with the lurid crime. Peavey was exonerated of the homicide theory, but rumors that Taylor may have been gay or bisexual have always remained.

With such rampant yellow journalism it was hard to piece together the truth. Taylor's neighbors, the MacLeans, told the police that their maid heard someone in the alleyway between their and Taylor's bungalows after seven on the fateful night. Later, when Mrs. MacLean heard a noise that sounded like a car backfiring, she had investigated and, from her front door, had seen a person emerge from the victim's house, close the front door, and walk calmly away. She described the individual as a "roughly dressed man."

The investigation was certainly not aided by Los Angeles district attorney Thomas Woolwine, who had many close ties to key film industry figures. One major L.A. newspaper insisted that the DA was guilty of "erecting a barricade of silence between the searchers for truth and the truth itself." As if the investigation were not being handled badly enough, some of the witnesses hindered the search for truth in efforts to protect their reputations. When questioned by the police Mabel Normand did her best to downplay her romantic relationship with Taylor. She remained deliberately vague on other issues involving herself and the victim, especially anything touching on her drug addiction and the deceased's efforts in assisting her to break the habit. (Other witnesses, however, claimed that they had seen Taylor chase away drug dealers who had been trying to feed Mabel's habit, and that the incensed Taylor had reported the dealers to federal authorities.)

In the rush for tantalizing headlines, journalists embroidered on the discovery of Mary Miles Minter's monogrammed pink lingerie at Taylor's place. Although the young star always strongly denied this—though later admitting she had once given him a monogrammed handkerchief—the distorted information suggested to the public that the couple was having a clandestine romance. (Supposedly, a pink nightgown had been seen among Taylor's effects by Peavey some time before his employer's death.) This perception of supposedly demure Minter having an affair with the much-older Taylor helped to destroy her film career.

The coroner's inquest on February 4, 1922, lasted a surprisingly short time (less than an hour), and not all the witnesses on hand were called to testify. The coroner's jury of six men quickly concluded that the director's death by gunshot wound to the chest was "by some person or persons unknown to this jury."

To many observers, the murder investigation appeared to be a medley of contrivances to hush up potential scandals. This led a *Chicago Tribune* article to state: "Twenty people are said to be under suspicion. Twenty theories of the crime are being aired, but there has been not one arrest and not one clue. It is believed the movie interests would spend a million not to catch the murderer, to prevent the real truth from coming out." To counteract such sentiment, the film studios established a special committee to "help" the press deal with the case, which the movie companies wanted forgotten as quickly as possible. The few reporters who did not cave in to the powerful committee's dictates were intimidated by the Los Angeles police.

As years passed—with the case never officially resolved—bits of truth continued to emerge amidst the exaggerated fiction and burgeoning filmdom legends. Speculation included the theory that perhaps a hired killer of a drug dealer did in Taylor, or even that a disgruntled World War I veteran, who blamed William for his having been court-martialed, carried out his delayed revenge. Other guesswork insisted that the murderer had been Mabel Normand, Mary Miles Minter, or the latter's highly manipulative mother who was, according to one theory, a jealous rival for Taylor's love.

Adding to the growing myths was research done by veteran filmmaker King Vidor in 1967. Having known the principals involved in the murder/scandal, he hoped to parse through the mire of (mis) facts and fiction to create a truthful screenplay that he could direct as a movie. In his extensive exploration he interviewed (retired) police officers assigned then or later to the infamous case. They claimed to Vidor that they had been told by their superiors, including later district attorneys Asa Keys and Buron Fitts, to lay off the investigation. Eventually, Vidor abandoned the project, convinced he had discovered the real culprit (the vicious Mrs. Selby) but concluding it was too painful to proceed further. King Vidor passed away in 1982. However, his research became the basis of a nonfiction account of the long-standing murder mystery.

Mabel Normand's career was destroyed by the Taylor scandal as well as by another incident not long thereafter involving her chauffeur and the murder of a Hollywood playboy. She made a few additional films, but, by then, her health was ruined and she had lost her verve. She died in 1930 of tuberculosis and pneumonia. Mary Miles Minter retired permanently from the screen in 1924, thereafter alternating between feuding and reuniting with her overbearing mother. The latter died in 1957, and the reclusive, vastly overweight Minter passed away in 1984.

Today the spectacular Taylor murder case still fascinates many Hollywood and murder buffs as an absorbing whodunit. This Tinseltown homicide is also an appalling example of how the once-powerful film studios were so easily able to obstruct and confound justice.

Wallace Reid: The Tragic Matinee Idol

"Normally he could have been sent to a sanitarium, a cure, or something—but he was altogether too good box office. There was too much more to be gotten out of . . . [him]. So in order to keep the services of this most popular of popular leading men alive, they [Paramount Pictures] kept him supplied with more and more and more morphine."

— Cinematographer Karl Brown, in 1979

The early 1920s were not good times for the mighty Paramount Pictures. Several of its prime stars were involved in major scandals that threatened the future of the company—let alone that of Hollywood. In 1921, the studio's famed comedian Roscoe "Fatty" Arbuckle went on trial for rape and manslaughter, and in 1922, actor-turned-director William Desmond Taylor was murdered at his Los Angeles home. Capping Paramount's run of enormous bad luck, in January 1923, 31-year-old Wallace Reid, the lot's exceedingly popular, all-American leading man, died at a Los Angeles sanitarium while undergoing treatment for morphine withdrawal.

Little wonder that Paramount, as well as the entire American film business, panicked at the tragic death of Wally Reid, the handsome, unpretentious matinee idol. His unfortunate passing gave morally conservative groups around the nation further ammunition to blast Hollywood for its out-of-control, "corrupt," and scandalous lifestyle. Reid's tragic end reconfirmed for industry leaders the wisdom of having set up, in 1922, the Motion Picture Producers and Distributors of America. The organization, under the leadership of Will Hays, former U.S. postmaster general, was chartered to regulate—in ways not yet fully determined—the content of screen fare as well as to be a moral watchdog over the private lives of Tinseltown's celebrated. It was a stopgap measure to prevent threatened government censorship of movie product and its players.

While thousands of shocked filmgoers mourned the loss of beloved Wally, rumors circulated in Hollywood that his studio had not been such an innocent bystander in his ongoing substance abuse. It was touted that the company had actually nurtured his addiction so that their workhorse star could maintain his enormous output—often six or more features a year!

William Wallace Reid was born on April 15, 1891, in St. Louis, Missouri. His father, James Halik (Hal) Reid, was an established stage producer and playwright who later became both an actor and director in silent pictures. His domineering mother, Bertha Belle Westbrooke, a former St. Louis socialite, was a leading lady of the stage who made occasional films. At age four, Wallace began appearing in his parents' act. However, they separated and it was Mrs. Reid who made sure that her beloved boy received a broad-spectrum education. He attended private schools in the East, where he displayed a talent for painting and music (including the saxophone and the violin). His thirst for book learning was balanced by his enjoyment of playing sports. The young man's true love, however, was automobiles, especially fast racing cars.

This jack-of-all-trades, under his mother's constant prodding, initially considered becoming a physician. Instead, after completing high school he hired on as the auto reporter for the *Newark Morning Star*. Later, having tried several career outlets, including being a government surveyor in Wyoming, he finally gave in to his heritage and turned to show business.

By 1910, Hal Reid, then in his late forties, had migrated into the film business and was working as actor, director, and writer for the Selig Polyscope Company in Chicago. He arranged for Wally, then 19, to find employment at the same studio. Thanks to his athletic prowess Wally worked as a stuntman in Tom Mix's short Western films, as well as a supporting actor and scriptwriter. Wallace found screen work so congenial that he abandoned thoughts of one day becoming a musician or a race driver.

Moving over to Vitagraph in 1911, young Reid worked as actor, scenarist, and cinematographer. When his dad went to Reliance Studio, Wallace joined him there for several entries. The next year, the rising talent made *His Only Son* at Nestor. His leading lady was 17-year-old Dorothy Davenport, from an illustrious theater family.

Initially, Dorothy, a striking but not beautiful young woman, was unimpressed by her virile costar. However, after a few days of working together she was smitten with the six-foot, one-inch Reid. When she discovered that he was a superior horseman who matched her skills in that arena, she fell in love with him. They wed on October 12, 1913. (In 1918 their son, William Wallace Jr., was born, and in 1922 they adopted a girl, Betty Ann. One source suggested this child was the result of an adulterous relationship Wally had with an unnamed woman.) Once Reid married Davenport, a tug-of-war developed between Wallace's suffocating mother and his self-willed wife to capture the actor's attention.

With his good looks and versatility, Reid kept busy grinding out films. If moviegoers in general were aware of Wallace only from the sheer volume of his work, the public took notice when he played the brief role of Jeff the fighting blacksmith in *The Birth of a Nation* (1915). By the middle of 1915, Wallace, 24, signed with Famous Players-Lasky (Paramount), where he was teamed in *Carmen* with opera singer Geraldine Farrar. The duo made several popular movies together. During this period, Reid also paired with his wife, Dorothy, in celluloid entries.

Square-jawed, pipe-smoking Wallace was an ingratiating romantic leading man, inspiring one fan magazine of the times to label this unmannered actor "the screen's most perfect lover." While such roles appealed to female moviegoers, it was in action and adventure tales that he truly excelled. He was especially pleased to make stories concerning car racing such as *The Roaring Road* (1919). For these movies, Reid enthusiastically undertook his own stunts.

Wallace's seemingly charmed life took a sharp turn when he went on location to the High Sierras for the lumber camp adventure *The Valley of the Giants* (1919). While traveling to a filming site, the production's special train derailed, and he was severely injured, with gashes to his head and damage to his back and leg. He was in such serious pain that a studio physician ordered morphine to help him endure the remainder of the physical shoot. Once back home, he recuperated for three months in bed before returning to the soundstages.

At the time, prescribing morphine for severe pain was not considered out of place, because few knew about the addictive consequences. While the drug had kept the almost completed feature from being shut down temporarily or being scrapped altogether, it also had longer-lasting effects: the medication became a crutch for the star, and he soon became addicted. (Some sources suggested that the addiction was more an escape from his unhappy domestic life. It was theorized that Reid, perhaps bisexual, was enduring great emotional stress over the confines of his marriage, particularly to such a forceful personality as Dorothy. Another avenue of thought focused on Reid's unhappiness with being forced by the studio to continue as an actor when he much preferred directing. In any event, in the years before his death, he began to drink and party heavily, relying on drugs to get him through the intolerable days at the studio.)

In Hollywood of that era, it was not difficult to obtain drugs. For example, there were people at the Mack Sennett studio—an actor, in particular—who had underworld connections for supplying customers with their needs. Then too, it was not unusual for drug pushers (part of a Los Angeles drug ring) to hang around the studios (a situation that came to public light during the investigation of William Desmond Taylor's murder), knowing that many film workers had the income to support their expensive habits.

It was not long before Wallace's substance abuse was known to his superiors at Paramount. Jesse Lasky, one of the company's founders, claimed that he had urged Reid to be treated for his drug abuse but that the star had ignored the suggestion. Others, as already noted, insisted that the film company made sure that their valuable asset was well supplied with his drugs of choice. It was their way of keeping him at his hectic filmmaking pace, turning out profitable product for the studio. In any event, Wallace kept promising friends that at the end of each new picture, he would take a long rest and cure his spiraling problem. It never happened.

Reid was crafty about obtaining his fixes. His wife insisted that he did not resort to underworld sources: "Wally could charm any doctor into giving him the tablets he wanted. He knew just enough about medicine to convince doctors that he knew exactly how many grams he could safely take every day. . . . And when he found that he couldn't put a stop or even a check to the morphine, he began to use liquor as a cover-up for what he was really doing."

Wallace made seven features in 1921 (the year in which he was America's top box-office attraction). Already the drugs had adversely affected his personality. Gloria Swanson, with whom he costarred in *The Affairs of Anatol* (1921), said, "I heard endless rumors that he was an addict, and although I never saw him take drugs, his behavior never seemed quite right. He gave me the jitters." Despite Reid's mounting problems, he continued the frantic filmmaking schedule in 1922. However, by then his dependencies had not only adversely distorted his nature but had also seriously impaired his health. He lost his robust looks, and his weight dropped sharply from his usual 180 pounds. Now just 30 years old and earning $7,000 weekly, he seemed a far different man. Yet he still refused to alter his ways.

By November 1922, Reid was in really bad shape and struggling to perform on the set of the comedy *Thirty Days*. Henry Hathaway, then an assistant director at Paramount, recalled, "He sort of fumbled around the set and bumped into a chair and then he just sat down on the floor and started to cry." After completing the silent picture, Wallace finally agreed to take a long vacation, going on a mountain trip with his wife and his trainer, Teddy Hayes. The studio made an announcement that Reid was recuperating from the stress of a heavy production schedule and from eye strain caused by the klieg lights on the set.

When Wallace returned to L.A., his condition had not improved so he agreed to seek treatment. He vowed, "I'll either come out cured—or I won't come out." When film industry censorship czar Will Hays learned of his treatment plans, he said, "I hope he comes back. I have nothing but sympathy for him. I have always greatly admired him on the screen." He also noted, "The unfortunate

Mr. Reid should be dealt with as a diseased person—not censured, shunned."

Wallace entered the Banksia Place Sanitarium in Hollywood. (There is some indication that this was not the first time he had tried the cure at that establishment.) The regimen at this private center was austere and utilized treatment methods far more spartan than those used today. As his wife detailed, "In the basement there were padded rooms adjacent to one another. Each room had a single light that burned overhead constantly, a sink, a toilet without a seat, and a small mattress on the floor. . . . In this confined space Wally was to cure himself. A doctor . . . looked at him from time to time. . . . A nurse would leave food only after Wally had spent the first 72 hours virtually all alone. And then the food was very soft. . . . All of the patients in that 72-hour period vomited, urinated, and defecated on themselves and on the floor. Only if the patient were deemed safe would anyone venture inside with a mop and a new hospital gown. Most of the patients stayed naked because they sometimes tore their gowns in anguish."

Appreciating how serious her husband's condition was, Dorothy Davenport, as well as her mother-in-law, candidly told the press of Wallace's drug problem, giving them frequent updates on Reid's life-or-death battle. The news was tremendously shocking to readers in an era when such disreputable matters as drug addiction were generally unknown to the general public or, at the most, discussed only in whispers. The outcry was enormous, with many fans writing letters of concern and sympathy to Mrs. Reid and to the studio. However, the patient was not informed that his loyal public knew of his plight. It was reasoned he was enduring enough hell and humiliation trying to overcome his severe habit.

In January 1923, the actor contracted influenza. His weight fell to 120 pounds, and he slipped into a coma. On the afternoon of January 18, the star slipped away, dying of lung and kidney congestion. The day Reid died, production stopped at Hollywood studios to pay tribute to the fallen star. When Wallace was buried at Forest Lawn Memorial Park in Glendale, California, the flag on the

Paramount lot flew at half-mast. Meanwhile, around the country, clergymen and newspaper editorials decried the vicious spread of drugs in the film capital and how it created dope fiends of such beloved, tragic figures as pitiful Wallace Reid.

When *Thirty Days* was released that December, the *Los Angeles Times* wrote of Reid's final picture: "The sympathy his illness engendered was denoted by the applause which first rippled and then rolled in a frenzy of enthusiastic clapping in the theatre." In the midst of all the fulsome tributes, Reid's mother rushed out a thin biographical volume about her late son.

Both in acknowledgment to her husband's deadly drug problem and to refill the family's coffers (high-spending Reid left an estate of only some $40,000), Dorothy Davenport (now billing herself professionally as Mrs. Wallace Reid) produced an exploitative, anti-drug feature (1923's *Human Wreckage*). By then Will Hays's industry watchdog group had banned the mention/use of drugs in American films, but Hays made an exception for this educational screen project. In the picture's preface, Mrs. Reid editorialized, "Dope is the gravest menace which today confronts the United States. Immense quantities of morphine, heroin, and cocaine are yearly smuggled into America across the Canadian and Mexican borders. The Dope Ring is composed of rings within rings, the inner ring undoubtedly including men powerful in finance, politics and society. But the trail to the 'men higher up' is cunningly covered. No investigator has penetrated to the inner circle."

Never referencing the industry's complicity in Reid's demise, Hays nonetheless used this latest calamity to push the harried American film business into greater compliance with his edicts designed to purify motion pictures and the movie colony. His efforts proved to be a mixture of surface cosmetics and careful ignoring of circumstances when powerful studio forces so dictated.

Even when the hue and cry over the drug scandal tapered off in subsequent months, the public remained stunned by Wallace Reid's untimely death. Many disheartened filmgoers would never again view Hollywood as the magical land of wonder and enchantment.

2

1930–1949

D uring the early 1920s, Hollywood had been rocked by such major scandals as the Roscoe "Fatty" Arbuckle case and screen idol Wallace Reid's drug-related death. The strong adverse reaction to these shocking events caused the American film industry to fear possible outside intervention. The concern was that federal and state governments, as well as powerful public groups, would step in to censor what type of screen fare was allowable. The film colony also feared that such regulatory legislation and watchdog groups planned to ride herd on the suspected immoral private lives of Tinseltown folk. This led the panicked film business to form a self-censorship administration (the Motion Picture Producers and Distributors of America, Inc.). However, it was not until 1934 that the association's regulations were strengthened to give the code real teeth. Thereafter, its regulations strongly affected the content of motion pictures as well as the off-screen behavior of film workers. (Although most studio contracts contained a morals clause, it was enforced only if the employee in trouble was not financially worth salvaging from the cloud of the personal problem.)

True to human nature, and stars being stars, notables still got into minor or major scrapes, despite the industry watchdogs. Such predicaments required the celebrities' all-powerful studios to rush into play with their internal police forces, crafty lawyers, and high-powered publicists to save the day and keep the stars' scandalous misbehavior from public knowledge.

During World War II, America was on a patriotic high and the film business was at its most profitable. Nevertheless, its talent still managed to get into trouble (e.g., Errol Flynn's 1943 statutory rape case). As in the past, celebrities had to be coddled through their annoying difficulties. Most often, *thanks to studio intervention, they emerged from such situations without much or any damage to their screen images.*

No sooner had the United States celebrated the armistice in 1945 than the Cold War began, with Russia again becoming America's enemy. *Paranoia about a possible Soviet takeover of America led, in the late 1940s, to the House Un-American Activities Committee (HUAC) savagely probing Hollywood for suspected Communists. The intimidated movie business succumbed to the government's reign of terror, instituting its own blacklist of alleged Reds within the business. This shameful situation caused industry chaos for many years to come.*

The Mob: Taking on Hollywood

"*The mobs moved in on Hollywood moviemakers during the reign of Al Capone, when the industry was still silent. Movie executives tended to be silent, too, when faced with Capone threats.*"
—CARL SIFAKIS, *THE MAFIA ENCYCLOPEDIA*, 1999

When the topics of Hollywood and gangsters are discussed in tandem, most people's initial thoughts immediately turn to such celluloid genre entries as *Underworld* (1927), *Little Caesar* (1931), *High Sierra* (1941), *Criss Cross* (1949), *Bonnie and Clyde* (1967), *The Godfather* (1972), *Scarface* (1981), *State of Grace* (1990), and *Cradle 2 the Grave* (2003).

The majority of Tinseltown chronicles and celebrity biographies and autobiographies hardly mention the pervasive influence mobsters often had on the daily operation of the studios and how underworld figures frequently rubbed shoulders with the movie colony elite by night and terrorized film company executives by day. Over the decades, while the likes of ambitious leading ladies (e.g., Clara Bow, Bette Davis, Deanna Durbin, Katharine Hepburn, Lana Turner, Rita Hayworth, Judy Canova, and Marilyn Monroe) were pitting themselves against the iron-handed wills of their film studio bosses (e.g., respectively, Paramount, Warner Bros., Universal, RKO, MGM, Columbia, Republic, and Twentieth Century-Fox), hoodlums were intimidating the same tough moguls into lucrative compliance. It was a bizarre and frightening situation, a major scandal that came to full light only years after the mob's influence had diminished in the movie industry.

The underworld's infiltration of the American film business—with its accompanying reign of threatened violence and extortion—has existed for decades. At no time was the mob's power more evident than during Hollywood's golden age (1920s–1950s), when the movie industry's power was centered in a few major studios and the tightfisted regimes of their dictatorial film lot bosses. As such, organized crime had well-defined targets to coerce and shake down—which they did with ruthless regularity.

By the 1920s, Hollywood was no longer a sleepy outpost of the once-dominant East Coast film business. The major studios were clustered around Los Angeles and thrived in the optimistic Roaring '20s. With Prohibition in full sway, the underworld found the ritzy movie colony to be an especially rewarding marketplace for bootleg liquor at very inflated prices. As revealed in the wake of the scandals involving the 1922 murder of movie director William Desmond Taylor and the 1923 drug-related death of film idol Wallace Reid, mob syndicates (and entrepreneurial individuals) were actively peddling narcotics to the film crowd, often having distribution centers at the less-vigilant studios.

With the repeal of Prohibition in the early 1930s, organized crime (particularly from New York and Chicago) sought fresh ways to bleed the film industry, beyond their usual loan sharking (when the Depression put many of the studios into financial peril). As the underworld further spread its control over the movie business, it helped to have an established toehold in Tinseltown. One such useful contact was George Raft.

Born George Ranft on September 26, 1895, the future movie star grew up in Manhattan's infamous Hell's Kitchen, where one of his childhood pals was Owney Madden. The latter grew up to be a vicious killer and was renowned for being a thinking man's hoodlum. Whether as a bootlegger, an operator of a laundry service racket, or an infiltrator into the boxing world, Madden was a respected/feared member of the New York crime world. (Besides his longtime friendship with Owney and his confederates, Raft mingled with other underworld figures during the 1920s as he worked first as a gigolo and then as a nightclub and Broadway dancer.)

Wanting to distance himself from a brewing gang war in the East, Madden vacationed in southern California in 1930 and brought George along. Raft had made an earlier trip to the West Coast under mobsters' orders to chaperone nightclub hostess Texas Guinan, who was about to make a Hollywood film. This time, Raft was told to stay in Los Angeles. Madden wanted to protect George from Manhattan underworld rivals; he also believed that his swarthy, good-looking friend (who wore shoe lifts to compensate for his below-average height) had screen star potential.

In films such as 1931's *Quick Millions* and 1932's *Scarface*, George quickly established his movie persona—a slick, well-dressed gangster. It was a part for which he had real-life experience. Of equal importance, studio executives appreciated that with Raft's off-camera affiliations, the mobs would look favorably and/or tolerantly on George's portrayals of movie hoodlums and would not be offended by Hollywood's celluloid representations.

Although Raft had been married to Grace Mulrooney since 1923, the union had quickly become loveless. However, being a staunch Catholic, George would not divorce. (Besides, he enjoyed being a suave playboy on the loose and feared making a substantial divorce settlement.) With his essentially single status and agility on the dance floor, the well-groomed, well-mannered actor was in constant demand on the Hollywood social scene. Many film people were intrigued by George's checkered past and his known underworld ties. His array of escorts over the years included such diverse performers as Billie Dove, Carole Lombard, Lucille Ball, Betty Grable, and Norma Shearer, as well as the shifty socialite Dorothy Di Frasso. However, his greatest love was socialite/fledgling actress Virginia Pine, with whom he unofficially lived in the late 1930s.

Eventually, their romance ended when she finally tired of his constant philandering.

In the early 1930s, George circulated on the Hollywood scene with, among others, Pasquale "Pat" J. DiCicco. Pat was a wealthy East Coaster who traveled in underworld circles for the thrill of it. Pat had become acquainted with New York gangster kingpin Charles "Lucky" Luciano before turning up in Los Angeles as a self-professed talent agent/manager. From 1932 to 1934, DiCicco was wed to beautiful, tragic movie actress Thelma Todd. She died under mysterious circumstances in late 1935, reportedly a death ordered by Luciano, her sometime lover, who intended to use her Los Angeles restaurant as the site of a gaming club for the Hollywood wealthy. Later, among other activities, DiCicco turned to film producing.

Another of Raft's pals was Benjamin "Bugsy" Siegel. In the late 1930s, Ben was dispatched to California by the East Coast crime syndicate. He was to assist the New York mobs in gaining greater control of the West Coast rackets. Southern California was then run by Jack Dragna, a crime boss known as "the Al Capone of Los Angeles." However, Dragna's organization—later jeeringly labeled the "Mickey Mouse Mafia"—was never especially well organized and was easy pickings for Siegel and his strong-arm associates. One of Ben's initial mandates was to take charge of the bookie business that drew a great deal of its profits from the movie crowd. As such, Siegel and his group schemed to consolidate the racing wire services upon which the bookies relied, as well as grab an interest in (or, better yet, control of) Los Angeles racetracks. (Another faction after the same target was the Chicago underworld contingent.)

Soon after Ben's arrival in Los Angeles, he and George were seen everywhere together, whether at Santa Anita Racetrack by day or on the Tinseltown party circuit at night where beautiful starlets gravitated to these two exciting men. It was Raft who not only instructed Siegel on sartorial matters but also introduced Siegel to many of the colony's elite. Before long, Ben was hobnobbing with the likes of Al Jolson, Cary Grant, and Gary Cooper, all thrilled to be in such dangerous company. Siegel set up headquarters in a Beverly Hills mansion once owned by opera/film star Lawrence Tibbett. With Ben's dapper looks, he was a magnet for movie industry love-lies who thrilled to be dating a real-life hoodlum.

One of Siegel's frequent girlfriends was British-born actress Wendy Barrie, who had become a Hollywood movie name. She hoped one day to marry the moody, elusive Siegel. Another of Ben's inamoratas was Marie "the Body" McDonald, a voluptuous person-ality who made several films in the 1940s. However, Ben was most smitten with Virginia Hill, a crime syndicate bagwoman. This tough dame's checkered career ran the gamut from carnival dancer to bed partner of a wide variety of underworld figures (e.g., Frank Costello, Joe Adonis, and Frank Nitti). Ben and Virginia had probably first known each other in New York. Their acquaintanceship heated up when she arrived in Hollywood in 1939, ostensibly to pursue a film career. (In actuality, the East Coast mob had dispatched Hill to keep an eye on the increasingly erratic Siegel.) Virginia attended A-list Hollywood parties, was a frequent figure on the swank nightclub scene, and was usually seen in the company of Siegel and his good buddy Raft.

During the 1940s, the New York and Chicago gang syndicates, who had an uneasy alliance and vied with one another for top con-trol, voted to expand their West Coast operations beyond bookmak-ing, drugs, prostitution, and extortion. Their new enterprise was to turn Las Vegas into a gambling mecca, one that would draw the free-spending Hollywood crowd and, in turn, lure other high roll-ers who wanted to gamble neck and neck with the glittery movie contingent.

Siegel was in charge of the Las Vegas project and in the mid-1940s set out to build the Flamingo (named after redheaded Virginia Hill, whose nickname was "Flamingo"). The hotel/casino was to be a flagship for the envisioned gaming capital in Nevada. A key to developing the sleepy town into a successful gambling oasis would be to have well-known entertainers perform there and draw in the crowds. Because of Raft's film community standing and his wide circle of show business friends, he was expected to help pave the way for getting name talent.

As construction of the plush Flamingo got under way, what had been envisioned as a $2 million project mushroomed to $6 million. Mob chieftains suspected psychotic Siegel was skimming from the construction coffers and having his mistress, Hill, cart the cash to Switzerland. Meanwhile, the Flamingo debuted in late 1946, and initially the hotel was not a success. Its underworld investors were infuriated. A deeply concerned Ben negotiated an extension for the mob loans that had made the building possible. (In a squeeze, Siegel turned to a Hollywood pal, publisher Billy Wilkerson, to provide the needed loan.) By mid-1947, the Flamingo had made a financial turn-around, and Siegel believed he had weathered the storm.

Ben's fate, however, was already sealed. The syndicate back East decreed that Ben must pay with his life for the Las Vegas near-failure. On June 20, 1947, while Virginia Hill was conveniently away in Europe, Siegel was gunned down in her rented Beverly Hills mansion on North Linden Drive. George Raft was distraught at the gruesome slaughter of Ben, but he was wise enough to remain silent as to any details or suspicions he had regarding the murder.

Thereafter, at the bequest of the mob, Raft became involved, at different periods over the next decades, as a front man/greeter at underworld casinos in Cuba and Las Vegas and, later, at the Colony Club in London, where he glad-handed high rollers, danced with their women, and signed autographs. George died November 24, 1980, the same year he made his final film appearance (*The Man with Bogart's Face*).

One of the most despised and feared members of the mob to reach Hollywood in the 1930s was Willie Bioff. The Russian-born, Chicago-bred hoodlum gained his initial reputation as a resourceful teenager who was a tough-minded procurer. His meanness brought him to the attention of Harry and Jake Guzik, two Windy City gang leaders. The burly and brazen Bioff was put to work as an enforcer, helping the organization maintain its cash flow from extortion and protection enterprises. As such he made a mark in

Chicago underworld circles, even coming to the attention of the city's underworld kingpin, Al Capone.

In the early 1930s, after Capone had been imprisoned on income tax evasion charges, his successor, Frank "the Enforcer" Nitti, paid heed to Bioff's latest activities. By then ruthless Willie had become acquainted with another short and pudgy strong-arm man named George Browne. The latter was already involved as a "business" agent for the Chicago Stagehands Local 2, which was linked to the International Alliance of Theatrical Stage Employees. (IATSE had several locals throughout the United States, and its large membership encompassed a wide range of crafts and professions in film distribution and exhibition.)

The deadly duo of Bioff and Browne concocted a twofold get-rich-quick scheme. First, they raised the dues of Stagehands Local 2 by $5 a week. This cash influx, which they laundered through a soup kitchen operation, was nothing compared to their major idea. They planned to shake down the Windy City's movie theaters. Their first target was the lofty Balaban and Katz movie house chain. They made the theater owners a hard-to-refuse offer: pay $50,000 into a union emergency fund and there would be no demands for costly pay raises for union members. The alternative would be to suffer a series of mishaps. When B & K balked initially, their theaters suddenly experienced a variety of misfortunes: projectionists running reels out of order, films unspooled without sound, stink bombs placed in the cinema, and so forth. The demanded $50,000 was handed over to Bioff and Browne's representatives.

Due to the devious pair's bragging, their lucrative, illegal efforts came to Frank Nitti's attention. He informed the duo that, henceforth, his organization was taking a 50 percent (later raised to 75 percent) cut of Willie and George's new scam. Nitti also announced that he planned to have Browne moved up from his local union responsibilities to presidency of IATSE, a job coveted by another troublesome local racketeer, Tommy Malloy. To accomplish his goal, Nitti called upon New York–based Lucky Luciano and his underlings. Lucky, who hated Capone/Nitti, a combination that threatened his supremacy as America's chief mobster, agreed to help upon certain conditions. Luciano, who had a thriving drug business in Los Angeles, wanted Nitti—and his West Coast henchman Johnny Roselli—to stop muscling in on that profitable enterprise. Also, greedy Lucky wanted a stake in the nightclubs/restaurants that Nitti, under Roselli's supervision, controlled in the L.A. area. Nitti reluctantly agreed to some of the demands but had little intention of letting the New York rivals push them out of the Los Angeles gold mine. (It led to recurrent bloody skirmishes between the opposing organizations.)

As a result of the unholy alliance, Browne was elected to the head of IATSE. Accompanied by Bioff, he next pressured New York City theater chains into compliance. Browne and Bioff's operation spread to other cities and finally moved on to Hollywood, the seat of the big studios. Through threatening production stoppage or sabotage action by the union affiliates on the film lots, Willie and George wrung huge extortions from the studio heads. (Reportedly, each major lot paid at least $50,000; the smaller movie firms were assessed $25,000.) To fulfill these annual financial demands, the studios invented creative bookkeeping schemes: sometimes paying off in cash, other times inflating film production budgets to bury the payoffs or creating elaborate phony expense accounts. Before long, with their 75 percent cut of the extortion, the mobs were exacting huge sums from the studios.

On the other hand, the studios generally felt such mobster-enforced overhead was cheaper than allowing the Conference of Studio Unions, a coalition of industry craft groups, to take hold within the film business. If the CSU succeeded with its demands regarding membership wages and benefits for studio workers, the agenda would have outweighed the cost of paying the underworld extortion. Thus, while pretending on the surface to be against the mob-infested IATSE, the studios largely preferred this corrupt scenario to the more expensive CSU version. This battle between the unions led to the 1945–1946 Hollywood film industry worker strikes in which mobster underlings performed dirty work on IATSE's behalf. In the bloody skirmishes that resulted, the CSU was routed.

This ended the potential of progressive trade unionism for several decades.

Interestingly, film industry executives were as intrigued as they were frightened by these mobsters. Not only did the executives fall into line on the underworld's ever-rising tariffs as well as usurious loan rates when studios periodically needed a financial bailout, but many of the industry bigwigs also associated socially with Bioff, Browne, and other hoodlums. It was at one such festive gathering that newspaper journalist Westbrook Pegler wondered what Willie Bioff, whom he remembered from Chicago days, was doing as the featured guest at a Tinseltown shindig. Pegler's investigation, as well as that of *Daily Variety*'s Arthur Unzer, led to a series of crusading articles which, in 1941, got Bioff and Browne convicted of violating antiracketeering laws. The two were sentenced to lengthy prison terms but, instead, made a deal to get early release if they squealed on the mob. Once freed, Browne vanished. In 1955, Bioff, living under an alias in Las Vegas, was discovered by his old mob enemies and blown to bits in a car bombing.

Johnny Roselli married movie leading lady June Lang in 1939. In the early 1940s, he spent a few years in prison as a result of Bioff and Browne's squealing to authorities. Thereafter, Roselli produced films (e.g., 1948's *He Walked by Night*). Later, he was based in Las Vegas to handle the Midwestern underworld's investments in the gaming city.

Another mob envoy in the Hollywood fray was attorney Sidney Korshak. After graduating from DePaul University Law School, he went into practice in Chicago, soon defending members of the Capone syndicate. By the late 1940s, he was in Hollywood, where he became a bridge between mob interests and Hollywood top guns. His huge fees for arbitrating union "problems" with the studios would be sent back to his Chicago office (where he was licensed) and then divvied up with underworld associates. Frequently, Korshak worked out of the Bistro, a swank Beverly Hills restaurant, where he conferred with the industry's powerful and, over the years, courted several screen lovelies (despite having a wife who, herself, associated with A-list Hollywood figures).

As has been well documented, entertainer Frank Sinatra enthusiastically counted several underworld figures among his intimates. In the 1930s, Frank was a struggling newcomer. Willie Moretti (aka Willie Moore), a northern New Jersey racketeer who had an underling reputedly related to Frank's first wife (Nancy Barbato), helped Sinatra gain important band bookings. The two diverse personalities stayed in touch until Willie's murder in 1951.

During the 1940s, Joseph Fischetti, a gangster from Chicago, was frequently in touch with Sinatra, and they met occasionally in both New York and Miami. In early 1947, the crooner accompanied Fischetti and his brother to Cuba, where they got together with deported mobster Lucky Luciano. It was Joseph who helped Frank gain club bookings in Chicago and Miami in the early 1950s when Sinatra's career was experiencing a downslide.

In the late 1950s, when Sam Giancana was top dog of the Chicago underworld, he and Sinatra began associating (first in Miami, then elsewhere). In 1962, when Giancana operated the Villa Venice Supper Club (part of an illegal gaming operation), Frank arranged for himself, Dean Martin, Sammy Davis Jr., and Eddie Fisher to perform at the Wheeling, Illinois, venue. Meanwhile, Sinatra was given ownership participation in the Cal-Neva Lodge on Lake Tahoe, a casino/club where he had performed previously. During a 1963 investigation, the Nevada State Gaming Commission revoked the singer's gaming license, based on his unsavory associations over the years (including his notorious associates on the Las Vegas gambling scene).

Jean Harlow was another Tinseltown name who mingled with underworld figures. In the early 1930s, Jean was cementing her career at MGM. The platinum blonde went on a promotional tour. While in New York, her stepfather, Marino Bello, introduced her to a past pal, Abner "Longy" Zwillman, who, in tandem with Willie Moretti, had a stranglehold on New Jersey underworld operations. Bello fostered an association between Jean and Longy, hoping to be recompensed for his efforts. Harlow and the love-struck, homely Zwillman became intimate, and, for a time, he sent her monthly checks to help support her relatives and maintain a proper Hollywood lifestyle. The relationship ended when Harlow wed producer Paul Bern in mid-1932. As for Marino, he, thereafter, attempted to become a Hollywood talent agent, following in the wake of a successful acquaintance, Frank Orsetti, a former bootlegger.

Such was the uneasy "alliance" between the power elite of Hollywood and the ruthless mobs over the decades, one that did not fully end with the disintegration of Tinseltown's studio system. The scandalous part of this activity has always been its pervasiveness throughout the Hollywood scene, its pernicious hold on the studio system and its stars, and its ongoing catering to the very worst desires and instincts of the Hollywood community.

Clara Bow: When Being "It" Was No Longer Enough

"I thought she was the most marvelous star of the 20s because she was the 20s. Garbo came from Europe, Swanson was already very sophisticated and dressy in DeMille films but Clara was the real jazzy baby."
—ACTRESS AND WRITER LOUISE BROOKS, IN 1979

Few movie personalities symbolized an era so totally as did hotsy-totsy Clara Bow. During the 1920s she reigned supreme. While she was not silent cinema's first flapper—Colleen Moore was—film-goers adored Clara's irrepressible naturalness and perky beauty. She had such verve that her energy seemed boundless. As one publication of the times described her: "She's just a red hot flaming little baby with sex appeal all her own." According to Adolph Zukor, head of Bow's studio (Paramount), Clara "was exactly the same off the screen as on."

Later, Hollywood would ballyhoo the "Platinum Bombshell" (Jean Harlow), the "Sweater Girl" (Lana Turner), and the "Oomph

Girl" (Ann Sheridan). But earlier, in the Roaring '20s, the Tinseltown publicity mill promoted Clara as the "Brooklyn Bonfire." That tag didn't stick, so she was redubbed the "It Girl." The new title referred to her *sexiness*, a word not considered proper to mention directly in that more circumspect era.

The term "It" was created by Madame Elinor Glynn, a British novelist who came to Hollywood in the '20s to adapt her fiction to the screen. One of her stories was *It*, which Paramount used as a basis for a 1927 Clara vehicle. Paid to promote the picture, matronly Glynn dramatically announced to the world that Clara was one of the few in Hollywood (besides Rex the Wonder Horse and the doorman at the Ambassador Hotel) to have "It." And what exactly was this elusive quality? According to Glynn: "To have 'It,' the fortunate possessor must have that strange magnetism which attracts both sexes. 'It' is a purely virile quality, belonging to a strong character. He or she must be . . . full of self-confidence, indifferent to the effect he or she is producing, and uninfluenced by others. There must be physical attraction, but beauty is unnecessary. Conceit or self-consciousness destroys 'It' immediately."

As the "It Girl," spirited Clara—a joyful new screen type—held sway at the box office in the later 1920s. Although most of her feature films were pedestrian productions carelessly tossed together, her many fans did not mind at the time. They flocked to see pert Bow powerhouse her way through her latest celluloid showcase.

The coming of talkies was especially traumatic for Bow, who was extremely self-conscious about her heavy Brooklyn accent. While making her first sound feature (1929's *The Wild Party*) she discovered that the primitive recording equipment required actors to curtail their movements in order to be captured better by the stationary microphones. This inhibited her buoyancy and fostered her paranoia about that dreaded microphone staring so accusingly at her.

In the midst of Clara's escalating career crisis, her private life—both actual and media exaggerated—suddenly was exposed to full public scrutiny. This occurred when she initiated a lawsuit in early 1931 against her former secretary Daisy DeVoe. In retaliation, devious Daisy told the media about Bow's undisciplined and disreputable private life, which was full of lovers, gambling, and other riveting tidbits—some true, some not. The press seized upon these breathtaking disclosures and embellished them with further innuendoes and fabrications to titillate their avid readers. By the time the trial ended and Daisy was sentenced, the media extravaganza had destroyed Clara emotionally and professionally. (Also, the ongoing Depression changed the public's tastes radically. Clara's unbridled image became a stereotype from the racy past. Somber moviegoers of the early 1930s wished to forget the indulgent Roaring '20s and everything associated with it—including Clara.)

Exaggerated "tales" about fun-loving, man-hungry Clara Bow and her "scandalous" lifestyle stuck in the public's mind long after the "It Girl" and her zesty screen appearances had been relegated to America's past. This was a cruel fate that Clara did not deserve.

Clara Gordon Bow was born on July 29, 1905, in a Brooklyn tenement, the child of Robert Bow, who sometimes worked as a busboy in slum eateries, and Sarah Gordon Bow. Sarah suffered from epilepsy and depression. Before Clara was born, Sarah had lost two baby girls soon after birth, and in Sarah's twisted view of life, she almost wanted the same fate for her new child. While Sarah was pregnant with Clara, heavy-drinking Robert vanished, coming back only when he discovered that his latest offspring had somehow survived.

In subsequent years Robert drifted in and out of his family's miserable life. Unstable, ill-equipped Sarah had to support the household. In desperation, she turned to prostitution, with mother and daughter frequently moving from one squalid dwelling to another. As Clara grew, she found escape at the movies. She soon fixated on becoming a film player, convinced that she would be safe in such a fantasy world. The youngster did not share her dream with her morose mother, who thought the cinema was ungodly and feared Hollywood's evil temptations.

As Clara matured, her dad occasionally popped up in her helter-skelter existence. During one stay, he sexually molested his daughter, a situation that recurred over the years. The insecure youngster rationalized his shameful acts—as she would his financial demands in later times—because she was so anxious for his affection.

It was in 1921 that Clara begged a dollar from her father to enter a film magazine contest. To her amazement, she won a screen test in New York City. In turn, this led to her debut that year in the silent feature *Beyond the Rainbow*. When Sarah Bow discovered that Clara was partaking in the devil's work (i.e., making pictures), she became manic. One night, 16-year-old Clara awoke to find her frenzied parent holding a butcher knife over her and shouting, "You'd be better off dead than an actress!" The girl escaped her mother's fury, but the traumatic event left her with a lifelong fear of sleeping.

In 1923, Mrs. Bow's medical and mental problems accelerated. She died just before she was to be recommitted to a mental asylum. By then, Clara's film career was progressing, and she was offered a Hollywood contract. She had been hired by B. P. Schulberg, the head of Preferred Pictures, an independent film studio. He built her career by thrusting her into many features, often on loan to other companies. Filmgoers took real notice of Bow in 1925's *The Plastic Age*. By this point, Schulberg had moved over to Paramount as associate producer, and he brought Clara with him. As the lead figure in *It*, Clara rose to stardom, a status confirmed when she played the lively Red Cross worker in that year's *Wings*.

When Clara first came to Tinseltown, she lived with her agent/lover Arthur Jacobson. The relationship ended when her shiftless dad came to Hollywood and drove a wedge between the couple. While making 1926's *Mantrap*, love-hungry Clara became enamored of much-older Victor Fleming, who was directing the comedy. This upset her then lover, actor Gilbert Roland. Bow's costar in *Children of Divorce* (1927) was handsome Gary Cooper, with whom she embarked on a torrid affair. In the long run, these amorous associations fell apart because each of these men wanted Bow's exclusive attention.

In 1927, Clara became fascinated by the hunky college athletes who constituted the Trojans football squad at the University of Southern California. She was soon an avid devotee of the "Thundering Herd" and invited them to Saturday night parties at her modest Beverly Hills seven-room bungalow. At these parties, there would be plenty of food (but no liquor) served and dancing thereafter. Sometimes the gatherings would get so noisy that neighbors would call the police to quiet things down, but these parties were basically harmless fun. When Bow's meddlesome father came back into her life, Clara began hostessing these weekend events at her getaway digs at the Garden of Allah. The weekly socials ended when her dad discovered her deception. In later years, these mild diversions would transform into legendary rumors about a supposedly insatiable Clara Bow involved in sex orgies with the entire USC football squad.

Naive and unsophisticated Clara was making huge profits for Paramount. However, the studio took advantage of her by not paying her the top salary she deserved and not providing sufficient budgets to showcase her on camera in a way that would ensure her screen future. While blithely exploiting her, they were, at the same time, exasperated by her gambling sprees, her rambunctious excursions to Mexico, and her impulsive abandon, which frequently put the indiscreet star into delicate situations. Another problem for the studio was that five-foot, three-inch Bow was prone to putting on weight. However, because Bow was such a money earner, the studio dealt with these inconveniences for the time being.

Clara had an appendectomy at L.A.'s St. Vincent's Hospital in February 1928. As she recuperated, she became intrigued with handsome intern William Earl Pearson. Despite Pearson's having a wife back home in Texas, Bow allowed a romance to develop. Before long, Pearson's wife, Elizabeth, learned of the situation and announced she was divorcing him for "alienation of affections." To quash this brewing scandal, Paramount settled quietly with the woman, who changed her divorce plea to "failure to provide." The studio paid off the irate woman with $30,000 from Clara's bonus salaries (funds the company held in reserve as leverage to ensure Bow did not misbehave too badly during the term of her contract). Pearson was then shipped off to Germany, where he continued to contact Bow, but she had had enough of him by then.

While critics and the public were not too enthusiastic about Bow's speaking voice in her early talkies, her pictures still brought in patrons. While making 1929's *The Wild Party* she met former boxer-turned-stuntman Jimmy Dundee, but that affair paled in comparison to her encounter with song-and-dance man Harry Richman. A braggart and a user, Richman latched onto Bow when he came West to star in *Puttin' on the Ritz* (1930). This opportunist exploited their affair, gaining tremendous publicity in the process. The unlikely romance ended in 1930.

Clara continued turning out pictures, but talkies had robbed her of any career enthusiasm (she wanted to retire, marry, and have a family). Hard living was eroding her once-youthful look. Further wearing her down was her obsession that she would end up in an insane asylum as her mother and aunts had. Meanwhile, her inability to control her actions and what she foolishly said to the press was fast turning public sentiment against her. Because Bow's box-office impact was tapering off, Paramount no longer felt inclined to protect her image as they had in the past. One of the few bright lights in Clara's life was actor Rex Bell, who had appeared with her in *True to the Navy* (1930). He seemed genuinely interested in their future together.

One person particularly unhappy about Bow's budding romance with Bell was Kentucky-born Daisy DeVoe. She felt her special friendship with Clara was being threatened by Bell's influence. DeVoe, who had never graduated high school, had been a Paramount hairdresser when she'd first met Clara on the studio lot. They became friendly, and soon Daisy was working on all of Bow's films. As the star's best friend, she went on holiday larks with Clara and was privy to confidential information about Bow's scattershot life. Later, DeVoe became the star's secretary and did her best to get her chum's finances and lifestyle into better order. Hoping to take advantage of Clara's new buddy, Paramount's B. P. Schulberg asked DeVoe to secretly report back to him on Bow's personal activities. Daisy's refusal angered the executive.

The rivalry between DeVoe and Bell came to a head in the fall of 1930. Daisy was seeking to prevent Clara from investing in wild moneymaking schemes that well-intentioned Rex kept pushing on her. One day DeVoe overheard Bell urging Bow to dismiss Daisy. Convinced she would soon be fired, the angered DeVoe grabbed an assortment of Clara's business papers, personal correspondence, and checkbook and placed them in a bank safe-deposit box. During the next days the situation spiraled out of control, as suspicious Bell became further convinced that DeVoe was nothing but a conniver. When Daisy couldn't arrange a meeting with Clara to explain the situation, she sought help from an unsympathetic Paramount studio attorney who brushed her off with a referral to another lawyer. Because Daisy felt Clara had abandoned her, DeVoe gave her new lawyer an ultimatum to pass on to Bow and Bell: "Tell Clara she can have her papers if she's willing to pay for them. Otherwise, I'm going to turn them over to the newspapers." Daisy's price was a staggering $125,000.

The next day a repentant Daisy found Clara at home and volunteered to withdraw her blackmail demands, even asking for her old job back. By now, confused and hurt, Bow could not differentiate Daisy from others in her life who'd taken advantage of her. With Bell backing her, Bow ordered Daisy to leave; Rex phoned the police, and soon there was no turning back. Los Angeles DA Buron Fitts (in the pay of the studios) took charge of the case, and the minor matter soon escalated into an explosive court case.

On November 6, 1930, Daisy was arrested. She was interrogated nonstop for more than a day but still refused to sign a confession that she had "stolen" $35,000. She was kept in jail and not allowed to have legal representation. She grew increasingly vindictive the longer she remained behind bars. Upon release, she filed a false-arrest lawsuit, using a shady lawyer to represent her in her demands for $5,000 in damages.

Even at this juncture, Paramount could have persuaded Fitts to stop convening the grand jury to bring an indictment against Daisy. If this had happened, the subsequent courtroom airing of Bow's wild life would not have occurred. However, self-serving Schulberg felt Bow's value to the studio had so diminished that he chose to do nothing to assist her. At the hearing in late November, the grand jury brought an indictment against Daisy on more than 30 counts of grand theft.

The media and public alike could not wait for the mid-January 1931 court case to begin, sure that the proceedings would reveal much dirt about Clara. (By then, even former friendly movie fan publications were alluding to Clara's unseemly, raucous private life.) While Daisy's attorney was grandstanding the jury with florid speeches, she remained poised and confident in the courtroom. However, Clara was the direct opposite. Just as she trembled at performing in front of the soundstage microphone, here she had to be on inspection and answer questions in front of a mob. It robbed her of whatever confidence she had.

When DeVoe came to the witness stand she did her best to distract everyone from the charges of theft and extortion leveled against her. She craftily added into her testimony derogatory statements about the star ("Miss Bow was drunk") and fabricated Clara's supposed threatening remarks ("If I had gotten into any argument with her she would have tried to kill me"). Daisy also worked into her testimony descriptions of Bow's excessive gambling binges (which DeVoe was forced to retract partially under cross-examination), and she listed the expensive tokens of affection Clara had given several of her men. DeVoe also detailed that she had helped Clara destroy old love notes from Gary Cooper and Victor Fleming, but she brought forth an assortment of Bow's messages to other men (the intern from Texas, Harry Richman, and Rex Bell) to provide "insight" into Clara's reckless, amorous nature. The cumulative effect of this "evidence" suggested that Bow was indeed a loose woman who had had several sex partners—sometimes in the same time span.

Adding further insult to injury, the defendant insisted that Clara had kept evidence of Mr. Bow's misconduct during the time he handled her finances. DeVoe claimed that Bow retained the data to use as leverage against him if the need arose. (This made the movie star seem disloyal to her own parent, even though, if all the facts were known, she had a full right to do so.) Despite these gross breaches of faith from her best friend, Clara never dreamed of besmirching DeVoe's reputation in court. She actually had plenty of ammunition: Daisy's dad was a jailed bootlegger; Daisy was then living with China-born cinematographer James Wong Howe. (An interracial relationship in those bigoted times would have discredited DeVoe with jurors.)

When a trembling Clara took the stand, her nervousness, combined with her Brooklyn accent and unrefined vocabulary—especially in contrast to Daisy's demeanor—made Bow the subject of courtroom laughter. Humiliated, the highly distraught star started crying. "I can't help it," she told the court. She wailed at how "my friend . . . my best friend in the world" could be doing this to her. Failing to regain control, the near-hysterical Clara kept apologizing for her crying jag and had to be led from the courtroom by Rex. (Later, an unremorseful Daisy snapped to the press about Clara, "She staged the fireworks, only because she's got to be the main drag. This is my trial, but she had to be the center of it just the same.")

By January 23, the jury reached its verdict. Daisy was found guilty of one charge of grand theft: a check for $800 that Clara claimed she had signed upon DeVoe's telling her it was for income tax, when Daisy had actually used it to purchase a fur coat. However, on the other 34 charges, DeVoe was found innocent. Later, the defendant was sentenced to 18 months in jail. (Ironically, good-hearted Clara felt sorry for Daisy and had written a letter to the judge pleading for him to be lenient in the sentencing. However, devious Buron Fitts, wanting to salvage a fuller victory from this embarrassing court case, did not pass on Bow's note to Judge Doran.)

So ended this case which the presiding judge labeled a "mud-slinging carnival" and one in which the average person would have difficulty determining "just who was on trial." Interestingly, DeVoe had been punished arbitrarily. Because the jury was in a state of indecision about Daisy's alleged wrongdoings amidst the jumbled testimony and confused bookkeeping, they arbitrarily picked one count. This was to pacify those jurors who thought DeVoe must have been guilty of at least one charge.

The real loser in this case, however, was Bow. Not only had her fans rudely scoffed at her in court, but the filmgoing public also had rejected her at the box office. During the much-publicized trial, her latest movie (*No Limit*) had opened to bad business. Already at the studio, features that had been planned as Bow vehicles were being refitted for other stars.

In the wake of the court trial and the complete loss of both studio and public confidence, exhausted Clara suffered a nervous break-down. She and the studio ended their pact. By the end of 1931, she and Rex Bell were married. The couple would have two sons. Bow made only two more features: *Call Her Savage* (1932) and *Hoopla* (1933), filmed at Fox. Clara's emotional problems accelerated over the years, leading to her and Bell eventually living separate lives. She spent her final years in near seclusion in Culver City, California. She died on September 27, 1965, never quite understanding how her wonderful dreams from childhood had gone so far amiss.

Jean Harlow and Paul Bern: A Deadly Marriage

"All I want is to be able to sit at Paul's feet and have him educate me."
—ACTRESS JEAN HARLOW, IN THE SUMMER OF 1932

In more recent times, the tragic chronicle of sex symbol Marilyn Monroe grabbed the public's interest. Many fans found it ironic that this beautiful screen goddess never enjoyed substantial roman-tic happiness during her trouble-plagued life. Earlier, the same fate befell another platinum blond bombshell, Jean Harlow.

In Jean's short life, she gained screen fame not only for her curvaceous figure and striking hair color but also for her sassy personality. She admitted readily, "I was not a born actress. . . . I have had to work hard, listen carefully, do things over and over and then over again in order to bring it out." She observed wisely of her cinema alter ego: "Men like me because I don't wear a brassiere. Women like me because I don't look like a girl who would steal a husband. At least not for long."

Besides her sharp comedic talent, Harlow had a knack for handling more serious screen moments. However, it was the unseemly drama in Jean's shocking private life that made her legendary, even before her untimely death in 1937 at age 26.

Harlow endured a disastrous marital record: she divorced two of her three spouses, and her second husband, MGM executive Paul Bern, died under mysterious circumstances in 1932, which placed his complex private life under intense scrutiny. Some observers at the time, and later, insisted that the claimed suicide was actually murder. In either case, the facts surrounding this explosive situation included one of Hollywood's most audacious cover-ups. When Bern died, personnel from the all-powerful MGM studio hastened to the Bern-Harlow home and boldly tampered with key evidence before belatedly summoning the subservient Los Angeles police. The film factory representatives also rearranged the chronology of "facts" and the "testimony" of crucial witnesses to protect their substantial investment in Harlow's movie career. With the facts surrounding Bern's death muddled, the deceased became a weird, much-discussed footnote in the history of Tinseltown.

Jean was born Harlean Harlow Carpenter on March 3, 1911, in Kansas City, Missouri. She was called "the Baby," a nickname that stuck with her for life. Her adoring father, Mont Clair Carpenter, was a prominent dentist, and her mother, Jean Harlow, was a homemaker. The latter detested being subordinated to the men in her life, which included her overbearing father, Skip Harlow, a thriving real estate broker. In 1922, Mont and Jean Carpenter divorced. The next year, Jean and her daughter moved to Hollywood, hoping to get lucky in pictures. After two frustrating years, they reluctantly returned to the Midwest because Skip Harlow had ordered that his granddaughter be returned to Kansas City or he would disinherit Jean.

Pampered Harlean attended private schools and led a privileged, refined life. By then, the divorced Jean had met Marino Bello, a dapper, married schemer who charmed his way into Mrs. Carpenter's life. While Harlean barely tolerated this slick immigrant, Skip Harlow abhorred him. However, he preferred that his willful daughter marry the conniving Bello than continue her tawdry affair with him. After Marino's first spouse filed for divorce, Jean wed him in early 1927.

While her mother was being romanced by Bello, Harlean attended a private girls' academy in Lake Forest, Illinois. By then the five-foot, two-inch student was stunning. On a blind date, she met Charles Fremont McGrew II, 20, the scion of a well-to-do family. For the bored girl, marriage to this playboy appeared a reasonable alternative to her humdrum academic life. Besides, it would give her freedom from her overly possessive relatives. Chuck and 16-year-old Harlean eloped to Waukegan, Illinois, in September 1927.

A few months later, the groom came into a portion of his inheritance. The newlyweds departed for L.A. and bought a Beverly Hills home. To the couple's regret, grasping Mama Jean and Marino soon moved to the West Coast to share in Harlean's affluent lifestyle.

As a young socialite, bright but unambitious Harlean was content with life. However, fate intervened. Through a movie-happy girlfriend, she was introduced to executives at Fox Films. Later, Harlean's pals wagered that she would be too shy to follow up on that studio's suggestion that she try movie acting. To prove them wrong, she registered at Central Casting (utilizing her mother's maiden name of Jean Harlow). As such, she made her movie debut in a bit part in 1928. Sensing an opportunity at hand, Mama Jean and Marino persuaded the young woman to seek a screen career. Jean soon was appearing in brief parts at Paramount and other studios. She was relieved to learn, in the spring of 1929, that she was pregnant. This would allow her to abandon acting. But Mrs. Bello insisted she have an abortion, which

Marino arranged. That June, the young performer suffered another loss. She and Chuck separated, and in 1930 they divorced. He could no longer cope with his meddling in-laws.

Having to support her household, Jean became more serious about her career. A brief role in Clara Bow's *The Saturday Night Kid* (1929) led to Harlow's gaining a lead in Howard Hughes's *Hell's Angels* (1930). In this World War I airplane epic, Jean looked stunning but was unconvincing as a refined British lady. Critics carped about her histrionics, but on a visceral level she registered strongly as the sexual predator.

Although Hughes had her under contract, he had no properties lined up for her and loaned her to other studios. Meanwhile, fed up with being under the thumb of Jean and Marino, she found escape in unrealistic love affairs, first with an L.A. stockbroker, then with New Jersey gangster Abner "Longy" Zwillman, whom she had met through Bello. The homely Longy became obsessed with Jean, lavishing gifts on her, including paying for a fancier L.A. home for Jean and her family.

If Jean was amused by Zwillman's mob world, she was more intrigued with MGM executive Paul Bern, who had been taking a strong interest in her career. He had arranged for her to first come to MGM on loanout, which he did again for *Beast of the City* (1932). Thereafter, Bern exerted his influence to get the studio to buy Jean's contract from Hughes. The deal was made, and, at $1,250 weekly, Harlow began her seven-year contract at MGM in April 1932.

Born in Germany, Paul Levy was nine years old when he arrived in New York in 1898 with his parents and eight siblings. The youth aspired to study psychiatry, but his father's death in 1908 ended those costly dreams. He supported his family as an office stenographer and later enrolled at the American Academy of Dramatic Arts, graduating in 1911. By then he'd adopted the less-ethnic stage name of Paul Bern. A jack-of-all-trades, he acted and stage managed in stock, wrote scripts for the silent screen, and managed a Manhattan film theater. His mother committed suicide in the fall of 1920. (He was so shamed by her deranged act that he often told others that her death was accidental. For the rest of his life, he feared that he had inherited her genes of mental instability.) Thereafter, Bern went to Hollywood. He readily found work at various studios. In 1928, he joined MGM as assistant to second-in-command Irving Thalberg.

Over these years, slightly built, short, and plain-looking Bern became infatuated with several screen beauties including resilient Joan Crawford and the tragic Barbara La Marr (who died from drug addiction in 1926). However, none of these passions led to any substantial romances. It was rumored that highly cultured Paul had several major problems courting women. It was said he had an undersized penis and/or was impotent. Another obstacle was his strong mood swings from optimism to melancholia. While generally chivalrous toward women, he also had a detached fascination with sex that led him into dark fantasies that he barely kept reined in. (Some sources have cited Bern as being a latent homosexual who occasionally had a gay affair.) With such a catalog of romantic shortcomings, it was little wonder that Tinseltown women much preferred Bern as a wise and overly solicitous friend than as a prospective love mate.

By May 1932, Jean was filming *Red-Headed Woman* (1932) and was being squired about town by Bern. Paul told associates he planned to marry Jean. His friends were amazed that gorgeous Harlow would marry this physically unprepossessing man who was 22 years her elder. It was assumed that she was playing the Hollywood game of wedding an industry mover to ensure her career. Even Mama Jean worried about her daughter linking with this strange man. However, she feared if she voiced her objections too strongly her daughter would want to marry him all the more. As for Harlow's former boyfriend Longy Zwillman, he confronted Jean and told her that Bern was reputed to be homosexual. None of these warnings changed the performer's mind.

On Saturday, July 2, 1932, the couple wed in a small ceremony at the Berns' home in Beverly Hills. To Jean's bewilderment, they did not consummate their marriage that night. Jean simply accepted this as another sign of Paul's tremendous respect for her.

She believed Paul's reasoning: "Sex is not the most important thing in our lives. We'll have a long life together and a long marriage." At the Sunday wedding reception at the Bellos', the bride seemed happy.

During the summer of 1932 there were delays on Jean's next MGM picture, *Red Dust*. On the social scene, Harlow confided to friends: "All I want is to be able to sit at Paul's feet and have him educate me." He did just that. He also attempted to wean her away from the negative influences of her mother and stepfather. Failing in this regard, Bern became angry when his wife mentioned she wanted to invest in Marino's gold mine scheme or that she'd like to give their Easton Drive home to her family so she and Paul could move closer to civilization.

During these early months of marriage Bern sank into another of his depressions. It was so prolonged that he consulted physicians about his impotence, began drinking heavily, and purchased a gun. Meanwhile, Jean seemed buoyant, even hoping to adopt a child.

By August, Jean was costarring in *Red Dust* with Clark Gable. The filming of this drama on the soundstages and back lot was difficult, but she remained in good spirits. At month's end, the Berns attended a small dinner party given by industry friends. During the evening, the host accidentally picked up Paul's coat and discovered it contained a pistol. Bern said offhandedly, "I intend to use it someday." (No one took him seriously.) The next day, Paul underwent a physical exam at the studio regarding an $85,000 life insurance policy he'd just bought.

On Friday and Saturday (September 2–3) while Jean was shooting *Red Dust*, Paul was developing *China Seas*, an upcoming Harlow vehicle. On Saturday night, because Harlow was delayed at the studio, Bern canceled plans for them to attend a celebrity party. Instead, Paul dined at a bungalow at the Ambassador Hotel with married MGM producer Bernard Hyman and his mistress, actress Barbara Barondess. Bern then went home and retired to bed to read. Harlow stayed at her mother's house that evening because it was closer to the studio where she had to return in the morning.

While Paul worked at home on Sunday, Jean went to MGM and then eventually back to her own house. She'd promised to stay with Mama Jean again that night, since Marino had planned a weekend holiday with Clark Gable.

When Jean talked with Paul at home on Sunday evening, she tried to convince him to come to her parents' for dinner. He refused, because he thought so poorly of the Bellos. When she suggested she'd stay home, he reportedly insisted that she go as planned.

The next morning, Labor Day, the Berns' cook and butler arrived at 11:30 to find Bern's nude body in a "puddle of blood" sprawled out in front of the dressing room mirror. Soon thereafter, the Berns' gardener, learning of the situation, phoned the Bello home where Mama Jean was told the bad news. In turn, she contacted Louis B. Mayer, head of MGM, without, allegedly, telling Jean of her husband's passing. The mogul immediately ordered Whitey Hendry (studio police chief) and Howard Strickling (in charge of MGM's publicity department) to the Culver City lot, along with Virgil Apger, a company still photographer. Hendry and Apger later went to the death scene, where the latter took shots of the death scene for future reference.

Strickling was supposedly the next to arrive at 9820 Easton Drive, and he spotted the deceased's guest book laying on a table. Flipping through the pages, Howard read a puzzling entry:

Dearest dear,

Unfortunately, this is the only way to make good the frightful wrong I have done you and to wipe out my abject humiliation.

I love you. Paul

You understand last night was only a comedy.

When Mayer appeared at the Berns', Strickling prevented him from removing the guest book, suggesting that without it authorities might think—even briefly—that Jean had killed her husband. The mogul agreed with this reasoning. Still later, MGM's Irving Thalberg came onto the scene. It was not until 2:15 P.M. that the police were finally alerted to the death; 15 minutes later, L.A. police detectives arrived. They discovered a revolver (a .38, which had been fired) in the dead man's right hand. Another .38 (which had not been fired) was found on a nearby table, next to the guest book. Some minutes later, Thalberg went to the Bellos' to tell Jean of her husband's death. Later, a hysterical Harlow had to be sedated by her physician. News of Bern's curious death was soon reported in the press.

The next day the MGM powers concluded that Mama Jean's refusal to allow the police to question the distressed movie star would look bad to the public, who, at the moment, were blaming Jean for being responsible somehow for her husband's killing himself. Thus, later that Tuesday, law enforcers were permitted to talk with Harlow. She insisted, "There was nothing between us that would have caused him to do this." Louis B. Mayer was on hand and, later, conferred with Harlow upstairs. Insisting that the screen sex siren must gain public sympathy in this tragedy, he told her to tell authorities about the sexual problems in her marriage. She refused and purportedly attempted to throw herself over the balcony but was saved by her studio boss.

On September 7, MGM asked Tallulah Bankhead to replace the still inconsolable Harlow in *Red Dust*. She refused. By then, Bern's brother, Henry, had arrived in L.A. Angered by rumors about his sibling's supposed sexual inadequacies, he insisted that he had access to a woman (whom he identified later) who could prove this gossip to be wrong. On the 8th, at the coroner's inquest, the jury reached a verdict that Paul's death was a suicide from an undetermined motive.

While this ostensibly ended the much-headlined case, it was really only the start.

As it developed, the woman Henry Bern was referring to was born in 1894 in Ohio as Dorothy Roddy. She had married a reporter in 1907. Her husband later moved out West, while she went to New York to be an actress, using the stage name of Dorothy Millette. She met Paul Bern while they were at the American Academy of

Dramatic Arts. They began a relationship that continued as they moved about the East Coast and Canada. When they took up residence at Manhattan's Algonquin Hotel, they registered as Mr. and Mrs. Bern. Under New York law, such acts transformed the non-Jewish Dorothy into Paul's common-law spouse. Meanwhile, Bern's mother, who always wanted to be the only woman in her son's life, learned of her "rival." That is when she committed suicide. Not long afterward, the guilt-ridden Dorothy was institutionalized for an emotional breakdown. While she was at a Connecticut facility, Bern moved to L.A., keeping information about Dorothy hidden from most of his new associates and friends. Those who did hear about Millette (which reputedly included Jean) had no idea of the full, tangled story.

Months later, when Dorothy had recovered to a degree, she returned to Manhattan where she again lived at the Algonquin. Bern provided a monthly stipend and occasionally sent her written notes. Even less often, he visited when he returned to New York on business. In the spring of 1932 she moved to San Francisco to be near to her sister (and perhaps to be closer to Paul and confront him about his break of faith by marrying Harlow). She spent the next months living in seclusion at a hotel in the Golden Gate City. After Bern's body was found and the death reported by the media, she vanished. A week later, her body was found in the Sacramento River; she had apparently jumped from a ferry. Meanwhile, on September 9, a funeral was conducted for Bern at Inglewood Park Cemetery in L.A., with Harlow sobbing throughout the service. Thereafter, the deceased was cremated. On Monday, September 12, Harlow returned to the *Red Dust* set, the studio having decided that public sentiment had turned in her favor and that she should continue in the assignment.

Putting aside wild conjectures published over the years about this lurid case, gradually new facts emerged (as can best be determined after the studio's intricate cover-up). Millette had come to Los Angeles the night before Labor Day to confront Bern about his marriage to Jean. Purportedly, Harlow had been at the house during the evening and had encountered Dorothy arguing with Paul. Both women left the house that night. The next morning, after Jean went back to the Easton Drive house from her mother's, Bern had shot himself. Allegedly, Harlow then phoned MGM's Strickling and then returned to Mama Jean's so she could be distanced from the scandal (and later pretend to first learn of her spouse's death from Thalberg). Under this scenario, Bern's puzzling death note actually was an apology that was to accompany flowers to Jean at her studio dressing room. As for Millette's drowning, it was theorized that she killed herself due to her guilt that had accumulated since Paul's mother's suicide in New York.

At the time, with the deceptions created by MGM working at cross-purposes to the lax L.A. police and with witnesses skewing their testimony to protect themselves and/or follow a studio-ordained script, it would have been nearly impossible to unravel the "real" facts. Only revelations years later by interested parties allowed for a revised hypothesis of the troubling case.

As for Harlow, she married MGM cinematographer Hal Rosson in September 1933 but divorced him in 1935. She later became romantically involved with MGM star William Powell. When she died of uremic poisoning in June 1937, speculation arose over those ultimately responsible for her lack of lifesaving medical attention. It made "the Baby" the center of yet another supposed studio-engineered conspiracy concerning the true facts about her passing.

With such ongoing controversy concerning Harlow's relatively brief life and career, little wonder that this vibrant screen talent became such an enduring but infamous Hollywood legend.

Thelma Todd: The Tragic Ice Cream Blonde

Thelma Todd: "You'll open a gambling casino in my restaurant over my dead body!"
Lucky Luciano: "That can be arranged."
—A CONVERSATION AT THE BEVERLY HLLLS BROWN DERBY
RESTAURANT IN THE FALL OF 1935

Everyone enjoys a good mystery, and nothing makes a crime story more intriguing in the retelling than a case involving a celebrity that has baffled authorities for decades. Like the puzzling 1922 murder of movie director William Desmond Taylor and the 1962 "suicide" of cinema sex siren Marilyn Monroe, the demise of actress Thelma Todd (once publicized by her studio as the luscious ice cream blonde) remains a Hollywood bafflement. Although ruled an accidental death from carbon monoxide poisoning, the true facts in this sensational case remain unresolved to this day.

Back in 1935, when Los Angeles district attorney Buron Fitts formally closed the Todd case, many in the Hollywood establishment were greatly relieved. After all, on the same day (December 16, 1935) that Todd's body was found in her garage in Pacific Palisades, film choreographer/stager Busby Berkeley was going on trial for three counts of vehicular manslaughter. Tinseltown executives as well as the film industry's self-censorship board worried that having yet another ongoing scandal—such as the Todd case—in the world's news could have devastating repercussions for the film industry. With Thelma's death ruled accidental, there was one less embarrassing situation about which to worry.

In the 1930s, due to corrupt L.A. civic and police officials, many unpleasant episodes involving movie colony personalities were swept under the carpet. After all, in a city whose chief industry was creating believable illusions on the screen, it was not that difficult for powerful studio officials to restructure shocking and shameful incidents into fabricated, more palatable scenarios for public consumption.

As the *Hollywood Citizen News* editorialized in October 1936: "The real and underlying causes of death of many well known Hollywood figures, past and present, will never be known because of cover ups by an oligarchical community, police and citizens alike, protecting its own and the millions of dollars in revenue such causes of death, if they were really known by the public, could be harmed. . . ."

Thelma Ann Todd was born on July 29, 1905, in Lawrence, Massachusetts, the first of two children of John and Alice (Edwards)

Todd. Thelma's father had progressed through the ranks of the police force and was in politics. Because the aloof Mr. Todd was so preoccupied with getting ahead, Thelma's frustrated mother channeled all her energies to daughter Thelma and her five-year-younger child, William. As a youngster, tomboy Thelma had a fascination with her dad's police revolver. Often she snuck the gun out of her parents' bedroom to play cops and robbers with friends. One day, during such a game, the gun discharged, blasting a hole in the living room ceiling. Receiving little rebuke from her mother, the youngster even "packed" the gun into her high school to impress classmates (who were unaware that the firearm was actually loaded!).

By the time Thelma was 10 her father had become director of pubic health and welfare for Massachusetts, a post that kept him even more away from his family. Thelma was developing into a pretty young lady. A shapely teen, she wore provocative outfits and found more pleasure in teasing her admirers than in spending quality time with them. But there was also a serious side to Thelma. In 1923, she enrolled at the Lowell State Normal School, planning to become a teacher. In 1925, the Todds' son was killed in an accident. Engulfed by the family tragedy, Thelma dreamed of moving away, somehow, from her oppressive home life.

Fate intervened when a local boy submitted Thelma's high school picture to a statewide beauty contest and she won. This led to a talent scout from Famous Players-Lasky (Paramount) inviting Todd to screen test for the studio's inaugural class at its new film school. She passed the audition and became one of the 16 enrollees, on condition that she lose 10 pounds before arriving at the facility in Astoria, New York, where the studio shot some of its films.

During her training program Thelma fell in love with a classmate (Robert Andrews), but the studio squashed the romance fearing gossip might taint its new school. This show of authority led always-rebellious Thelma to gain her revenge, by being extra sexy around studio executives. (It was this devil-may-care aspect of her nature that led to her nickname, "Hot Toddy.") With her class-mates Thelma made her screen debut in the 1926 silent feature *Fascinating Youth.*

Initially Mrs. Todd had been thrilled by her daughter's career opportunities. However, she had second thoughts when she saw a publicity pose of her five-foot, four-inch girl in a flimsy costume. Alice Todd rushed to New York to voice her strong moral disapproval to studio executives. Already exhausted by defiant Thelma, Paramount gave the contractee an ultimatum: relocate immediately to Paramount's Hollywood studio or go home. Todd went West.

Under a five-year, $75-per-week Paramount contract, Thelma made features on the home lot and on loanout, and she made the transition to sound pictures easily. However, Paramount discharged her in 1929. Comedy maestro Hal Roach offered her a new movie deal that would allow her to freelance as well. Mrs. Todd, widowed since 1925, was in Hollywood on one of her frequent visits and urged her daughter to accept the pact. Thelma agreed reluctantly because the agreement required that (1) she must bleach her hair platinum blond, and (2) she must abide by a "potato" clause. The latter meant she was being contracted at a particular body weight, and if she gained more than five pounds, it was grounds for instant dismissal. Before reporting to the Roach lot for her first assignment, her mother supervised the bleaching of Thelma's hair and guided her daughter through a stringent diet.

Thelma bounced back and forth between comedy shorts and occasional features. Always up for partying when not on the sound-stages, Todd found it difficult to avoid liquor and food, both of which were fattening. Friends on the Hal Roach lot introduced her to diet pills, and she soon became hooked on the tablets.

Restless with her life and career, Todd was more than pleased when producer/director Roland West showed a strong interest in her, even though the unattractive man was 20 years her senior and married to silent screen actress Jewel Carmen. They began a romance, with West promising her a lead role in Howard Hughes's *Hell's Angels* (1930), but that role went to Jean Harlow instead.

To make amends to his mistress, West cast Thelma as the leading lady in *Corsair* (1931), a picture he was producing/directing for United Artists. When released, *Corsair* was a misfire. Still engulfed in pills and booze, Thelma returned to her heavy work schedule. Although Todd was no longer romantically drawn to West, they remained friends. By then he had lost interest in moviemaking and suggested they open a restaurant catering to the film colony. She promised to consider the venture.

Meanwhile, Thelma crossed paths with Pasquale DiCicco, a handsome New York playboy who associated with East Coast gangsters for the thrill of it. The suave Pat, new to Hollywood, promoted himself as a talent agent/manager and began networking on the chic restaurant and nightclub circuit. The industry's rich and powerful knew he associated with mob boss Lucky Luciano back in Manhattan, making him intriguing to them. Todd also was amused by Pat and thought associating with him gave her life a touch of welcome danger.

The whirlwind Todd-DiCicco romance progressed, despite his temper and penchant for beating her, and the couple eloped on July 10, 1932, to Prescott, Arizona. However, marital problems quickly occurred as DiCicco refused to be domesticated and often left his wife alone at their Brentwood home while he was out on the town. To blot out her frustration, she increasingly relied on liquor and diet pills. Todd also turned back to West, who was now "permanently" separated from his wife. During this time, one night when they were out clubbing, DiCicco introduced Thelma to Lucky Luciano. Thelma was thrilled to be in the presence of this renowned criminal, although Pat was upset to observe the gangster's strong interest in Todd.

By 1933, Pat was frequently away on business in New York while Thelma was churning out films, including her new comedy shorts series with Patsy Kelly. Reportedly, she and Luciano were seeing a good deal of each other. By February 1934 Thelma filed for divorce, labeling her spouse rude and quarrelsome. That August her prior plans with Roland West to open a restaurant at the beach came to fruition. With funding from Roland's spouse, supervision by West himself, and Thelma's name to lure in the film crowd, Thelma Todd's Sidewalk Café opened.

Located at 17535 Roosevelt Highway (today's Pacific Coast Highway), the establishment occupied the ground floor along with a drugstore. On the second level were a bar/lounge (also used as West's business office) as well as two apartments, in one of which West and Todd lived "separately." Nearby, at 17531 Posetano Road, was the big house where Roland's wife, Carmen, sometimes lived, along with her brother (the café's business manager) and his wife. Thelma stored her car in one of the garages of the Posetano Road house. To reach the garage required a climb of 270 cement steps behind the restaurant.

In mid-1935, 35-year-old Thelma was spending much of her spare time operating the restaurant. She was still on her diet of liquor and pills. Her hectic life was further complicated by a rash of threatening letters demanding a sizable blackmail fee (which proved to be the work of a deranged stalker back in New York). More disconcerting was the pressure she was receiving from Lucky Luciano to turn over the café's third-story storage room (used unofficially for wealthy customers to gamble) to the hoodlum. Todd kept refusing Luciano's request, and he had become violent with her. In late November during one of their dinners at the Beverly Hills Brown Derby she had threatened to take her plight to the L.A. district attorney (not knowing that Buron Fitts was already a mob pawn). In response, the sinister Luciano obliquely threatened her life. (Luciano's representatives had also been pressuring West to accede to the gambling takeover. In turn, Roland, bewildered as to how to handle the situation and by his own downward spiraling life, had been urging Todd to buy out his interest in the café.)

Thelma arranged an appointment with Fitts's office for December 17, 1935. To spite Luciano she began converting the third-story café space into a steakhouse. Meanwhile, Pat DiCicco turned up one day to suggest that he wanted to manage the restaurant. Todd wondered if this was his way of getting back into her life or if he was on a mission from Luciano.

A few years earlier Thelma had made a movie with Stanley Lupino, the English stage comedian and father of Hollywood actress Ida Lupino. Stanley and his wife were in town, and Ida was hosting a small dinner party for him in honor of his friend Thelma at the Café Trocadero in Hollywood on Saturday, December 14. When Todd informed West (who was not invited) of the engagement, he was angry that she would be out gallivanting on what would be a busy evening at the restaurant. A few days before the festivities, DiCicco encountered Ida Lupino at the Trocadero, which prompted an invitation for the fete. Later, Ida informed Thelma that she had invited Pat.

On the afternoon of December 14, Thelma and her mother went out holiday shopping, driven by chauffeur Ernest Peters. Later she returned home to change while her parent did further errands. At 7:30 P.M. Peters, with Mrs. Todd, picked up Thelma. The actress was a wearing a blue satin evening gown with lace and sequins, expensive jewelry, and a luxurious mink coat. Before leaving, she and Roland had had another of their arguments, he threatening to lock her out of the apartment if she were not home by 2:00 A.M. She refused to be intimidated and departed. After dropping Thelma at the Trocadero, Peters took Mrs. Todd home and then made himself available to drive Todd back to her residence after the party.

The Lupino gathering was a great success, except that Pat did not arrive as planned. Later that evening, he showed up in the Trocadero escorting actress Margaret Lindsay. (Some later surmised that this snub was his way of spiting his ex-wife.) At the dinner, Thelma told Ida that she was in love with a man from San Francisco but refused to go into details. At one point in the evening, Todd left the group to make a phone call and use the powder room. When she returned, she seemed unexplainably moody. Around 1:15 A.M. DiCicco and Lindsay left without bidding good night to the Lupino gathering. (About an hour before Pat's departure, he made a mysterious phone call at the club that left him jittery, but he refused to comment on it.)

While Thelma waited for her summoned chauffeur to arrive, she asked industry friend Sid Grauman to call West and say she was on her way home. Sid made the call, telling West that Todd should be back at the Pacific Palisades apartment after 2:30 A.M. It was not until after 3:00 in the morning that Thelma actually left the establishment. The car reached its destination about 3:30 A.M. As usual, Peters offered to escort Todd to her door, but she said it wasn't necessary. Wrapping her coat closely around her on the cold, windy night, she headed off into the dark.

That is the last that anyone officially saw Thelma Todd alive.

One version has Thelma going up to the second-floor apartment entrance only to find it locked as West had threatened. The two supposedly argued loudly through the door. Then, in a snit, the somewhat drunk woman climbed the many stairs to the garage preparing to drive off in her 12-cylinder Lincoln convertible touring car to another party. There she fell asleep at the steering wheel as the motor ran. Another premise suggests that the angered Roland may have followed his beloved to the garage. While she was warming up the car, he closed the garage door (possibly locking it). Either thinking this confinement would be sufficient punishment for his errant love *or* deliberately intending that she should be overwhelmed by the car's carbon monoxide fumes, he retired to bed.

An alternative hypothesis, one chosen by the coroner's investigation, was that, in her drunken stupor, Thelma had gone to the car to sleep until West let her in. She turned on the motor to keep warm and then fell asleep. As a result, she was asphyxiated by the noxious fumes. (This still left unexplained why, when the corpse was discovered, the ignition key was turned on, but the motor was off and there were two gallons of gas in the tank.) The conclusion that Todd died accidentally countered initial lurid media rumors that the cinema performer had committed suicide.

A more dramatic interpretation suggests Luciano was waiting in a car down the street from the café that evening. When Thelma returned home, he'd ordered her into his vehicle. Needing to find out what she had already told the DA about his demands for the café's casino concession, as well as anything about other illegal matters she might have overheard him discuss, he had his driver take them up the coast toward Santa Barbara. Along the way, they stopped to have drinks from the liquor cache in his trunk. The next morning they continued talking as they drove in downtown L.A. Later in the day, it is conjectured that the strange couple was in Beverly Hills, where they dined that evening with an associate of the gangster. Thereafter, in the early hours of Monday, December 16, the mobster dropped Todd at her Pacific Palisades home. As Thelma walked to her garage, Luciano's hired killer emerged from the shadows, choked and slugged her, and put her in the car. The hit man then turned on the car ignition, closed the wooden garage door, and let the carbon monoxide fumes snuff out her life.

What is next known is that after 10:00 A.M. on Monday, December 16, Thelma's maid, Mae Whitehead, discovered Todd's body (still wearing Saturday night's outfit) in the garage. The police were called, and there followed the law's fumbling (or cover-up) of the crime scene. How bloodied and battered Thelma's corpse actually was depended on whether the coroner's report, the court inquests, or contemporary newspaper accounts were to be taken as gospel.

In the subsequent coroner's examination and later grand jury investigation, there were many conflicting statements and conjectures by witnesses and contradictory "facts" presented that, if fully examined, defy logic. Although the confused (or devious?) authorities eventually concluded that Thelma had expired on Sunday around 5:00 P.M., several witnesses insisted that they had seen the star driving in a car in L.A. with a swarthy stranger or that they had talked with the victim on the phone during that fateful day. (Some sources insist such startling testimony confirmed the Luciano murder theory; others conjecture that the auto companion with Todd could have even been Pat DiCicco.)

As the slipshod investigation proceeded, some nervous witnesses claimed to have received ominous threats and, in turn, recanted part or all of their original statements. In another peculiar twist, when Thelma's mother first reached the death scene, she maintained that someone had murdered her offspring. (At a later time she insisted her daughter had died accidentally, but still later in life she indicated that some unstated, terrifying person was responsible for Thelma's murder.) When Mrs. Todd was told that Thelma had supposedly climbed the many steps to reach the garage, she responded that her daughter had a heart condition and never would undertake such a strenuous hike. (The unreliable report from the coroner, however, stated that there was nothing wrong with the deceased's heart organ.)

Investigators on the scene re-created the "accident" by retracing the victim's supposed climb to the garage. They noted that a woman could *not* have made the trek without badly scuffing her shoes. (Thelma's slippers were unscuffed.) While a result of carbon monoxide poisoning could cause traces of blood to collect around the deceased's upper lip, more blood was found on and about Todd's body than should have been there. Then too, at one point, the maid insisted to authorities that the body was not in the same position when found by the police as when she had earlier discovered the corpse.

Throughout the investigation, the distraught Roland West was a model of contradictions, changing to one degree or another the facts of his activities on that crucial weekend. Moreover, several times on that telltale Sunday people had called or come by the café asking for Thelma, and he had replied that she might be with her mother. This was untypical of the controlling man who always wanted to know everything about Thelma. Later, some sources who have studied this complex case point to the fact that West had close ties to industry mogul Joseph M. Schenck and that the latter may have used his major clout to help his friend avoid being charged with Thelma's homicide.

What *is* known is that Roland West never directed another film in his remaining years. He and Jewel Carmen divorced soon after Thelma's passing. Later he sold the café, and by 1950 he had suffered a debilitating stroke and endured a nervous breakdown. On his deathbed in March 1952, he confessed to actor Chester Morris that he was responsible (directly or indirectly) for Todd's passing. He provided an assortment of frenzied recitations to explain his part in her demise, a tragedy that hounded him to the end.

As for Todd, her body was cremated and her mother took her ashes back to Lawrence, Massachusetts. When Mrs. Todd passed away at 92, she had Thelma's urn placed in her own coffin and buried with her. Thus, even in death, Thelma could not escape her demanding mother. Nor could the beloved movie comedian find peace from all the inquisitive individuals who, over the many years, have sought to solve the mystery surrounding Hollywood's legendary ice cream blonde.

Loretta Young and Clark Gable: The Baby That "Wasn't"

"When I see his humor and warmth on screen, I think, 'Gee, I would like to have known that man.'"

—JUDY LEWIS, DAUGHTER OF LORETTA YOUNG AND
CLARK GABLE, IN 2003

Elizabeth Taylor said of her MGM teammate Clark Gable: "He was the epitome of the movie star—so romantic, such bearing, such friendliness." Director John Huston observed of "the King": "Clark Gable was the only real he-man I've ever known, of all the actors I've met."

Despite his enormous success over several decades of filmmaking, Oscar-winning Gable was modest about his global popularity. "All this 'King' stuff is pure bulls***. I eat and sleep and go to the bathroom just like anyone else." As to his acting acumen, he noted, "I worked like a son of a bitch to learn a few tricks and I fight like a steer to avoid getting stuck with parts I can't play." Clark insisted, "The only reason they come to see me is that I know that life is great—and they know I know it."

If Gable was straightforward, such was not the case with his occasional cinema costar, Loretta Young, also an Oscar winner. This amazingly beautiful leading lady, who enjoyed a lengthy tenure in films and on TV, was a far more complex personality. She was deeply ambitious: "If you want a place in the sun you have to expect a few blisters." Yet she shrewdly hid her pushiness in the prefeminist age under a veil of gentility and decorum. To sustain her manufactured public image, she created rigid rules of proper conduct (on the surface), and to her, they were everything: "Wearing the correct dress for any occasion is a matter of good manners." She was also an extremely devout Catholic and constantly proselytized her religious beliefs.

On the other hand, Young's commanding public persona did not appeal to everyone. Screen siren Marlene Dietrich noted wryly, "Every time she 'sins,' she builds a church. That's why there are so many Catholic churches in Hollywood." Actress Virginia Field once confessed, "She was and is the only actress I really dislike. She was sickeningly sweet, a pure phoney."

Gable and Young were also polar opposites in their views on love. He preferred the chase-and-seduction scenario to long-term emotional commitments. As one ex-flame quipped, "Of course, Clark [who wed five times] never really married anyone. A number of women married him, he just went along for the gag." On the other hand, twice-wed Loretta had a more dreamy approach to romance: "I believed all those love stories—the hero was the hero—because that's what I grew up with. I loved the romance and the roses, but when it came to a more realistic life, I would back away." For Loretta, the act of marriage was "a step into paradise."

That these two disparate luminaries shared a heated romance in the mid-1930s was astounding by the standards of the day. That their adulterous union led to a love child titillated the Hollywood crowd in an era when life's established moral codes meant far more than they do now. That Young should bluff her way through the scandalous situation by formally adopting her infant girl astounded those who knew the actual facts and later amazed and shocked her public when the particulars became generally known. That, later, Young should ignore her daughter's questions about her lineage or, thereafter, refuse to confirm for the offspring whether, as most all of Hollywood knew, Gable was her real father was selfish and cruel. It was an astounding story that could have happened only in Tinseltown and one that flabbergasted movie fans of classic Hollywood when the long-circulating rumors were finally substantiated only fairly recently.

William Clark Gable was born on February 1, 1901, in the coal-mining town of Cadiz, Ohio. Although Clark's father, an oil prospector, was Methodist, his wife, Addie, had their six-month-old baby christened in the Catholic church. A few months later, the long-ailing mother died. While the father pursued his luck in the oil fields, his boy stayed with relatives. In 1903, after Mr. Gable remarried and settled in Hopedale, Ohio, Clark lived with his father and stepmother. By the time Clark was 15, he was six feet tall and weighed 155 pounds. The strapping youth quit high school the next year. Thereafter, he was a tire salesman, a telephone lineman, and, to appease his dad, an oil field worker. Between jobs, he pursued his love of the theater with various stock companies. (Mr. Gable was perplexed at his son's career interest and constantly told Clark he should be doing real man's work. His opinion never changed, even after Clark became a superstar.)

By 1922, Clark was part of a theater group in Oregon. He fell in love with Franz Dorfler, an aspiring actress, but he dropped Franz when he met Josephine Dillon, an acting coach 13 years his elder. With Dillon's guidance, the two moved to Hollywood. They wed in 1924.

In the mid-1920s Clark did extra bits in silent movies but found stage work more satisfying. His masculinity appealed to his leading ladies (usually much older than he), and he had affairs with several of them. By 1930, Gable had appeared on the Broadway stage and was back on the West Coast. He had divorced Dillon and was living with Ria Langham, a rich Texas socialite, 17 years his senior. His stage success in *The Last Mile* led to an MGM contract. He made 11 movies that year, quickly becoming the studio's key male performer. To avoid possible scandal, the studio convinced Gable to wed Ria, which he did in June 1931.

Being married did not stop Clark from his affairs. One of his most intense was with frequent MGM costar Joan Crawford, then wed to Douglas Fairbanks Jr. Another was with Elizabeth Allan, a British import, who was featured with him in 1934's *Men in White.* Later came Virginia Grey, who worked with Clark in such films as 1938's *Test Pilot.*

MGM loaned Gable to Columbia Pictures for the screwball comedy *It Happened One Night* (1934). To express his disgust at working at second-rate Columbia, Clark arrived drunk on the set and was surly to director Frank Capra. Before long, however, Gable came to appreciate the filmmaker's talent and settled into his assignment. His performance earned him an Oscar.

During 1934, Gable considered separating from demanding, status-driven Ria, but he insisted to Crawford and others that he never wanted to wed again. Toward the end of 1934, the studio assigned Clark to star in an adaptation of Jack London's *The Call of the Wild.* The shoot would provide him a breather from his bickering wife and her annoying fancy dinner parties. Gable looked forward to working with Loretta Young, his beautiful, 21-year-old costar.

Loretta was born Gretchen Michaela Young on January 6, 1913, in Salt Lake City, Utah, the third child of John Earl and Gladys Young. About 1916, the father, a railroad auditor, abandoned his family (turning up later briefly). In 1917, Gladys relocated with her three girls and a boy to L.A. and opened a boardinghouse. Through her brother-in-law, an assistant production manager for a film studio, Gladys maneuvered screen roles for pretty young Gretchen in 1917 and 1919. However, Mrs. Young decided that movies were frivolous. She wanted Gretchen to focus on her education and religious faith. (Mrs. Young, like her husband, had converted to Catholicism in 1909, when their first child, Polly, was christened.) As such, Gretchen boarded at Ramona Convent School in Alhambra, California, and later attended the Immaculate Heart school in Hollywood. In 1923, Mrs. Young remarried, this time to a Los Angeles businessman, George Belzer. (The couple had one child, Georgiana, and divorced in 1935.)

In late 1926, Gretchen reactivated her film career with a small role in a Colleen Moore movie. This quickly led to a First National Pictures contract where, as Loretta Young, her starting salary was $50 per week. She moved over to talkies easily, and by the end of the 1920s the five-foot, four-inch ingenue was constantly busy on her home lot. While making *The Second Floor Mystery* (1930), she became infatuated with her costar, Grant Withers, almost nine years her senior. (In the mid-1920s he had wed, had a child, and divorced.) In a burst of independence, Loretta eloped to Yuma, Arizona, with Withers. Her shocked mother begged her to have the civil union with the non-Catholic annulled; Loretta refused. However, by 1931, Loretta had had enough of her frivolous spouse and divorced him.

One of Loretta's nine features in 1933 was made while she was on loanout to Columbia Pictures. Her costar in *Man's Castle* was Spencer Tracy, an Irish Catholic. She was 20; he was 33 and married, with two children. From the start, there were romantic sparks between the two. She revered this intense, virile actor. When the picture wrapped, the two continued to date, even though his recurring drunken binges (during which he disappeared for days at a time) frightened her.

One night at church, Loretta confessed to a priest about her affair with Tracy, and he refused to give her absolution unless she ended the situation. Thereafter, she seesawed between her devotion to God and to Tracy (then separated from his spouse). Eventually, pressures from all sides caused her to end the situation with Spencer, leaving him bereft for months to come.

In 1934, Loretta had joined the newly formed Twentieth Century Films. Late that same year, studio head Darryl F. Zanuck assigned her to *The Call of the Wild*. With the Spencer Tracy affair just over, Loretta was excited to leave Hollywood and go on location to Mount Baker, Washington. She and her costar, Clark Gable, first met during costume fittings for the picture, and there was an immediate rapport. Clark had long admired Tracy as an actor and was intrigued to find out what there was about Loretta's personality that had so caught Spencer's fancy.

Initially, director William Wellman planned to spend just six weeks shooting in Washington. Unfortunately, blizzards hit the area, and the cast and crew of 100 were forced to remain there for three months. When outdoorsy Gable was not carousing in the nearest town with coplayer Jack Oakie, Clark and Loretta began an affair. The fling caused problems on the set. According to Wellman, "Gable wasn't tending to business, not the business of making pictures. He was paying a lot of attention to monkey business, and I called him on it."

After *The Call of the Wild* ended, Young and Gable continued to date, although the still-married Clark was also quietly seeing British-born actress Elizabeth Allan. While Loretta was at Paramount making *The Crusades* (1935), she learned she was pregnant. When she told Clark, his response was, "I thought you knew how to take care of yourself." Shocked by his reaction, Young was equally amazed by Gable's next move. "He kept calling and calling, wanting to see me, and I kept telling him to go away, go away. I was so terrified someone would see us together. All I could think of was keeping him away."

Being Catholic, an abortion was not an option for Loretta. To deal with her increasingly obvious pregnancy, she concocted a ruse that due to a serious unspecified illness, she was putting aside all her upcoming film projects to recuperate abroad. On June 30, 1935, she and her mother departed for England, not realizing the scope of her international fame. Even in London, the press hounded her. After several weeks, Young and her mother snuck back to America. Loretta hid away at a house she owned at 8612 Rindge Street in Venice Beach, only a few miles from both her and Clark's studios.

Because the media and public were eager to know what had happened to the "vanished" leading lady, enterprising Loretta devised another scheme. She and her mama staged an exclusive get-together at Loretta's swank Bel-Air home for gossip columnist Dorothy Manners. The star was interviewed in her bedroom, buried under mounds of comforters so that only her head showed. The subterfuge worked.

Meanwhile, Gable contacted Loretta, volunteering his help. She ordered him "to leave town. I thought maybe if he was away all the gossip would stop." Perplexed Clark did as instructed and embarked on a promotional tour to South America.

On the morning of November 6, 1935, at the secluded Rindge Street house—with all the window shades drawn down tight—Loretta gave birth to her love child. Three thousand miles away, Gable was in New York, recouping from his exhausting South American trip. He received a telegram that read, "Beautiful blue-eyed blond baby girl born, 8:15 this morning." After digesting the news, he flushed the note down the toilet. (Young always denied that she had sent the telegram.)

By November 18, Gable was back in L.A., informing the press that he and his wife had separated officially. He called Loretta asking to see their child but was told the infant was not in town. By month's end, a healthy Loretta reemerged in public and resumed her career. The baby was cared for by a nurse at the Venice Beach home with Loretta making occasional visits. In December, the girl was baptized at St. Paul the Apostle Church in Westwood. The priest was made aware by Young's representative of the truth of Mary Judith Clark's parentage and that William and Margaret Clark were fictitious names for the real parents.

In late January 1936, Loretta allowed Gable to visit their child. When he snuck into the Rindge Street house late one night, Judy was asleep in a bureau drawer. After studying his offspring, Gable handed Loretta $400, telling her, "The least you can do is buy her a decent bed." Clark visited his child once more during this period.

Months later, Loretta dispatched her child to St. Elizabeth's Infant Hospital in San Francisco. Judy remained at this home for unwed mothers for five months. Then, Young took the next step in "officially" adopting her own child. She confided to gossip columnist Louella Parsons in June 1937 that she had just adopted two little girls: three-year-old Jane and 23½-month-old Judy. (There was no Jane, and Judy was actually five months younger.) Weeks later,

Young regretfully announced that the natural mother of the older girl had reclaimed Jane.

Certainly in a sophisticated city such as Los Angeles and in the tight social circle of the film colony, Loretta's elaborate deception fooled few for very long. However, the consensus was, "If she wants this badly to be a single parent, then so be it."

In the first years of the adoption, Loretta avoided having Judy photographed in public for fear someone would spot the child's resemblance to Gable. Because the girl had inherited Clark's prominent ears, Young always had the tyke in bonnets or her ears covered by her brushed-down curly hair. Later, Judy underwent cosmetic plastic surgery to pin back her ears.

In March 1939, newly divorced Gable wed his third wife, actress Carole Lombard. The next year, in June, Loretta married writer/producer Thomas Lewis. (They would have two sons in the mid-1940s.) Lewis agreed to adopt Judy, continuing the fiction that the girl was not actually Loretta's. As the child grew up, many of her peers were aware of her real parentage but were too embarrassed to tell her or assumed she must already have known the truth.

MGM's *Key to the City* (1950) reunited Young and Gable for the first time since *The Call of the Wild*. As they performed together in this romantic comedy, both pretended to the world that their amorous past did not exist. It was also around this time that 15-year-old Judy met her father, although she still had no conscious understanding that he was her parent. One afternoon Gable came to Young's home and spent a few hours politely chatting with his offspring, asking her about her daily life. Without knowing why, she felt surprisingly comfortable in this movie giant's presence. She was thrilled when, as he left, he kissed her on the forehead. It was the last time they ever met.

When Judy was going abroad in 1956 she required a passport. The complexity of obtaining the needed birth documentation led her to suspect that Young was indeed her biological mother. (It was a subject, however, she dared not broach with her imperious, self-focused mother, for fear of incurring her wrath.) Two years later, when Judy was about to marry, her husband-to-be confirmed what much of Hollywood had known: Clark Gable was her father.

There began an open battle of wills between controlling Young and her actress daughter who never received industry help from her competitive parent. As Loretta's career as a TV star wound down in the late 1950s, Judy's professional success on the small screen (as an actress, later as a producer) was rising. This caused unspoken rivalry and resentment between the two women. Young continued to hide behind her all-encompassing religious faith, as well as her regal status as a legend, eventually shutting out her offspring.

The one thing Judy craved most was to have Loretta acknowledge her publicly as her own. Another bone of contention—rather than a bond—between Loretta and Judy was that each had ended their unhappy marriages. Throughout these domestic changes, Young maintained a barrier of formality that left her daughter (now a mother herself) feeling an outsider.

It was around 1986 that Judy Lewis first met her half brother, John Clark Gable. John, the offspring of Clark and his fifth wife, Kay Williams Spreckels, had been born in 1961, five months after his dad succumbed to a heart attack. When Judy was introduced to John, who then owned a car repair shop in San Diego, he was totally unaware of their special link. He also gave no indication that he even knew who Loretta Young was.

In the 1990s, Judy, now an L.A.-based therapist and family counselor, wrote *Uncommon Knowledge* (1994), which revealed her stressful life as Young's daughter. Loretta was deeply offended by this public airing of family "secrets." However, the two women came to a truce before Loretta died of ovarian cancer in 2000. That same year, in *Forever Young*, an authorized biography of the star by Joan Wester Anderson, Loretta at last publicly acknowledged the mortal sin she had committed decades before and which she had gone to such tremendous length to hide for so long to avoid any breath of public scandal.

Joan Crawford: The Demon Mother

"It was a 'first': the first story of family violence from the child's point of view in modern times; the first to shatter the myth that child abuse happened only to the poor and disadvantaged; the first to expose deviant celebrity behavior toward family behind closed doors and lay bare the lie of public image versus personal conduct, later to be copied by other writers and labeled 'tell-all' by the press. The title became a new American slang term in its own right, and changed the connotation of the word 'dearest' from one of endearment to one of abuse."

— CHRISTINA CRAWFORD, IN 1997

In 1957, Edward G. Robinson Jr.'s autobiography, *My Father, My Son*, recounted his escalating difficulties as the actor son of the famous on-screen gangster. Also that year, Diana Barrymore published *Too Much, Too Soon*. In that confessional tome, the actress exposed the bewildering dynamics of her dysfunctional family life. She focused on her tenuous relationship with her womanizing, alcoholic dad, John Barrymore, the legendary stage and film star. Diana's graphic-book shocked readers who were then unaccustomed to such titillating revelations from celebrities. However, that successful autobiography was only a warm-up to the astonishment generated by the 1978 publication of Christina Crawford's *Mommie Dearest*.

Christina's tell-all volume appeared less than a year after the death of her parent, Hollywood movie queen Joan Crawford. In this explosive bestseller, Christina explicitly recounted her years of physical and emotional abuse at the hands of her monstrous mother. In reaction, many industry figures as well as fans sprang to Joan's defense. They insisted that Christina's numbing recollections were highly exaggerated. They also chided the daughter for having published this profitable exposé when her parent could no longer defend herself. (Christina's revelatory tome led to a 1981 screen version of her Grand Guignol tale in which Faye Dunaway portrayed the out-of-control screen legend.)

Subsequently, it was proved that the essentials of *Mommie Dearest*—Joan's sadistic brand of mother love—were scandalously all too true. (This dismayed the faithful who had believed the carefully construed image of the perfect mother that Joan and studio publicity departments had promoted.) Processing these astounding disclosures prompted discussion as to how such cruelties could have gone on publicly unnoticed for years. (It should be remembered that this situation occurred in the 1940s and 1950s, before the rise of child advocacy groups. Also, at the time, only a small bit of Crawford's mania for parental control was known to her peers.)

The answer lies in the fact that as a top box-office personality, the Oscar winner (for 1945's *Mildred Pierce*) was an exalted industry celebrity. As such, people rarely questioned her stringent behavior, particularly in such a personal matter as parenting skills. (Screen leading lady Jane Greer once recalled for this author visiting Crawford's Brentwood home in the late 40s. During the dinner party, Jane used the upstairs powder room. When she passed by the children's bedroom, the door was ajar and she could not help but see young Christopher strapped into his bed so he would remain there throughout the night. Greer thought this strange parenting but did not feel it appropriate to bring up the situation with the empress of the manse.)

If anyone dared to criticize Crawford's child-rearing skills, her immediate, angry response was, "Don't tell me how to raise my children!" Or, to close friends (such as actor Cesar Romero) she might reason, "I was a kid once, and I didn't have a damn thing. Those kids are going to appreciate everything they get!" (As to the household staff and private school personnel who witnessed Crawford's bizarre relationship with her offspring, they felt powerless—in status and authority—to confront the issue directly.)

Then too, it was not as if the five-foot, four-inch, glamorous celluloid empress made a secret of her strong beliefs in strict parental supervision. This single mother proudly informed the media that she spanked her children whenever necessary. "Yes, with a capital S. I spank them almost daily. Spare the rod and you have brats." She further explained with single-minded intensity, "I intend that my children grow up to be ladies and gentlemen."

The future star was born Lucille Fay LeSueur on March 23, 1904, in San Antonio, Texas, the thirdborn of Thomas and Anna Bell (Johnson) LeSueur. (Daisy had died in infancy, while Hal had been born a year before Lucille.) The father was a sometimes contractor who abandoned the family when Lucille was quite young. This left the angered, unskilled mother to support her household, scrabbling to keep her kin from true poverty. They soon relocated to Lawton, Oklahoma, where Mrs. LeSueur married Harry Cassin, owner of the town's opera house.

When Billie (as Lucille was nicknamed) was 11, her mother discovered her sexually precocious daughter having intercourse with her 34-year-old stepfather. It led to Anna's divorcing her husband and forever blaming her girl for losing their meal ticket. Next, the trio relocated to Kansas City, Missouri, where Mrs. Cassin, for a time, managed a seedy hotel. By then Billie was as sexually active as her unhappy mother was. One of the girl's sex mates was her brother, whom she had persuaded herself was only her half sibling. When the mother discovered this, she punished both offenders, but it was Billie whom Anna held responsible for this latest family trouble.

By 13, Billie, who had been turned into a slave by her harsh mother, was attending St. Agnes School where she did drudgery to earn her tuition. At 15, she transferred to Rockingham Academy, a boarding school. (By then, Mrs. Cassin had a new live-in boyfriend and feared having Billie at home.) After Billie's difficult years of being a social outcast at Rockingham, she enrolled at Stephens College in Columbia, Missouri, where she worked as a campus waitress. However, between suffering from a spotty educational background and feeling socially inferior to her classmates, she quickly dropped out of school.

Despite an unpromising start, Billie was determined to make something of her present shoddy life. Returning to Kansas City to live with her mother and the latter's boyfriend, Billie became a department store worker. She dated a local young man who treated her with kindness. However, the relationship remained platonic because he was homosexual. (Some have put forward that the trauma of this experience led Billie to experiment with lesbianism to feel closer to her gay friend. It is also suggested that she continued to dabble in the alternative lifestyle in subsequent decades.)

Having an attractive figure and a striking face, Billie hoped to parlay her rudimentary dancing skills into a show business career. She joined a vaudeville troupe as a chorine. Later, Billie relocated to Chicago, where the worldly-wise 19-year-old used the casting couch to win a chorus job in a nightclub and, later, at a Detroit venue. Along the way, she allegedly was arrested on prostitution charges, but well-connected pals got her out of the legal scrape.

To get ahead, Lucille submitted to the advances of Broadway producer J. J. Shubert when he passed through town. He offered her a chorus assignment in his 1924 New York revue, *Innocent Eyes*. Once in Manhattan, Lucille LeSueur, as she was billed, continued her man-hungry ways but circulated with a richer class of men. One of her brief distractions was musician James Welton, whom she married and divorced that year.

By late 1924, Lucille LeSueur had met 42-year-old Harry Rapf of MGM. The married film producer had come East on a talent hunt for the studio. Lucille convinced Rapf to arrange a screen test, which led to a modest studio contract. En route to L.A., Lucille stopped in Kansas City to share the good news with her mother, but the two fought constantly.

As a Hollywood newcomer, Lucille quickly learned the rules. Whether agreeing to change her professional name (to Joan Crawford), sleeping with visiting exhibitors at the "request" of her studio bosses, or sexually accommodating MGM executives, Joan was passionately dedicated to getting ahead. For relaxation, she entered dance contests on the Tinseltown night scene, winning prizes for her adeptness at dancing the Charleston. Before long, Joan went from playing an unbilled extra (as in 1925's *Pretty Ladies*) to being a cinema leading lady (as in 1926's *Tramp, Tramp, Tramp*).

Joan set her sights on society figure Michael Cudahy, but his upper-crust parents discouraged their entanglement. Undiscouraged, Crawford pursued handsome, young Douglas Fairbanks Jr. His father (swashbuckling movie star Doug Sr.) and stepmother (the screen's perpetual ingenue Mary Pickford) were not in favor of the couple's marrying, but, nevertheless, they did in June 1929.

Eventually, Crawford won over her in-laws, but she soon became bored with her pompous, unambitious spouse, five years her junior. She found her married leading man Clark Gable much more appealing, and they had an affair while Doug Jr. found his own diversions. The Fairbanks divorced in 1933. Two years later, she wed Franchot Tone, her frequent on-screen coplayer. Joan was fascinated by his swank upbringing and his stage training at the innovative Group Theater. It prompted her pretentious phase, when she became a sophisticated lady of "culture." The union soon fell apart, with Franchot turning to drink and other women. Meanwhile, sexually voracious Joan dallied with Spencer Tracy, her costar in *Mannequin* (1937), and studio producer Joseph L. Mankiewicz. By 1939, Crawford and Tone had divorced.

As Joan, a devout Christian Scientist, fought and prayed to resurrect her failing screen career in the late 1930s with such vehicles as *The Women* (1939), she pondered having a child. Having suffered several miscarriages and abortions and still unsure whether she wished to disturb her career and figure with a pregnancy, she decided to adopt a baby. (Part of the allure of becoming a parent was to soften her aggressive public image.) However, at the time, legitimate agencies in California did not allow single parents to adopt. Undeterred, Joan contacted mob connections from her Midwestern nightclub days. It was underworld big shot Meyer Lansky who arranged for a girl—born on June 11, 1939, at Hollywood Presbyterian Hospital—to be placed with the star. Initially named Joan Jr., the tyke was pampered by the new mother and exploited via studio publicity. In May 1940, the actress went to Las Vegas where the baby could be officially adopted. By then, Crawford had decided that one Joan in the household was sufficient. Thus, the 11-month-old was renamed Christina.

After 1943's *Above Suspicion,* Crawford left MGM and moved over to Warner Bros. studio. Meanwhile, she had been auditioning potential new husbands, thinking that a perfect household required a perfect mate. The men who measured up to her high standards were disinterested in overly aggressive Joan. Instead, she settled for handsome, accommodating Phillip Terry, a minor film actor. She and the unassertive Terry, five years her junior, wed in July 1942 (six weeks after she'd first met him). The couple adopted a baby boy, Phillip Jr., from the same black-market ring that had supplied Christina.

Between 1943 and 1945 Joan searched frantically for the perfect screen vehicle at Warner Bros., all the while mangling her marriage to the overshadowed Terry. Just as she had fiercely carved out a screen persona, so she became a super mother—all within the confines of what she determined went into that domestic role. (Her domestic guidelines were based on surface, material things; emotional qualities rarely entered the equation.) As long as her two attractive children were small and compliant, everything went reasonably well. She and Christina dressed in identical mother-daughter outfits. Mother was the faultless hostess of elaborate birthday parties for her offspring.

Things changed in 1945. Her comeback showcase, *Mildred Pierce,* landed her an Academy Award and, once again, made the 40-something screen veteran a top Hollywood commodity. With her career thriving, she had little time for a husband (especially one so beneath her in the Tinseltown pecking order), and she divorced Phillip Terry in 1946. Crawford immediately renamed her boy Christopher. In 1947, Joan adopted two additional blond children, two girls. Cathy and Cindy, born a month apart, looked nothing alike, but Crawford insisted on calling them "the twins." To complete the fantasy household, Joan had acquired a small white poodle named Cliquot, whom she fanatically trained to be neat and obedient.

Life with Crawford was not easy for the children, especially as they grew older. Christina, the eldest and the most similar to her mother, became alternately perturbed by and embracing of Joan, and, in the process, somehow became somewhat spoiled. Christopher proved to be the most rebellious, frequently bridling at living in such an unreasonable dictatorship in which no one's wishes or needs counted. The twins were always the most compliant. Accordingly, they received the most attention and least abuse from their domineering caregiver. If governesses or servants showed too much "compassion" for her charges and disobeyed any of Joan's demands (or her methodical daily schedule for carrying out each minute task), they were immediately discharged without a reference.

In reaction to her tawdry early life, Joan was a tremendous believer in "proper" etiquette. Thus, every least action by her offspring had to fit within her specifications of how well-bred Hollywood youngsters should behave. This included always being "on" whenever guests—and especially the press—were present. Accordingly, each child learned the ritual of providing a polite good night and curtsy (or bow) to each visitor before retiring. They also knew they must always complete the ceremony with, "Good night, Mommy dearest. I love you."

If her older children did something out of bounds (such as wanting to stay up later than usual, not finishing their meal, and so forth), it was typical of Crawford to conduct their punishment in front of onlookers. Frequently, young Christopher would have his pants pulled down before astonished guests as Joan jubilantly spanked him.

As part of her martinet practices, Joan dealt out sadistic penalties. Once, Christina accidentally slammed a door on Christopher's hand. Crawford's justice demanded that the frightened girl place her hand in the same door, with the star pressing it tight, while the youngster screamed in pain. Once the young Christina, who was frequently complimented on her long blond hair, prattled on about her best feature. In retaliation for her girl's vanity, Joan grabbed a pair of shears and cut off the lauded locks. Another time, on her birthday, the girl made the mistake of contradicting her mother. This prompted Joan to lock her in her room while guests assembled on the lawn for the elaborate birthday celebration.

If Christopher, who was naturally left-handed, happened to use the "wrong" hand to cut his meat at the dinner table, Joan thought nothing of leaning across the table and knocking the food out of his hand, followed by smacking him in the face. When the movie star caught Christopher playing with matches, his punishment was to hold out his hand over matches she had lit.

Heaven help the youngsters if they did not keep their rooms clean according to Crawford's fanatical rules of tidiness. Infringements of her neatness mandates led to spankings and, for the worst abuses of all, a withering look and a stern lecture from their commander in chief. After bedtime, the children had to be on their best behavior, never crying out for attention during the night. Because Christopher was naturally restless (and increasingly rebellious), Joan restrained him in his bed at night with a truss so he could not jump out to misbehave. This also meant that if he needed to use the bathroom during the long night hours he was out of luck. (Eventually, Christina began sneaking over to her brother's bed to untie him so he could race to the bathroom and be back under the sheets with the truss rearranged before their mother might make her next surprise inspection.)

By the end of the 40s, middle-aged Joan was fretful about her lack of a full-time mate to accompany her to social functions and to share her bed. Increasingly, she turned to alcohol to bolster her lonely evenings and to gird herself as she fought to salvage her once again sinking box-office standing. Deeply unhappy and often inebriated, she took out her fury on her household staff and, of course, her easiest targets—her older children. One evening, during a surprise inspection of her children's highly organized clothes closets, Crawford discovered that Christina had disobeyed her mother's edict of never using wire hangers. In retaliation against this major infraction—which reminded Joan too vividly of the wire hangers in her childhood shack where her mother ran a makeshift laundry—Crawford yanked her daughter out of bed and dragged her to the closet. There the trembling girl watched as the offending hangers were dispatched, leaving the youngster to spend the rest of the night reassembling her clothes in the orderly fashion demanded by Joan.

In 1952, Crawford made another successful comeback with *Sudden Fear*, receiving her third and final Oscar nomination. By the mid-1950s, Christopher had been largely excised from Joan's life, shipped off to boarding schools. Christina, who loved, feared, and tried to emulate her unique parent, proved to be such a handful that she was sent to private school (later boarding at a Catholic institution although she was not of that faith). Crawford loved the freedom of not dealing with Christina face-to-face, but she could not deal with abdicating control of her girl to school staff whom she feared would steal the girl's loyalty to mom. As such, Joan used intimidation, guilt, and the threat of cutting off financial support to keep the cowering girl constantly in line. So great was Crawford's fame and so overwhelming her personality that school instructors generally bowed to the woman's peculiar and malicious dictates regarding her neglected, intimidated daughter.

In May 1955, Joan married Alfred N. Steele, 53, the head of the Pepsi-Cola Company. Initially he was drawn to Crawford's mystique, her sexual voraciousness, and the prestige factor she added to his business world standing. But as she badgered him into huge expenses for their elaborate new Manhattan digs, he fell into debt and became yet another victim of her totalitarian ways. Meanwhile, Christina dropped out of college to jump-start her acting career. Despite her mother's belittling and refusal to help her open show business doors (Joan reasoned, "Who the hell helped Lucille LeSueur"), the fledgling persisted in her craft. Although Christina was an adult, the strenuous battle of wills continued between mother and daughter, with Alfred relegated to the sidelines. Frequently, the two women, who had come to physical blows in past years, did not speak for months. When communication between the two reopened, it was frosty and full of recriminations for past real and fancied offenses.

Steele died of a heart attack in spring 1959. Suddenly alone, and with no financial reserves, Joan returned to screen work that year in *The Best of Everything*. She made a remarkable last comeback in *What Ever Happened to Baby Jane?* (1962), teamed with her longtime rival Bette Davis. Meanwhile, for a long time after her husband's death, Crawford continued as a Pepsi spokesperson, thriving on the perks of her globe-trotting job.

In her senior years, Joan still could not get along with Christina. By the late 1960s, the latter was a regular on the daytime TV soap opera, *The Secret Storm*. When Christina required emergency stomach surgery, Crawford agreed to substitute for her daughter on the daily TV show. Ignoring the fact that she was in her mid-sixties, Joan portrayed a character nearly 40 years younger. It didn't help matters that she was somewhat sloshed throughout her several appearances on the network soap opera. Nevertheless, the event created great publicity that pleased everyone—except hospital-bound Christina, who cringed as she watched her mother cavorting on the TV screen and, once again, pushing her into the shadows.

As the 1970s progressed, Joan became increasingly reclusive in her New York City life. She kept in polite contact with daughters Cathy and Cindy, but her communications with the married Christina were constantly fractious. When Christopher, who had served in Vietnam, returned to New York, he sought to visit his mother. He was told by her doorman, "Miss Crawford says she is not at home to you, sir." (As had been the case with her mother and brother—both now deceased—Joan had a way of putting offending souls such as Christina and Christopher out of mind.)

When Joan Crawford died on May 10, 1977, she had been ill for some time with cancer. Christina and her other siblings (including Christopher) had a reunion at the funeral. But if Christina, who by then had abandoned acting for a business-management career, thought that the long war with her parent was finally over, she was wrong. In the will, Crawford decreed, "It is my intention to make no provision herein for my son Christopher or my daughter Christina for reasons which are well known to them." (The two nonbeneficiaries sued Crawford's estate and eventually received a settlement.)

Summing up the life and times of the remarkable Joan Crawford, one observer noted that she had been so preoccupied being Joan Crawford the movie star that she never had time to become a human being. Actress Helen Hayes, a longtime Crawford friend (and Christina's godmother) observed wryly, "Joan tried to be all things to all people. I just wish she hadn't tried to be a mother."

Errol Flynn: The Relentless Swordsman

"Well, he just walked over to the bed, pulled down the covers and pulled up my slip and pulled down my pants. . . ."
— ALLEGED RAPE VICTIM PEGGY SATTERLEE, IN JANUARY 1943

Right or wrong, the public often has believed that Hollywood's highly paid, pampered talent could do as they pleased—regardless of laws or commonly accepted moral standards. A degree of these misconceptions about Tinseltown and its "indulged" citizens was a reaction to the fantasy propaganda fed the media about movie notables. In addition, some of the public's notions were tinged by envy and jealousy of these beautiful people who enjoyed charmed lives. There was also the belief (often true) that powerful film industry forces could bend the truth and buy off officials and law enforcers to protect erring contractees.

With such slanted views of the film colony, whenever a celebrity got into legal difficulties, public sentiment regarding the suspected miscreant was biased long before all the facts were known or the dispensation of justice made. For example, in 1921, when beloved, rotund comedian Roscoe "Fatty" Arbuckle was implicated in the San Francisco death of a minor movie actress, the local district attorney and the tabloid press molded public sentiment against the indiscreet but innocent movie star. After three (!) trials Roscoe was proved innocent, but his screen career was ruined.

On the other hand, in early 1943, when handsome, swashbuckling cinema star Errol Flynn was placed on trial for statutory rape, public sentiment quickly tipped in favor of the dashing star whom women swooned over and many men emulated. Unlike the Arbuckle case, of course, there was no death involved in the Flynn case. But in the morally restrictive 1940s, the charge of which the defendant was accused was against the law and certainly not sanctioned by much of the population. There was every possibility that the 33-year-old celebrity could go to prison. In fact, footloose Errol was sufficiently worried about this dire possibility that he made a contingency plan should he be convicted: a plane and pilot sat in constant readiness at a local airport to fly the star out of the country should the jury verdict go against him.

He was born Errol Leslie Thomson Flynn on June 20, 1909, in the seaport city of Hobart, the capital of Tasmania. His father, Theodore Thomson Flynn, was a well-regarded marine biologist/professor. His mother, Mary Lily "Marelle" Young, was pushy and self-focused, and she devoted herself to assorted male friends. While there was always a tenseness (later bitterness) between son and mother, the boy got along well with his father. But even over-indulgent Theodore admitted that his offspring was "not a manageable child." When the boy was 11, his sister, Rosemary, was born. Under Mrs. Flynn's prodding, the family moved to Sydney, Australia, because it offered a far more sophisticated environment. (Subsequently, bored Mrs. Flynn abandoned her spouse, relocating to France to pursue new romances.)

Like his dad, young Errol was a ladies' man and, early on, was endlessly fascinated by the opposite sex. The youngster was not, however, intrigued by academics. As his well-educated parent noted, "There was never any chance of Errol following in my footsteps in an academic career—school to him was a place to let off high spirits not a place where knowledge could be gained." By age 16, the boastful young womanizer had been booted out of several schools for prankish behavior. Thereafter, he had to flee a clerical post his dad obtained for him in Sydney because he'd pilfered the petty cash to bet (and lose) at the racetrack.

At this turning point in life, Errol learned of a fresh gold strike in Australian New Guinea. Deciding to make a clean start, he headed there. He never found gold, but in his four and a half years in New Guinea, the restless young man held a score of jobs, including bird trapper, pearl diver, newspaper correspondent, charter boat captain, and diamond smuggler. In 1932, an Australian filmmaker spotted Flynn's handsome profile in a Sydney newspaper and cast him in the feature *In the Wake of "The Bounty."*

Oppressed by mounting debts, Errol was anxious to move on to fresh turf. At this juncture he encountered the mysterious Austrian Dr. Hermann Erben, who had been in New Guinea, ostensibly looking for gold. The two sailed to Hong Kong in the spring of 1933, quickly moving on to Saigon, India, and, eventually, Marseilles, France. There the two pals parted company, with Flynn moving on to London. (It later developed that Erben had been working for German intelligence. A few sources have alleged that, during World War II, Erben, who recurrently turned up in Errol's wild life, convinced Flynn to undertake espionage activities to assist Hitler's Third Reich.)

Before long, spendthrift Errol found himself broke in England. He drifted into acting with a repertory company in Northampton but was later fired. Moving back to London, he came to the attention of the British division of Warner Bros. Pictures. Flynn was hired for a leading role in the studio's low-budget entry *Murder at Monte Carlo* (1935). This resulted in the movie newcomer's being dispatched to Warner Bros.' film plant in California.

Sailing to the United States, Flynn encountered French-born screen actress Lili Damita, a former model, dancer, and music-hall performer who had appeared in movies in France, Germany, and the United States. Petite and vivacious, the tempestuous Lili and the hell-raising Errol embarked on a shipboard romance. When they reached L.A., they settled at the Garden of Allah hotel. Despite their essential incompatibility, volatile Lili cajoled hedonistic Errol into matrimony in June 1935. She was eight years his senior and unable to control his persistent womanizing. Before long, Errol and Lili chose to live apart but agreed to share her bedroom when the mood suited them.

After a few minor roles at Warner Bros., the studio cast six-foot, two-inch Errol in the title role in *Captain Blood* (1935), which made him a major star and set the path for further swashbuckling screen assignments, including *The Adventures of Robin Hood* (1938). By then, his marriage to Damita had become one long quarrel, and they frequently separated. In the midst of their breakups and reconciliations, he bedded a bevy of willing Tinseltown lovelies. (There were also rumors that dashing Errol was bisexual and indulged his penchant for men when opportunities allowed.)

During one of the Flynns' increasingly infrequent cease-fires in 1940, Lili became pregnant. She gave birth to Sean on May 31, 1941. By then the couple had reached a domestic deadlock that resulted in their bitter divorce on March 31, 1942. In the settlement, she received custody of their boy. Now legally a free man, Errol resided in his $125,000 customized mansion (Mulholland House) in Beverly Hills. (Purportedly, to satisfy voyeuristic Flynn, the house contained many peepholes and listening devices to spy on guests' sexual activities.)

Among Errol's group of best buddies were character player Guinn "Big Boy" Williams, screen leading man Bruce Cabot, movie stuntman Buster Wiles, and club owner Johnny Meyer (who had underworld connections and was noted for "finding" girls for Flynn and others). In 1942, Cabot, along with wealthy British sportsman Freddie McAvoy and actor Stephen Raphael, was sharing a Spanish-style mansion (built by silent movie star Colleen Moore) at 345 St. Pierre Road in Bel-Air. On September 27, the rambunctious trio, joined by Flynn, hosted one of their wild parties at the Bel-Air house. Among those attending the revelry was 17-year-old Betty Hansen, a drugstore waitress who had gate-crashed the party, along with other young acquaintances (two of them minor employees at Warner Bros.). Betty had been told that she might meet someone of importance there who could help her get a job on the lot. During the afternoon, she watched Flynn and others play tennis. Later, she chatted with Errol, even sitting on his chair and then on his lap. However, by then she had drunk too much liquor and soon threw up. Flynn assisted her upstairs to clean up and to recuperate. Supposedly, he helped her find a vacant bedroom in which to lie down and then allegedly raped her.

Days later, this gal from Lincoln, Nebraska, who had initially come to L.A. to visit her sister and then had disappeared, was picked up by the police at a seedy Santa Monica hotel where she was staying. Detained on vagrancy charges, she was removed to Juvenile Hall, where a custodian, while examining her personal effects, found several phone numbers, including the unlisted ones of Errol Flynn and Bruce Cabot. Betty claimed that Flynn had had sex with her twice. This led two plainclothes L.A. law enforcers to Mulholland House in early October, and they brought Flynn in for questioning regarding a charge of statutory rape. If convicted of the allegations of ravishing a minor girl, he could be imprisoned for 10 years. After searching his mind, he vaguely recalled his accuser, referring to her as a "frowsy little blonde," and then made the error of saying, "I hardly touched her."

Later, Errol and his lawyer (Robert Ford) went to Juvenile Hall where, as a legal necessity for the prosecution to proceed, Hansen's police custodian confronted Flynn and restated the accusations. During subsequent interrogation, when asked by Errol's attorney if she had put up any resistance to the claimed seduction, the plain-looking girl replied, "No. Why should I?"

By now Flynn and Warner Bros. had retained the services of high-ranking defense counsel Jerry Giesler. With Giesler as Errol's clever legal representative, the grand jury threw out the case. Usually, that would be the end of the matter.

Flynn's reprieve, however, was short-lived. A few days later he was again arrested. This time the charges not only involved the Betty Hansen matter but included a claim that on the weekend of August 2–3, 1941, he had induced 15-year-old Peggy Satterlee to join his party aboard the *Sirocco* for a cruise off Santa Catalina Island. Purportedly, the movie idol had had sex twice with the attractive young lady aboard the yacht. When Peggy's mother learned of the supposed sexual activity, she attempted to press charges against the star. (Later, there would be allegations that the family had initially sought to persuade Flynn to buy their silence.) At the time, the police concluded (or, perhaps, were encouraged by Warner Bros. to conclude) that there was insufficient evidence. The Satterlees had been convinced to drop their allegations because if they pursued the action, the prosecution would prove humiliating for their teenager.

Once the Betty Hansen matter had occurred, the new L.A. County district attorney, "Honest" John W. Duckweiller (who replaced the crooked Buron Fitts), thought he could use the 14-month-old Satterlee case to help gain a victory against Flynn. (Observers thought the DA was grandstanding to show Hollywood he meant business; more cynical onlookers thought he was reacting to Warner Bros.'s not making it worthwhile for him and other city politicians to find other priorities.) On October 16, 1942, Errol was arrested, booked, fingerprinted, and, later, formally charged. When eventually released on $1,000 bail, Flynn spluttered, "I'm bewildered. I can't understand it." The dismayed, irresponsible actor found it hard to focus on his latest Warner Bros. vehicle, *Edge of Darkness.*

For usually devil-may-care Errol, the pending prosecution seemed a hopeless situation, even with well-experienced Giesler as his chief counsel. In the star's estimation, "Even if I win I lose." As he reasoned, "If the jury thinks I screwed her—then I'm screwed." If the prosecution team of Thomas W. Cochran and John Hopkins could prove in court that he had indeed had sex with the two underage girls (the key issue being their underage status, *not* their willingness), he would end up behind bars for several years. This was more than Errol could bear, thus his fallback plan of a getaway plane to take him to Mexico and then on to Venezuela if he lost the case.

Although news of World War II commanded priority attention, as Flynn's trial date of January 11, 1943, drew near, the case grabbed headlines around the world. Everywhere, people were taking sides, and bets, whether the screen's great Casanova and legendary off-screen playboy would be found guilty. (There was a segment of the public who despised Errol because he had been classified 4-F and was not serving in World War II. Because Flynn vainly refused to acknowledge publicly that his defective heart was the cause of his deferment, many patriotic souls thought this screen hero was a draft dodger.)

Putting on a brave face, Errol continued with his studio work. His close friends (including Warner Bros. stars Ida Lupino and Ann Sheridan) showed their support. However, many others in Hollywood kept their distance, afraid of being tainted by associating with and/or championing the accused. Meanwhile, the studio, with its huge investment in Flynn, worked overtime to present their prize asset in the most favorable light possible to the public.

When the trial opened at the Hall of Justice, a mob was on hand to see dapper Flynn—accompanied by short, pudgy, and bald Giesler—enter the L.A. County building. Many cheered the defendant as he made his way into the overflowing courtroom. Very quickly Giesler proved that he was worth his $50,000 fee (of which $20,000 went for expenses). In gathering his facts, the sharp lawyer had uncovered much more than the prosecution had (or would ever admit).

Betty Hansen proved to be her own worst enemy on the witness stand. She came across as dumb and crude, which, in tandem with her unpleasant dental overbite, won her no support from the jury, nine of whom were women and nearly all of whom were smitten by the handsome defendant. (During the proceedings, two female jurors were removed from duty for being openly biased in Flynn's favor.)

In Giesler's cross-examination of Hansen, he quickly exploded her claimed sexual naïvéte and innocence:

Q: "Did you tell him you objected to his locking the door?"

A: "Yes, I did. . . . I objected."

Q: "Did you object to lying down on the bed?"

A: "Yes, I did. . . . I told him I wasn't feeling all right and wanted to go downstairs."

Q: "Didn't you have any idea about what he wanted you to lie on the bed for?"

A: "No."

The defense team followed up with:

Q: "When did you first think about sexual intercourse?"

A: "When I had sexual intercourse with him."

Thereafter, the supposedly inexperienced victim detailed that she had not resisted Flynn's undressing of her because she had no idea what was to follow. She explained that the impressive sexual activity lasted about 50 minutes and that she took part in the performance of the act. Hansen let slip that her ulterior motive was to gain material rewards from her liaison with Flynn and that, indeed—which the women jurors refused to believe—she liked Errol neither as an actor nor as a person.

Subsequently, Giesler smashed Betty's pure image by bringing to the jury's attention that she was far more experienced in sexual matters than she had indicated. It was disclosed that she had indulged in oral sex with her boyfriend (a Warner Bros. studio messenger), an act then considered not only perverted but illegal. The couple was facing a possible felony charge for this activity, which could lead, she was told, to a four-year jail stay. As hoped, this suggested to the jury that Hansen had a motive for her alleged seduction fabrication. Also, apparently Hansen had indulged in sex with the young men who had accompanied her to the party.

As for Peggy Satterlee, at the time of trial 17 and a dancer at Hollywood's Florentine Garden, she had caught Errol's roving eyes when she was an extra on his Western, *They Died with Their Boots On*

(1941). (Flynn would describe Peggy as having "sensational uphol-
stery" and said that she "could have passed for anywhere between
20 and 25.") When she appeared on the witness stand, Satterlee
wore pigtails, a young girl's dress, and flat shoes, and she talked in
a babylike whisper, trying to make an impression on the jury. The
defense sarcastically pointed out that this demure outfit was not her
usual dress style.

As to the pivotal weekend cruise, Peggy insisted that the first of
her two seductions by Flynn occurred in her cabin on the *Sirocco*.
She claimed she had gotten into bed, taken off her clothes including her bra, and then put her slip back on. However, she was forced
to admit that she usually slept with nothing on. When asked whether
she had resisted Errol's advances when he entered her cabin, she
said she had. When questioned why she had not shouted for help
from the crew or other passengers (which included stuntman Buster
Wiles and a *Life* magazine photographer), she responded, "When it
was happening I did not care whether I screamed or not, but after
it was over I felt very ashamed."

The defense proved that after the first alleged incident Satterlee
not only stayed aboard the yacht for the rest of the weekend cruise
but seemed content and was photographed looking quite congenial. (Flynn would testify that she said she'd had "a wonderful
time" that weekend and that "it had been like a dream.") As for
her allegations that Flynn had forced her to later have sex a second
time aboard the vessel, she stated she had been lured to his yacht
stateroom by Errol's telling her that she could see a wonderful view
of the full moon from his porthole. Giesler proved that from the
position of the *Sirocco* that night, the moon could not be seen from
that side of the boat. Having attacked her credibility, the defense
soiled her reputation by revealing that she had once had an abortion (an illegal act for which she could be prosecuted—suggesting
that, like Hansen, she had been coerced by the prosecution into
going forward with the case). It also came out that she and her
sister shared an apartment paid for by a 43-year-old former Royal
Canadian Air Force pilot. She and the aviator, apparently, had once

pranced around a mortuary yanking the sheets off corpses and had even pressed their faces against the naked bodies. The jury was stunned and outraged.

When Flynn took the stand, he gave the performance of his life, leading Giesler to tell his client later that he was the best witness he ever had. Errol earnestly insisted that he had never had "an act of sexual intercourse" with either Betty Hansen or Peggy LaRue Satterlee.

On February 6 at 11:19 A.M., following deliberations that lasted two days, the jury acquitted Errol on all counts. The verdict was greeted by much courtroom cheering. In closing the proceedings, Judge Leslie Still said to the jury, "I have enjoyed this case, and I think you have." A much-relieved Flynn enthusiastically shook the hands of each jury member and later beamed to the press, "This just goes to show that there is justice in the United States." One of the jurors (a female) told a reporter, "We knew Flynn was not guilty all the time, but we didn't want to come out too soon because we wondered what the public would think if we did."

As for Peggy Satterlee, she moaned theatrically, "I don't know what I'm going to do. Here I am, just two days less than 17 years old, and I feel like a broken old woman." Regarding Betty Hansen, her mother sighed, "Oh well, nobody got hurt. . . . I have no hard feeling toward Mr. Flynn. Betty is the cutest little thing you ever saw—a clean little Christian girl."

At trial's end Flynn released the waiting pilot and went out to celebrate. Meanwhile, a special party was held in the ninth-floor press room of the Hall of Justice for reporters, with Warner Bros. providing the serving staff and other accommodations. Days later, Agnes Underwood, city editor at the *Los Angeles Herald-Express*, held a festive gathering/reunion at her home for the journalists who had worked the past months on the "notorious" Flynn case.

Over the course of the lengthy trial, a reporter had come up with a saying, "in like Flynn," to suggest the status of a man getting his way with a woman. The expression became popular. Years later, Flynn wrote of his courtroom ordeal: "I knew that I could never escape this brand that was now upon me: that I would always be associated in the public mind with an internationally followed rape case."

However, at the time, randy Flynn had another matter on his mind: 18-year-old redhead Nora Eddington. The pretty teenager was the daughter of the sheriff of L.A. County. At the time, she worked behind the cigar counter at the L.A. County Hall of Justice. Each day as the famous defendant passed by she flashed him a bright smile. Errol and Nora became much better acquainted after the trial and married in Acapulco, Mexico, in August 1943. They had two children: Deirdre and Rory.

Before Errol Flynn died of a heart attack on October 14, 1959, he made several dozen more films, divorced and married again, and valiantly lived up to the title of his 1959 autobiography, *My Wicked, Wicked Ways.*

The Blacklist: Shame of a Nation

"Don't present me with the choice of either being in contempt of this committee and going to jail or forcing me to really crawl through the mud to be an informer. For what purpose? I don't think it is a choice at all. I don't think this is really sportsmanlike. I don't think this is American. I don't think this is American justice."

—ACTOR LARRY PARKS, ON MARCH 21, 1951

One of the most pernicious periods in U.S. history began in 1938 with the establishment of the House Un-American Activities Committee (HUAC). During its decades of authority, it was particularly active in the post–World War II period. Its reign of tyranny reached its full height in the early '50s, spurred on by the activities of Wisconsin Republican senator Joseph McCarthy, who then headed the Senate's Permanent Subcommittee on Investigations.

HUAC's initial thrust in the 1930s was to investigate suspected subversive fifth columnist activities in the U.S. government. The Committee, however, soon branched out. It scrutinized the entertainment industry and, in particular, the film business. Some felt that movies, as a powerful means of communication, had an enormous sway over the public and that those who controlled the medium could subvert filmgoers' political stance. (In particular, this was of concern to HUAC because many screenwriters of the era were intellectuals with ultraliberal political viewpoints that often veered to the left.) Then, too, because motion picture actors were such revered icons who led envious, pampered lifestyles, and because several of these talents had extremely liberal—even leftist—sympathies, they were a ripe target for "exposure." The Committee knew that its probe of Hollywood would give a desired high visibility to its activities.

The resultant scandal, as seen through today's eyes, is that, before the Committee's frenzied purge ran its course, it did a tremendous amount of damage: ruining many artists' careers and personal lives, forcing Hollywood filmmakers to become fearful of expressing variant opinions on screen, and, most of all, subjecting moviegoers to a narrow, approved political philosophy that fell in line with the Cold War mentality of the '50s Eisenhower era. The repercussions of HUAC's attack on Tinseltown have been long lasting, always affecting the public's perceptions of Hollywood to some degree. While there were grounds for accusations of leftist, even Communist, influence in several aspects of Hollywood life, the actual effects on movies were greatly exaggerated at the time for political purposes. And, of course, the shame is that many artistic reputations were permanently soiled in the process.

In 1934, the Soviet government opened a consulate in San Francisco. Part of its plan was to stir up dissent among economically depressed workers on the San Francisco waterfront. (Its activities helped to foment a subsequent dock strike in that metropolis.) Meanwhile, Soviet Communist Party agitators were riling the unhappy labor force in Hollywood where the Great Depression had taken a toll on film industry jobs and salaries. (By 1938, due to the U.S. economic downswing, nearly 40 percent of Tinseltown employees were without work.)

In Hollywood, Communist Party workers and sympathizers were among those to tout loudly the formation of a new federation of craft guilds. They wanted an alternative to the powerful International Alliance of Theatrical Stage Employees (IATSE), then mob-infested and extremely pro–studio management. This anti-IATSE movement spawned the founding of the Conference of Studio Unions in 1941. (The CSU would suffer a fatal blow during the violent 1945–1946 film workers' strike against studio administrations. Aided by underworld forces, the motion picture companies smashed the strike and ended CSU's potential.)

In 1938, in the midst of President Franklin D. Roosevelt's second term of office, liberal Democrats controlled the government and set most American policy. At the time, with the growing power of Nazi Germany, there was increasing congressional concern about pro-Nazi groups influencing and sabotaging America. In this zealous patriotic climate, U.S. Representative Samuel Dickstein from New York suggested the formation of a committee on un-American activities. The resolution passed by a substantial margin in the House in May 1938. Martin Dies, a Texas Democrat, was named its chairman. One of Dies's first activities was to focus the Committee's attention on the German American Bund. Among other results, it led to the closure of German consulates in the United States.

Because of the June 1939 Nazi-Soviet nonaggression pact, it was reasoned that if Hitler's Third Reich was an enemy of America, so too was the Soviet Communist Party and its U.S. branches. Dies pointed out: "The agents of Russian Communism have been at work in the United States three times as long as the agents of German Nazism." The anti-Red investigation heated up as it was learned that many attorneys representing the U.S. government's National Labor Relations Board were members of the National Lawyers Guild, a Communist Party–controlled organization. Soon, Dies's group pried into the American Federation of Labor regarding members' loyalties to the United States.

As part of its surveillance process (aided by the FBI), Committee staff members scanned both domestic and foreign

Communist-affiliated publications as well as membership lists of suspected subversive organizations. This led Dies to announce there were suspected anti-American forces at work within the film community. One of the first "suspects" to be questioned by the Committee was screenwriter John Howard Lawson, who, like other scripters summoned before the investigators, swore under oath that he was not a Communist.

Dies next had "chats" with actors Humphrey Bogart, James Cagney, and Fredric March, as well as scenarist Philip Dunne, all in preparation for planned congressional hearings in Washington, D.C., at which newsreel cameras would be in full use. Eager to avoid subjection to such public dissection, Dunne and the others presented evidence to Dies that they were not Communist sympathizers. Dies was pacified for the time being. Later, a concerned Dunne helped to form Americans for Democratic Action, which, with its Hollywood contingent, challenged such pro-Communist groups as the Progressive Citizens of America (PCA), an organization with a heavy Tinseltown membership.

During the height of World War II, Dies's Committee was preoccupied with largely non-Hollywood investigations. In 1944, J. Parnell Thomas, a New Jersey Republican, became the congressional group's new chairman. Two years later, by a heavy margin, Congress voted to revitalize the Committee, and HUAC snapped back into action.

Since HUAC's formation, America had undergone many dramatic changes: Germany's invasion of Russia in 1941, the death of President Roosevelt in 1945, Vice President Harry S. Truman's taking over the Oval Office that same year, and the end of World War II in 1945, which signaled the start of the Cold War. It was now clear that the Russians had again become America's mortal enemies. Thus, an escalating Red scare engulfed much of the United States in the '50s.

Revving up their activity, J. Parnell Thomas's group went after Gerhart Eisler, alleged by his sister and other informants to be a major leader of American Communism. Gerhart was soon charged with contempt of Congress, passport fraud, and so forth. Meanwhile Eisler's brother, Hanns, a noted musician then writing scores for RKO Pictures, was also brought under investigation. When Hanns refused to cooperate with Thomas's minions, the latter sought corroborating evidence from others in Hollywood. As a result of such preliminary testimony, a recommendation was made to Thomas to hold public hearings about Communist infiltration into the film industry. (Like Dies, Thomas was well aware of the high publicity quotient of attacking the movie business.)

Fueling Thomas's fire were organizations like the liberal PCA, whose membership boasted director John Huston and such notable performers as Katharine Hepburn, Edward G. Robinson, John Garfield, Gregory Peck, and Gene Kelly. Groups such as these (and including the Hollywood Independent Citizens Council of the Arts, Sciences and Professions) were deemed by conservatives to be merely stooges of the Communist Party. (A 1945 U.S. Chambers of Commerce report on "Communist Infiltration in the U.S." warned of inroads made by the Reds in the entertainment industry, especially within the Screen Writers Guild.)

While this threat of exposing Hollywood's Communist underbelly was gaining momentum, the film industry was reeling from several other problems, leaving it too vulnerable to really oppose the investigation. Economically, there had been a downward trend of movie attendance since the war had ended. In 1945–1946 there had been a costly labor strike in Hollywood, which had slowed down production. Meanwhile, congressional antitrust legislation (geared to separate film production from distribution) was readied to further fragment the picture business, as was the growing success of actors combating the studios' contract systems. (There was also the emerging TV industry that offered the public free entertainment.) In addition, anti-Semitic factions in the United States and, in particular, in Congress were anxious to target the Hollywood film business, which they characterized as being run by autocratic Jews.

To appease the contentious congressional committee, Eric A. Johnston, the newly appointed head of the Motion Picture

Association of America (MPAA), informed Congressman Thomas that the movie business welcomed such public hearings, at which time it would demonstrate that Hollywood was *not* Communist-dominated. Initially, it was Johnston's policy that exposing supposed Reds in the film business was fine but should not lead to suspects being fired. (Later, when Johnston's high-paying MPAA job was in jeopardy, he went along with scared industry leaders who created an informal blacklist of suspected anti-Americans.)

On October 20, 1947, in Washington, D.C., a standing-room-only crowd (including newsreel camera operators) watched as Thomas opened the much-hyped hearings. The chairman insisted the proceedings would be "conducted in an orderly and dignified manner at all times" and were in no way to be construed as "an attack on the majority of persons associated with this great industry." Among those who volunteered to speak before the Committee were studio heads Jack L. Warner, Louis B. Mayer, and Walt Disney, as well as veteran actors Adolphe Menjou, Gary Cooper, and Robert Taylor. These friendly witnesses sang the patriotic praise of the United States, decried the making of (and/or their participation in) such past Soviet-friendly Hollywood films as MGM's *Song of Russia* and Warner Bros.'s *Mission to Moscow* (both 1943), and casually tossed out the names of a few Red suspects (in particular, scripters John Howard Lawson and Lester Cole). Director Sam Wood, founder of the Motion Picture Alliance for the Preservation of American Ideals (MPA), proclaimed: "These Communists thump their chests and call themselves liberals, but if you drop their rompers you'll find a hammer and sickle on their rear ends." Virulent anti-Communist novelist Ayn Rand (*The Fountainhead*) was another key speaker. Others who paraded before Thomas's austere assemblage were directors Leo McCarey and Fred Niblo, as well as actors George Murphy and Ronald Reagan. (Reagan intoned: "I abhor the Communist philosophy, but . . . I hope we are never propelled by fear of Communism into compromising any of our democratic principles." Nevertheless, both Reagan and his brother Neil later served as government informants on suspected Reds in Hollywood.)

Still others who spoke to the Committee—but in private—were Roy M. Brewer, an IATSE representative and a strong anti-Communist labor head, as well as actors James Cagney and Robert Montgomery (who also talked in public session). The two stars, backed by Brewer, explained that frequently Communist Party organizers added the names of well-known Hollywood figures to the rolls of Red-oriented causes and political gatherings without the individuals' being aware that this had happened.

With such a high-profile start, there was no question that full hearings focused on suspect Hollywood personalities would soon get under way. Fearing this major attack on individual liberties, a Hollywood coalition was formed called Hollywood Fights Back. Among its participants were actors Lauren Bacall, Humphrey Bogart, Henry Fonda, Marsha Hunt, Danny Kaye, Burt Lancaster, Myrna Loy, Groucho Marx, Burgess Meredith, Gregory Peck, Frank Sinatra, and Jane Wyatt, as well as directors John Huston and William Wyler, and producer Walter Wanger. (Later, HFB changed its name to the Committee for the First Amendment, but it was defunct by the end of the 40s, beaten into compliance by the power of HUAC.)

Next in line to come before Thomas's Committee were 45 subpoenaed unfriendly witnesses. Of that number, only 19 were called. Of this group, 13 were Jewish and also had not served for one reason or another in World War II. Two were involved in the making of 1947's *Crossfire*, an attack on anti-Semitism, and two others participated in the filming of *Mission to Moscow*, considered a pro-Soviet tribute.

Of the 19, only 11 testified. One of them, Bertolt Brecht, the German-born playwright and screenwriter, fled the United States immediately after giving his testimony. The remaining number became known as the Hollywood Ten. They included directors Herbert Biberman and Edward Dmytryk and screenwriters Alvah Bessie, Lester Cole, Ring Lardner Jr., John Howard Lawson, Albert Maltz, Samuel Ornitz, Adrian Scott (also a producer), and Dalton Trumbo. Members of Hollywood Fights Back (Bogart, Bacall, and Kaye) flew to Washington to demonstrate against the congressional proceedings. While the protest created much publicity, their support proved ineffectual at the inquiry, and several of their number, including Bogart, later recanted their "un-American" behavior.

At these congressional hearings, with the media again in full attendance, the Hollywood Ten boldly presented a united front, choosing—in a tactical error—to cite their constitutional rights under the First Amendment (i.e., freedom of speech) rather than relying on the Fifth Amendment (i.e., protection from self-incrimination). Brought before his accusers, Lawson was asked what became the Committee's trademark question: "Are you now, or have you ever been a member of the Communist Party of the United States?" Lawson had his own agenda, which included such statements as, "This committee is on trial here before the American people," and he decried that it was shameful that "I have to teach this committee the basic principles of American[ism]." Lawson was forcibly removed from the proceedings. Thereafter, his Communist Party registration card was entered in "evidence," as were compiled listings of his other suspect affiliations and activities. As with Lawson, when the other witnesses were interrogated, they were shouted down by gavel-wielding Thomas when they refused to respond with a "yes" or "no" to his accusatory questions. Before being removed from the hearings, witness Dalton Trumbo shouted, "This is the beginning of the American concentration camp!"

Thereafter, the Hollywood Ten fought these congressional proceedings in federal district court in mid-1950, but they were found guilty of contempt. The Supreme Court refused to hear the case on appeal. As a result, the defendants went to jail, a few for six months, most for a year.

Meanwhile, 50 film executives from the major Hollywood studios held a clandestine meeting at Manhattan's Waldorf-Astoria Hotel in late November 1947. There, in a fourth-floor suite, they reached a tacit agreement to not employ any of the Hollywood Ten until such time as they were either acquitted for their contempt citations or swore they were not Communists. From this crucial conference arose the "blacklist," in which it was agreed by the studio heads to not employ named or suspected Reds at their film factories. (That same year, the Congressional Taft-Hartley Act stipulated that all labor union officers must sign anti-Communist affidavits for their unions to remain certified as legitimate bargaining bodies. This caused the quick dismissal or non-reelection of film industry guild and union leaders who were suspected of being and/or actually were Communists.)

In November 1950, Canadian-born Edward Dmytryk was released from prison. Having had a sharp change of political and intellectual heart, and determined to again work in the Hollywood film industry, he was ready to make amends. (By then the Korean War had begun and America was undergoing another wave of anti-Communist hysteria.) One step toward Dmytryk's redemption was to have a "friendly" meeting with IATSE's Roy Brewer, the virulent anti-Red. Another was working with writer Richard English on a *Saturday Evening Post* article (May 19, 1951) titled "What Makes a Hollywood Communist?" This published Dmytryk interview set off a battle royal between the director and the remaining Hollywood Ten, who felt he had betrayed them. Dmytryk, who had been nominated for a Best Director Oscar for *Crossfire* (1947), was back directing Hollywood films by 1952. Two years later, he was at the helm of mainstream major films such as *The Caine Mutiny*.

By 1951, HUAC was ready for its next series of hearings. J. Parnell Thomas was no longer in charge. He had pled no contest to embezzling government funds and was serving three years behind bars. John S. Wood was chosen as the chairman of these federal inquiries. (Also by this point, Senator Joseph McCarthy was running rampant with his scurrilous campaign to dig out the hundreds of alleged Communists in the State Department and the U.S. Army. It was not until 1954, with the televised Army-McCarthy hearings, that the tide of support turned against loose cannon McCarthy and his largely unfounded witch hunt. He was censured by the U.S. Senate, losing his once-huge power and standing.)

Among the first Hollywood personalities to testify before HUAC's new session in March 1951 was Larry Parks, one of those subpoenaed in 1947 but not called before the session. At this point, the Committee demanded that this star of *The Jolson Story* (1946) and *Jolson Sings Again* (1949) not only humble himself but also humiliate himself by naming other alleged Reds. (It was not that HUAC did not already have any names that Parks might reveal. However, it was a way to show the Committee's power by making the recanting witness a stool pigeon, thus debasing the individual completely.) While Parks acknowledged that he may have been misguided in his political viewpoints and misled in his political affiliations (e.g., joining the leftist Actors Laboratory) in his younger days, the actor insisted that it was his American right to make such personal decisions without fear of recrimination and in order not to be a "cow in the pasture." He reiterated, "I do not believe that I did anything wrong." At later interrogations (held in executive, private sessions, but with the results leaked to the press), he named names, squirming with self-hatred in the process. As a result of his sweated confession, he made only one more major film (1962's *Freud*). The blacklist (and the later backlash of those who felt betrayed by him) forced this broken man to eke out his living with occasional stage and TV assignments. (Parks's torturous situation led to a splintering within the Motion Picture Alliance for the Preservation of American Ideals. Its then president, actor John Wayne, spoke out in sympathy for Parks, while, on the other hand, another Alliance member, gossip columnist Hedda Hopper, opined that once a Commie always a Commie.)

Parks's abject mortification set the tone for subsequent witnesses in the hot seat. They included performers John Garfield, Sterling Hayden, José Ferrer, and Edward G. Robinson. If Dmytryk's recanting in April 1951 marked a low point for many in the shotgun hearings, the nadir came when stage/film director Elia Kazan took the stand in April 1952. He buckled under in a grand manner, providing names as requested. Because he kowtowed so strongly to the Committee, Kazan continued to direct major studio features such as 1953's *Man on a Tightrope* and 1954's *On the Waterfront.* Forty-five years later he won an honorary Oscar for his career achievements. Recalling Dmytryk's 1952 stance, several in the Hollywood community felt Kazan did not deserve the accolade and booed him at the Oscar festivities.

HUAC's investigation of Communist infiltration in the entertainment industry was *not* limited to just the movies but also dealt with the mediums of radio, TV, and Broadway (where many leftist-inclined organizations such as the Federal Theater Group had thrived in the 1930s). Reputations were sullied by merely being listed on the roll of subpoenaed witnesses, let alone being named by a frightened testifier who may or may not have spoken accurately. Once-potent Hollywood names (e.g., Edward G. Robinson, John Garfield, Anne Revere, Howard da Silva, Marsha Hunt, J. Edward Bromberg, Zero Mostel, and Gale Sondergaard), tainted and shunned by the Hollywood establishment, fled to the Broadway stage, where producers were more willing to risk hiring them. Or they traveled abroad to make movies. Or, in those days when TV was still the film industry's arch enemy, they made forays into that "lesser" medium. Scriptwriters who had not decamped to Mexico, Europe, or South America were reduced to accepting a pittance of their usual wages to write screenplays anonymously, with the credit going to a "front" (as detailed in the Woody Allen–Zero Mostel movie *The Front*, 1976). The same situation befell once-esteemed Hollywood film directors (e.g., Jules Dassin and Joseph Losey).

As the '50s moved onward, HUAC eventually ran out of big show business names to embarrass and torment. By then, witnesses were frequently invoking their Fifth Amendment rights to not incriminate themselves.

Since that bleak period, Hollywood has made only a scant few features (e.g., 1991's *Guilty by Suspicion*) dealing with this dark era. However, there have been myriad books on the complex subject (including the pathfinding *Only Victims*, 1972, by actor Robert Vaughn) and several documentaries (e.g., 1976's *Hollywood on Trial* and 2002's *Scandalize My Name*).

The hope that such an age of persecution as the 1950s' anti-Red witch hunt could never again happen in America was frustrated, to a degree, as the United States endured the terrorist attacks of

September 11, 2001, leading to the wars in Afghanistan and, later, Iraq. One had only to observe the vicious sniping, boycotting, and so forth that befell entertainers such as Sean Penn and the Dixie Chicks, who dared to speak out against the 2003 war against Iraq, to be discouraged once again about individuals' civil liberties.

Robert Mitchum: Hollywood's Literate Rebel

"It has been common gossip for months that a dope scandal was hovering dangerously over the film colony. Luncheon crowds discussed it freely wherever film folks and newspaper correspondents gather. . . . What will Hollywood do now, officially, to clean its house and try to win back some of the public confidence it has destroyed in the disgraceful mess of the past few weeks? . . . Right now Hollywood has the biggest problem of all on its hands. The public never did—never will—laugh off a dope scandal involving a favorite screen performer."
—REPORTER HAROLD HEFFERNON, IN THE *INDIANAPOLIS STAR* ON
SEPTEMBER 19, 1948

Today, with heroin, cocaine, ecstasy, and other deadly drugs of choice so easily available throughout the world, it seems almost "trivial" that a drug bust about a few joints of marijuana once should have caused such furious repercussions. However, in the far more moralistic, conformist climate of 1948, this was, indeed, shocking news to the public. That the arrest involved a major Hollywood star—Robert Mitchum—made the scandal that much more electrifying. Adding fuel to the mix, the Los Angeles police had long been hunting for a big-name catch to help restore their credibility after years of police corruption, and they did their best to play up the situation for all it was worth. Meanwhile, the press seized on this tantalizing episode to heighten circulation and, in the process, sensationalize the coverage.

Hollywood moguls reeled at the September 1, 1948, arrest of Mitchum (and three noncelebrities) for, among other things, conspiracy to possess marijuana. They remembered all too well when several silent screen notables (including Wallace Reid, Mabel Normand, Barbara La Marr, and Alma Rubens) suffered drug-addiction-related deaths in the '20s and early '30s, as well as the furor of moral watchdogs across the country. At that time, such "debauchery" inspired attempts at federal control of Hollywood movies and its stars. Such drastic action had been avoided only when movie executives formed an industry self-censorship administration to keep Tinseltown on a higher moral plane—at least on the surface.

In the post-World War II climate, the Hollywood studios were extremely vulnerable. Movie attendance had diminished dramatically and would get worse as the spread of commercial TV would provide viewers with free entertainment. Moreover, the government had started the separation of film production and exhibition that hurt the studios' profit margins. In addition, the American entertainment business was cowering from the congressional anti-Communist witch hunt. The battered picture industry dreaded what this latest scandal might do to their sagging financial bottom lines. (On a more direct economic level, Mitchum had three completed features awaiting release at the time of his arrest. Two of the pictures were made for his home lot, RKO, and one was for Republic. These studios, as well as independent producer David O. Selznick, who controlled a piece of the star's RKO contract, panicked at the thought of losing their substantial investments in the popular actor.)

Robert Charles Durman Mitchum was born on August 6, 1917, in Bridgeport, Connecticut, the second child of James Thomas Mitchum and Norwegian immigrant Ann Harriet Gunderson. While Ann was pregnant with her third child, the family moved to South Carolina, the father's home state. There, in February 1919, while working in the Charleston navy yard, James was killed in a railroad accident. Mrs. Mitchum took her children back to her family in Connecticut, where, in September, she gave birth to John. Later, she married a raucous New York newspaper reporter, Bill Clancy, whose sideline activities included bootlegging. The union ended when Clancy erupted in a drunken rage, almost killing Ann and then disappearing. To support her clan, Mrs. Mitchum worked as a Linotypist at a local newspaper.

Robert shared his mother's love for poetry and the other arts. By age eight his poems were being published in the *Bridgeport Post-Telegram*. Like his younger brother, John, Mitchum was a rowdy, restless youth, frequently getting into mischief. When Robert was nine, he and John were sent to live with relatives on their farm in Woodside, Delaware. In 1928, Mitchum ran away from home for a time with a pal. The next year, he and John were shipped off to stay with their sister, Annette ("Julie"), in Philadelphia. Thereafter, the boys were reunited with their mother in Manhattan. (By then, she had wed for the third time.) The year 1932 found the prankish Mitchum brothers removed from temptations of city life to live with kin in Delaware. There, in Rising Sun, precocious Robert accelerated through high school academics. However, he left Felton High before graduation to once again take to the road.

His vagabond life led to his being arrested for vagrancy in Savannah, Georgia, in the summer of 1933. After 30 days on a chain gang, he escaped and returned to his mother, then living in Delaware. Later he tramped around the country, working at odd jobs (e.g., prizefighter, punch-press operator, coal miner). By the summer of 1937 the former hobo was in Long Beach, California, where his sister resided. He became involved with a community dramatic group and appeared on stage there; later, he authored a play. However, his wanderlust frequently kept him on the move. In the autumn of 1939, he worked for astrologer Carroll Righter, who was making an East Coast tour at the time.

Back in 1933, Mitchum had met Dorothy Spence at a swimming hole in Camden, Delaware. They fell in love, and he promised to marry her one day. They wed in March 1940 and moved to California, where he became a sheet metal worker at Lockheed Aircraft in Burbank. Their first son, James, was born in 1941. (Son Christopher arrived in 1943 and daughter Petrine in 1952.) Abhorring the grind of conventional work, Robert drifted into film acting. A talent agent decided he was made for cowboy pictures, as

Mitchum was six feet, one inch, beefy, and ruggedly handsome. As such, Robert made his screen debut as an actor/stuntman in the Hopalong Cassidy Western *Hoppy Serves a Writ* (1943).

Because sleepy-eyed Mitchum would accept any type of screen assignment, by the end of 1944 he had appeared in 23 releases— sometimes in bit parts, other times in more substantial roles. By then, Mitchum had signed an RKO Pictures contract, and independent producer David O. Selznick had purchased part of this pact for his Vanguard Films.

In April 1945, Mitchum was drafted into the army and spent seven months at service camps in California. Meanwhile, that June, Robert's *The Story of G.I. Joe* premiered to excellent reviews. As the tough but caring army officer, Robert received a Best Supporting Actor Oscar nomination.

In the next few years his movie career mushroomed with, among others, prestigious leading parts opposite Katharine Hepburn (1946's *Undercurrent*) and Greer Garson (1947's *Desire Me*), as well as a key assignment in a controversial murder yarn (1947's *Crossfire*). Now earning more than $100,000 yearly at RKO, Robert and his family purchased a modest four-bedroom home near Universal Studios. Everything *seemed* to be going well for the Mitchums.

However, there were conflicts. Levelheaded Dorothy was wary of the Hollywood lifestyle. At the same time, she was disturbed by her husband's casual attitude toward his career and his seeming disinterest in building financial security for their future. (Robert left pesky financial matters to his business manager—and best friend— Paul Behrmann.) Moreover, Dorothy was upset by Robert's devotion to a variety of "undesirables," hangers-on such as bartender Robin "Danny" Ford. She also disapproved of her husband's smoking of marijuana joints, which were illegal. Moreover, she was well aware that her spouse, who enjoyed too many nights out on the town with his leeching pals, was an easy target for attractive women seeking a quick fling.

One day in late 1947, Mrs. Mitchum needed cash for household expenses. Unable to reach Paul Behrmann (who usually doled out a small weekly sum to the actor), she went to their bank. She was flabbergasted to discover that only $58 remained of what should have been around $50,000. When Robert confronted Behrmann, the latter acknowledged that the funds were gone, but he refused to give details of the situation. Dorothy was furious when Mitchum would not press charges against Paul. The actor reasoned that his best friend's actions had left him "more hurt than angry," and he let the matter drop, which infuriated Mrs. Mitchum. Robert's relatives were so nonplussed by his strange reaction to the betrayal that they pressured him to see a psychiatrist. The latter informed Robert that he was suffering from "a state of overamiability." He shrugged his shoulders and went home.

Within months, con artist Behrmann resurfaced into the Mitchums' lives. He was accused of swindling $10,000 from a Burbank housewife. In the court case, the prosecution subpoenaed the Mitchums to testify. Paul was furious at his former friend for agreeing to testify and was especially aggravated that Dorothy had supposedly volunteered damaging information against him. Behrmann vowed retaliation. During the courtroom proceedings, Robert testified. As a result of his and others' testimony, Behrmann was sentenced to San Quentin Prison. Thereafter, Robert received anonymous threats.

The accumulation of stress over the Behrmann matter, their emptied bank accounts, as well as Mitchum's seedy friends and carousing pushed Dorothy into action. She demanded they return East to stay with relatives in Delaware. Because Robert was between pictures, he sheepishly complied. However, Mitchum grew restless immediately. He convinced Dorothy to drive into New York for several days, where he met with David Selznick about possible new projects. Then Mitchum had to return to L.A. to start a film at the end of May. Dorothy refused to go. As such, he traveled westward alone while she and the boys remained in Delaware—for the time being.

As Robert was returning to the West Coast, Howard Hughes was negotiating the takeover of RKO. Once that coup was accomplished, production ground to a near halt as Hughes put a new regime in place. Mitchum found himself with too much spare time that summer. To keep busy and, he hoped, to woo Dorothy and the boys back to Hollywood, he carried through on his pledge to find the family a better home in a more appropriate neighborhood. Figuring he could assist a pal, he turned to Robin Ford, who was now trying his hand at real estate. He asked Ford to help him sell the Mitchums' current place and locate their new residence.

Together they made a few forays in search of a new home. However, Robert was more intrigued when Robin introduced him to Lila Leeds, an attractive young actress who had spent short tenures at MGM and Warner Bros. At loose ends, this Lana Turner look-alike frequented the nightclub circuit where she often got into arguments with other patrons. More recently, she had attempted suicide with an overdose of sleeping pills. Robert and Lila hit it off and began dating, with neither expecting the relationship to be more than just fun. They both enjoyed smoking pot and discussed having a marijuana party at her place sometime in the future.

By the end of August 1948, Leeds was subletting a ramshackle, three-room cottage with 25-year-old dancer Vicki Evans at 8443 Ridpath Drive in the Hollywood Hills. On Tuesday, August 31, Robert and Robin spent the day house hunting. That evening, when he and Ford returned to Mitchum's home, his secretary conveyed a phone message from Lila Leeds. He called her and she invited them to see her new digs that evening after 10:00. He said they might. While Robert and Robin continued drinking at Mitchum's, Lila called a contact to purchase marijuana sticks.

Late that moonlit evening, Mitchum and his pal drove up Laurel Canyon to Lila's place. The two men joined their blond hosts inside, where Lila, Robert, and Robin smoked marijuana sticks, using the ones Mitchum had brought in a partially filled pack of regular cigarettes. Soon thereafter, Evans, who was not smoking, thought she heard a noise on the porch and went to check. When she unlocked the kitchen door, two L.A. police officers, who had been hiding outside, rushed in and placed the quartet under arrest.

Within minutes, other law enforcers as well as an investigator from the Federal Narcotics Bureau arrived. Photos were taken, evidence was gathered (including three marijuana cigarettes and Benzedrine tablets found in Lila's bathrobe pocket), and the four individuals were hustled off to jail, the men in handcuffs. Each was booked on a felony charge of possessing narcotics, an offense that carried a penalty of up to six years behind bars. Photographers and reporters rushed to the lockup to capture this hot story.

In the first onslaught of newspaper accounts of the bust, one of the arresting police detectives claimed that the actor had been shadowed for months as he visited clubs and bars around town and attended parties at friends' homes. He pledged, "We're going to clean the dope and the narcotics users out of Hollywood. And we don't care *whom* we're going to have to arrest! This raid is only the beginning!"

Later that night, Howard Hughes arranged for Mitchum's bail. The next morning, Robert told the congregated press, "I was framed." This contradicted the statement released by the police that had the actor saying, "Yes, boys, I was smoking the marijuana cigarette when you came in. I guess it's all over now. I've been smoking marijuana for years. The last time I smoked was about a week ago. I knew I would get caught sooner or later. This is the bitter end of my career. I'm ruined." Meanwhile, the film player kept a cool demeanor. (At the time, the actor, branded a "dope fiend," was less than jovial about his plight. He feared the studio would invoke the morals clause in his contract and he would be out of work. So convinced was he of this, that when he was booked, he listed his occupation as "former actor.")

While formulating damage control, Hughes hid Mitchum at a studio staff member's home. Soon a joint statement was issued by RKO and Selznick: "Both studios feel confident the American people will not permit Mr. Mitchum's prominence in the motion picture industry to deprive him of the rights and privileges of every American citizen to receive fair play." Famed industry attorney Jerry Giesler, hired by Hughes to represent Mitchum, offered, "There are a number of unexplained facts and peculiar circumstances surrounding the raid." Meanwhile, RKO convinced Dorothy Mitchum to return immediately to the West Coast with her sons to show support for her husband.

At the county grand jury proceedings, the four defendants were indicted on two charges: possession of marijuana and conspiracy to possess marijuana. At the September 30 hearing before superior court Judge Thomas Ambrose the four pleaded not guilty. The subsequent trial date was twice postponed when Giesler was injured in an October 2 auto accident and required time to mend. Meanwhile, many newspapers across America published sanctimonious editorials berating the immorality of Hollywood and demanding action be taken to clean up the town (including the ending of Mitchum's film career).

Meanwhile, deciding they had far too much invested in Mitchum's career, RKO chose not to fire Robert for moral turpitude. As such, that fall RKO released its two completed Mitchum pictures: *Rachel and the Stranger* and *Blood on the Moon*. Both films did well. RKO's gamble had worked.

On January 10, 1949, Mitchum, Ford, and Leeds appeared in the courtroom of Judge Clement D. Nye. (Evans had disappeared back East.) Initially, Giesler strategized to have his client plead not guilty by claiming a frame-up and showing that Mitchum had been lured to the bungalow as part of the setup. However, the attorney altered his plan when prosecutors mentioned they intended to reveal unsavory information about Robert's carousing that would have destroyed his screen standing. Thus, it was agreed that the possession charge would be set to one side if the accused waived a jury trial, offered no defense, and allowed the testimony from the grand jury proceedings to be made part of the new record. As a result, the judge found the trio guilty with a February 9 date set for sentencing.

Howard Hughes made good use of Mitchum's free time. He rushed *The Big Steal* (1949) into production. It was a slapped-together story of a chase across Mexico to corral heist crooks. Hal Wallis at Paramount agreed to loan out Lizabeth Scott as Robert's colead, then changed his mind, fearing her working with a felon would taint her career. Next, Hughes assigned and then canceled his studio's prize female star, Jane Russell, for the vehicle. Instead, the mogul called on RKO contract leading lady Jane Greer (with whom he was feuding) to take on the part. She had teamed with Mitchum in *Out of the Past* and gladly agreed to the rematch.

After days of rushed filming on the RKO lot, Robert returned to the courtroom on February 9. Mitchum and Leeds were sentenced to a year in jail, but the judge suspended the order. He placed them on probation for two years, with the defendants to spend 60 days in the county jail. (Ford's sentencing was postponed because of other problems he was having with the law.) In making his determination, Judge Nye said, "I am treating it the same as I would any case of a similar nature. This sentence must serve as an example for hundreds of thousands of fans."

Following a week in the county jail, Mitchum, prisoner number 91234, was transferred—thanks to pressure from RKO and Mitchum's attorney—to the Wayside Honor Farm in Castaic, 40 miles north of Los Angeles. In the midst of his long workdays of manual labor, his captors allowed the press to photograph the star milking cows, working at the cement plant, and so forth. Among his occasional visitors at the facility were his wife and Howard Hughes. The latter brought the prisoner a large sack of vitamins and agreed to make his employee a $50,000 loan to buy his family a new home and to pay his attorney bills.

By March 24, Mitchum had been returned to the county jail, and on March 30, he (as well as Leeds) was released (10 days early because of good behavior). When asked about his prison farm time, Mitchum quipped, "I feel wonderful. I worked hard, slept well and batted .800 on the softball team. . . . [It was] like Palm Springs, without the riffraff." Once Robert was back home, the RKO publicists coordinated photo sessions featuring Mitchum and his family. It was business as usual.

Trim and tanned Robert soon flew to Mexico to undertake location filming for *The Big Steal.* To appease filmgoers who had not yet forgiven the star's much-publicized misadventure, the May 1949 issue of *Photoplay* magazine carried an article ("Do I Get Another Chance?") in which the contrite star reflected, "Now I am facing life with a new sense of responsibility to the world, to myself, and above all to my wife and our two sons. No matter what is cooking for me in the future, I am dedicating my life to dispelling the cloud hanging over my family. . . ."

A coda to Mitchum's bizarre misadventure occurred in January 1951 following the L.A. County district attorney's investigations of allegations that the star had been framed. Superior court Judge Nye, in reviewing Mitchum's case, entered a plea of "not guilty" to replace the actor's earlier plea of *nolo contendere*. He then expunged the case from the court records. For many reasons, the unusual results of the new inquiry went unpublicized, but Robert was glad to let the difficult matter drop. (Years later, Mitchum acknowledged that when Hughes had investigated the situation he'd found there had been a connection between the ongoing Paul Behrmann extortion case and a major L.A. blackmail operation spearheaded by organized crime figure Mickey Cohen. Among those implicated in the Cohen extortion ring was Lila Leeds. There was also evidence that Leeds's bungalow had been wired with microphones as part of Mitchum's entrapment.)

This contorted legal case and its repercussions followed the prolific actor until his death on July 1, 1997. Thereafter, it became part of Mitchum's legend as the larger-than-life Hollywood bad boy who once "calmly" faced a career-shattering catastrophe that potentially threatened the entire film business.

Regarding Robert's landmark moment under pressure, Mitchum's longtime friend Jane Greer had a special take on his stance. She said in the early 1990s, "To the people who knew him well, the gesture of remaining himself was the greatest piece of acting Mitchum had ever done. It was the toughest job in his career. For we could see that—far from the impression given by the newspapers—Bob was intensely upset by what had happened. He was upset for himself and he was even more upset for his wife and two sons. This latter fact came out just once: when he asked the photographers not to take pictures of him behind bars because his kids might see them. Otherwise, he did not show his extreme discomfort—and the fact that he did not, was a very special sort of heroism to those who love him. . . ."

Ingrid Bergman: Tarnished Saint

"Mr. President, now that the stupid film [1950's Stromboli] about a pregnant woman and a volcano has exploited America with the usual finesse to the mutual delight of RKO and the debased Rossellini, are we merely to yawn wearily, greatly relieved that this hideous thing is finished and then forget it? I hope not. A way must be found to protect the people in the future. . . . When Rossellini the love pirate returned to Rome smirking over his conquest, it was not Mrs. Lindstrom's [i.e., Ingrid Bergman's] scalp which hung from the conquering hero's belt; it was her very soul. Now what is left of her has brought two children into the world—one has no mother; the other is illegitimate."
—SENATOR EDWIN C. JOHNSON, ON THE FLOOR OF THE U.S. SENATE
ON MARCH 14, 1950

B randing screen star Ingrid Bergman, "a free-love cultist [and] an apostle of degradation," the U.S. senator from Colorado dramatically proposed a congressional bill granting the Department of Commerce jurisdiction to license films, performers, and producers based on moral decency. While Johnson's diatribe—made part of the congressional record—did not result in the demanded legislation, it reflected the attitude of much of the outraged American public at the start of the morally conservative, conformist 1950s. The target of this mass hysteria was Swedish-born Bergman, a wife, mother, and top international movie celebrity, who had indulged in a love fling with married Italian filmmaker Roberto Rossellini. At the time, her daring activity shocked the sensibilities of traditionalists. What made her liaison even more reprehensible to some was that her affair had been played out so openly (and brazenly) in the public eye.

As the robust leading lady of such successful Hollywood features as *Casablanca* (1942), *For Whom the Bell Tolls* (1943), *Gaslight* (1944—for which she won her first Oscar), *Spellbound* (1945—the first of her movies made with director Alfred Hitchcock), and *Notorious* (1946), Ingrid was beloved by both critics and filmgoers. Having already appeared on screen as a nun in *The Bells of St. Mary's* (1945), she had recently portrayed a saint in 1948's *Joan of Arc*. As a result, the viewing public had placed this radiant, natural beauty on a pedestal of idealism, confusing her screen roles with the real person.

The actual Bergman was much more complex than her concocted wholesome and impeccable screen image suggested. A dedicated, talented actress, her creative ambitions were not being satisfied by her Hollywood career. Nor were her emotional needs being met by her controlling Swedish husband, Petter Lindstrom, a dentist turned physician. So anxious was she to escape the confining Hollywood studio system and the suffocating bounds of marriage (which had produced a daughter, Friedel Pia, in 1938) that she latched onto Rossellini—the famed director of Italian neorealistic pictures—as both her professional and personal savior.

The key problem was that the outspoken actress was far too direct—and much too naive—to hide her personal feelings from public scrutiny. To deny her need for Rossellini was not an option for the highly charged Bergman. By bringing her love affair (which resulted in an illegitimate child) into the open, she violated a then key precept of Tinseltown: keep your follies hidden from public view. By being so blatantly indiscreet, impetuous Ingrid caused the movie studios great embarrassment, unwanted governmental scrutiny, and, the worst sin of all, lost box-office revenue. For her recklessness, Bergman was banished from the film colony (and the United States) for the next several years. It was a stringent punishment for disreputable behavior, one that had *never* been doled out before by Tinseltown.

Today, with our changed moral standards, it is hard to appreciate the scope of the worldwide furor, shock, and disappointment that Bergman's illicit romance ignited. It was an emotional earthquake rivaled only by the 1930s' romance of already twice-married Mrs. Wallis Simpson and the Duke of Windsor, which led the latter to abdicate the throne of England.

Ingrid was born on August 29, 1915, in Stockholm, Sweden, the daughter of Justus Bergman and the German-born Frieda Adler. In 1918, Frieda died, leaving Justus to raise his only surviving child with the help of kin as well as the young mistress he later acquired. Although Mr. Bergman was a camera shop proprietor, he had many creative interests and ambitions that would become realized through his daughter. As a youngster, Ingrid was highly imaginative and enjoyed acting out skits. When she attended a performance at the Royal Dramatic Theater in 1926, she instinctively knew she had found her life's work. Tragedy struck again, in 1929, when Justus died, and Lutheran-born Ingrid went to live with one of her aunts. The next year the woman died, and the 14-year-old moved again, this time forced to reside with stern relatives.

In 1932, Ingrid made her film debut as an extra in *Landskamp*. The next year she was accepted at the Royal Dramatic Theater School. While learning her craft, the teenager had her first affair. Her lover was 41-year-old actor Edvin Adolphson, a married man and a father. She was sufficiently practical to realize that the relationship could not endure. Later, she dated dentist Petter Aron Lindstrom, nine years her senior. Of this situation, Ingrid said, "It was not love at first sight, but it grew into something which, to both of us, became very important and impossible to live without." The couple wed in July 1937.

In the mid-1930s, Ingrid not only acted on stage but made several feature films. With her natural beauty and refreshingly direct personality she quickly became a leading light of the Swedish movie industry. In early 1938, she went to Berlin to make a picture. (Curious about many aspects of life, Ingrid was, however, largely apolitical, and she saw no reason not to work in Nazi Germany.) Following this project, she gave birth to Pia in the fall of 1938. While considering film offers in her homeland, Germany, and elsewhere, Ingrid was contacted by a representative of Hollywood producer David Selznick. He was aware of her striking screen performance in *Intermezzo* (1935) and wanted to remake it for U.S. filmgoers. Bergman signed a $2,000-per-week contract with Selznick. In abandoning her homeland, she felt that if the Hollywood experience proved unsuccessful, she could always return to Swedish and/or German picturemaking.

Upon becoming captivated with the nearly five-foot, eight-inch Bergman, Selznick said, "She had an extraordinary quality of purity and nobility and a definite star personality that is very rare." However, he immediately wanted to remold the blond talent with a Hollywood look. She refused to have her facial features adjusted and he, surprisingly, gave in. Ingrid made *Intermezzo* (1939), which pleased both reviewers and the public. Her Selznick agreement was extended, and, when she wasn't making pictures, she acted on stage (including in 1940's *Liliom* on Broadway). While playing the street tart in *Dr. Jekyll and Mr. Hyde* (1941), she experienced a close personal relationship with much-older married director Victor Fleming, one that aroused the resentment of already wed costar Spencer Tracy, who had become enamored with the Swedish import. Sparks reportedly flew between Ingrid and Gary Cooper when they made 1943's *For Whom the Bell Tolls*, a situation that supposedly heated up when they were rematched for 1945's *Saratoga Trunk*.

However, the real romance of these years for Bergman was her involvement with daring war photographer Robert Capa, a widower. It began in May 1945 in Paris where she had traveled to meet the victorious Allied troops. He was 31, and she was entranced because he was "worldly and wise, and yet . . . still vulnerable." Capa visited her in Los Angeles and they later rendezvoused in 1947 in Germany, but the couple concluded that the obstacles of her fame and marital status were too great to overcome.

Meanwhile, Ingrid had grown tremendously restless with her Hollywood picture assignments made on a freelance basis after her Selznick pact ended in 1946. Moreover, she was bored by her stifling home life with her husband, then working on his physician's license. Bergman had seen *Open City* (1945) and *Paisan* (1946) and thrilled at these raw, newsreel-style studies of everyday people coping with life's great forces. She was so tremendously inspired that, in April 1948, she wrote the films' director, Roberto Rossellini, in Rome. "If you need a Swedish actress who speaks English very well, who has not forgotten her German, who is not very understandable in French, and who in Italian knows only 'ti amo' [I love you], I am ready to come and make a film with you." Within weeks, the 42-year-old Italian filmmaker wired her, "It is absolutely true that I dreamed to make a film with you and from this moment I will do everything that such dream becomes reality as soon as possible."

With no sense of what lurked in the future, Bergman's husband was an equal supporter of Ingrid's making a picture with Rossellini. Petter and Pia were with Ingrid in London in the summer of 1948 where she was filming *Under Capricorn* (1949). She arranged a weekend visit to Paris. There, with her husband at her side, Ingrid met with Roberto on August 28, the day before her 33rd birthday. Despite her husband's concerns about the financial terms of the deal, Ingrid agreed to work with Rossellini on a movie.

What Ingrid was totally unprepared for was the muddled nature of Roberto's frenzied personal and professional life. One of four sons of a Rome architect, he had abandoned school to pursue his love of the cinema. At 20 he was confined for nearly a year to a mental asylum, perhaps because of a nervous breakdown or because of his parents' concern about his fast and furious lifestyle. A born Casanova, with an explosive, unpredictable temperament, he did not abandon his wild ways when, in 1936, he wed the aristocratic Marcella de Marchis.

Having survived Mussolini's regime during World War II, Rossellini charmed both his wife and his then current mistress to help finance *Open City* in 1945. Among the other women in Roberto's complicated romantic life was tempestuous, famed Italian actress Anna Magnani, who had starred in several of Roberto's recent movies.

This Italian's ways of filmmaking were equally unruly. He relied on his creative genius to overcome an overriding lack of discipline, preparation, and focus. With such casual work habits,

Roberto was unequipped and disinterested in directing in the Hollywood studio system style, one in which the highly disciplined Bergman had been nurtured. However, he was eager for the fame, money, and respect that working with a major Hollywood notable would bring him.

Emotionally committed to going abroad for this exciting new project, Ingrid was propelled into action by events. In early 1949, her cherished friend director Victor Fleming died of a heart attack at 65, cutting off one of her close ties to the movie colony. Her recent pictures, including 1948's *Arch of Triumph*, had been problematic at the box office, which increased her concerns about her future. In mid-January 1949, Rossellini arrived in L.A., seeking American financing for the Bergman vehicle. After staying with the Lindstroms for several days, Roberto realized he had fallen in love with his hostess. Buoyed by her great belief in Rossellini's craftsmanship, Ingrid was flattered by his devout attention (in direct contrast to her somber husband, who never complimented her on her acting talents). The couple began their affair, to which several in the movie colony (but not Petter Lindstrom) were privy.

Eventually, it was playboy billionaire Howard Hughes who helped to finance the Bergman-Rossellini screen collaboration. Having acquired controlling interest of RKO Pictures, Howard hoped his support of her international film venture would, one day, lead to a romance with Ingrid. As part of Hughes's deal for the American release rights to Roberto's new opus, Ingrid agreed to subsequently make a picture for Hughes's studio.

Overjoyed at the prospect of filming in Europe and excited about her temporary escape from her husband, Ingrid embarked for Rome on March 11, 1949. Initially, she thought she would be abroad for about three months.

Days after arriving in Italy, the suddenly liberated Bergman was heading to Amalfi with Roberto. As they toured that southern Italian city, a *Life* magazine photographer snapped a picture of them holding hands, fueling the already growing rumors that the duo were no longer just creative teammates. By April 3, Ingrid was writing to

Petter in L.A. about her grand passion for Rossellini: "I would like to ask forgiveness, but that seems ridiculous. It is not all together my fault and how can you forgive that I want to stay with Roberto." What Bergman had not calculated on was how much of a blow this public humiliation was to the Swedish doctor's ego. Becoming intransigent in the coming months, Lindstrom used 10-year-old Pia as leverage against his love-struck wife.

While the maelstrom of scandal was gathering force, Rossellini shot *Stromboli* on the title island near the coast of Sicily. The production was conducted in his usual haphazard method. This meant working without much or any script and largely using amateurs to fill roles in his somber drama. Highly professional, well-organized Bergman quickly became disillusioned with Roberto's work style as they filmed their bleak tale set in a fishing village and against the backdrop of Stromboli, a still-active volcano. However, throughout the venture, she was sustained by her love for Roberto and his past cinematic achievements.

By the first of May, Lindstrom was meeting his wife in Italy to discuss their future. Although he knew better, Petter insisted to the press, "There will be no divorce." In actuality, he and Ingrid were already talking about a permanent split. But he was playing for time, procrastinating in resolving this scandal that had become the talk of the world. Meanwhile, Bergman, appreciating that her bolt from the United States had cut off her ties and resources in Hollywood, told the press that a statement about her status with Roberto would soon be forthcoming. Money-minded Hughes used the accelerating circumstances to fan the gossip and, he hoped, increase the film's ticket sales in the United States.

In early June, Ingrid discovered she was pregnant. Because of a lava burst on Stromboli she was unable to meet her husband in London as planned. He returned to L.A., unaware that she was expecting a child in January or February. Trying to counter her spouse's crafty campaign to win their daughter's loyalty, Bergman wrote frequently to Pia. However, because matters dragged on and especially because Ingrid refused to brave the growing moral outcries in the States by flying home to see Pia, the girl became embittered toward her mother.

In the midst of all this, Ingrid became the target of Hollywood's Motion Picture Production Code Administration. Its director, Joseph I. Breen, wrote her that she *must* not divorce her husband to marry Rossellini, as this breach of decorum could cost Bergman her career. Producer Walter Wanger sent the star a similar letter, begging her to consider the financial fate of their *Joan of Arc*. That epic was in general release and was doing poorly because moviegoers refused to accept Ingrid as the noble peasant leader.

Beset by the spiraling situation and lack of proper communication with Lindstrom, Ingrid struggled through the early August completion of *Stromboli*. Thereafter, she and Rossellini returned to his Rome apartment. Regaining confidence, she bravely announced that she was quitting pictures to enjoy a private life and that her attorney was proceeding with her divorce from Lindstrom. Meanwhile, Roberto convinced his obliging wife to end their marriage. While many around the world were condemning Ingrid as a whore and home wrecker, the locals in Rome were largely enthusiastic toward their new celebrity resident.

Thanks to undiplomatic statements fed to the media by her self-absorbed lawyer, Ingrid lost points with the American public. Matters were made worse because Lindstrom had become a U.S. citizen, while Ingrid was still the "foreigner." As 1949 ended, Ingrid went into seclusion, fearful that her pregnancy would be all too obvious to the ever-pursuing press. However, Bergman's cover was blown when Howard Hughes (back in Hollywood) learned of her condition and leaked the sensational information hoping to build interest in *Stromboli*. The shocking news made headlines during the Christmas season. Branded a scarlet woman, Bergman observed, "Having been so loved, I was now deeply hated."

On February 2, she eluded the persistent paparazzi as she was rushed from Rossellini's apartment to a Rome medical clinic. That evening she delivered a baby boy, Robertino. The news created major headlines around the world. Thereafter, the determined press did everything possible to break into the private health center to snap a shot of this infamous love child. Meanwhile, Bergman received a steady flow of hate mail. Back in the United States, Senator Frank Lunsford of Georgia spearheaded a resolution to ban all of Rossellini and Bergman's movies in the Peachtree State because they "glamorized free love." He labeled Ingrid's actions as "a stench in the nostrils of decent people." Various church forces in America followed suit, lambasting Ingrid for her ungodly actions. In mid-month, *Stromboli* was released to poor reviews. Part of the hypocrisy of the times found exhibitors canceling the remainder of their bookings of the feature when audiences failed to be drawn to this laborious, somber tale. As an excuse for backing out of their exhibition contracts, they claimed that they refused to continue showing a picture starring such a disgraceful performer. (On the other hand, in the few locales where *Stromboli* did attract moviegoers, exhibitors sang a different tune: they were bravely defending their right not to stand in moral judgment of the picture's star.)

On May 24, Bergman and Rossellini were wed—by proxy—in Juarez, Mexico, with two men standing in for the notorious couple. The bizarre nuptials amused Ingrid. Finally, on November 1, 1950, Petter undertook his divorce suit in Los Angeles. Charging his spouse with desertion and cruelty, he berated his wife. The crushed actress agreed to all his divorce terms to end the ugly matter and in hopes of repairing her tattered relationship with Pia. (Ingrid's attempts to make peace with her daughter failed.)

As the '50s wore on, La Scandal ended. However, its aftermath lasted for years. Bergman struggled through such uninspired Rossellini features as *Europa '51* (1951), *Journey to Italy* (1954), and *Fear* (1955). In these years, often filled with financial uncertainty, she lived an increasingly tenuous existence with her volatile husband. As was the case with his undisciplined moviemaking, their domestic life became equally unstable. In 1952, the couple had twin daughters (including Isabella, who became a supermodel and actress). However, reckless Rossellini could not curb his philandering. In a career stalemate, Ingrid turned to the Paris stage in 1955 for a production of *Tea and Sympathy* and, thereafter, made a French movie, *Elena et les Hommes*. In July 1958, Bergman's long-dead marriage to Rossellini was annulled in Italy on the grounds that, according to Swedish law, Bergman was still wed to Lindstrom. Rossellini's career never regained the strength of his 1940s' work. He died in 1977 at 71, by which time he and Ingrid had cemented a truce.

Finally, rapprochement developed between Hollywood and the exiled Bergman. She was hired by Twentieth Century-Fox to star in the film version of the hit play *Anastasia*. The 1956 movie, shot in Paris, was well received in the United States and earned her a second Academy Award. At the Oscar ceremony, her friend and costar Cary Grant accepted the trophy on Bergman's behalf, saying, "Everyone here tonight sends you congratulations and love and admiration and every affectionate thought." On April 6, 1959, Ingrid was a presenter at the Academy Awards in Los Angeles. Coming on stage to announce the Best Picture award, she was given a tumultuous ovation. She tearfully told the enthusiastic crowd, "It is so heartwarming to receive such a welcome. I feel that I am home. I am so deeply grateful."

During the remainder of her life, Ingrid wed (1958) and divorced (1975) Swedish theatrical producer Lars Schmidt. She reestablished a relationship with daughter Pia and was close to her three children by Rossellini, whom she had raised. She won another Academy Award for her role in *Murder on the Orient Express* (1975) and earned a posthumous Emmy for portraying Israeli prime minister Golda Meir in *A Woman Called Golda* (1982). Bergman died of cancer on her birthday in 1982.

Years after her scandalous affair, a landmark in Hollywood's social history, Ingrid acknowledged, "Seeing *Open City* [in 1948] and the consequences of it was the most important event of my life." She also affirmed, "I have no regrets. I wouldn't have lived my life the way I did if I was going to worry about what people were going to say."

3

1950–1979

With the breakup of the studio system and the acceleration of the rival TV industry in the 1950s, Hollywood lots ceased being ruled by just a few power figures. As the once-almighty studios became shells of their former selves, high-priced talent was no longer at the mercy of long-term contracts. On the other hand, actors lost the benefit of the film factory system, with its buffering power to protect them from exposure/career damage when their escapades got out of hand.

In the Me Generation of the 1970s, independent production rose to an artistic and commercial height in Hollywood's fragmented power structure. (By then the industry's production and morality codes had lost much of their clout.) The new breed of Tinseltown figures often felt themselves above the law. Such an indulgent atmosphere–enhanced by the growing drug culture–nurtured conceited narcissists who often lacked good sense in their hedonistic activities (e.g., the bravado and womanizing of a Jack Nicholson or Warren Beatty). Sometimes, these pampered notables crossed the bounds of legally acceptable behavior, as in the case of director Roman Polanski's dallying with a minor female and being reported to the police. In the post-studio system era, troubled celebrities relied on their talent agents, management firms, and attorneys to come to their aid.

From the 1970s onward there was also acceleration in the number of print and TV tabloids. These media outlets catered to the public's unending fascination with the ins and outs of their favorites' personal lives, especially when something scandalous occurred. No longer could superstars present a fantasy of their existences and expect the world to readily accept it as gospel truth. It became common practice to print or air sordid details and speculation involving any facet of a notable's existence.

Lana Turner: One Man Too Many

"I raced down the stairs in panic. . . . I ran through the kitchen door. On the sink lay a gleaming butcher knife. . . . I grabbed the knife, ran upstairs, and had it beside the door."

—CHERYL CRANE (DAUGHTER OF LANA TURNER),
IN HER MEMOIR, *DETOUR* (1988)

"**I** find men terribly exciting," insisted glamorous movie star Lana Turner, "and any girl who says she doesn't is an anemic old maid, a streetwalker, or a saint." With a 35-23-35 figure and a beautiful face, five-foot, three-inch Lana definitely had no problem attracting men. But she had special requirements. If it was for a quick bedroom tussle, she wanted well-endowed beefcake. (One executive at MGM, Turner's home studio, said, "She was amoral. If she saw a stagehand with tight pants and a muscular build, she'd invite him into her dressing room.")

When it came to serious romances, the "Sweater Girl" had particular goals, especially in her prime. According to Turner: "A successful man is one who makes more money than a wife can spend. A successful woman is one who can find such a man." Later in life, the cinema legend acknowledged that her eight marriages to seven different men were, perhaps, a bit excessive. She blamed it on her old-fashioned ways: she usually wed the man with whom she thought she was in love.

One of Turner's lovers in the 1950s was 32-year-old Johnny Stompanato. He was handsome, courtly, and well equipped to satisfy her sexually, and he represented danger. She was excited by the knowledge that he was a member of Los Angeles gangster Mickey Cohen's entourage. However, her relationship with Stompanato took a sour turn and eventually became a deadly situation that resulted in a very public scandal. On Good Friday, April 4, 1958, Johnny was stabbed to death at Lana's Beverly Hills home. It was alleged that 14-year-old Cheryl did the deed, terrified that this gigolo planned to disfigure and/or kill her mother.

With highly connected Los Angeles attorney Jerry Giesler representing Cheryl, everyone anticipated a stellar defense in this scandalous case. Nothing proved more tantalizing than Lana's appearance on the witness stand. Thanks to coverage by newspapers, TV, and radio, the star had a huge audience hanging on her every word, observing her least gesture. Rising to the challenge, Turner gave the performance of a lifetime—and well she should with so much at stake. Many insisted that Lana's testimony provided her finest showcase as an actress. . . ever!

Turner had a hardscrabble childhood. She was born Julia Jean Mildred Frances Turner on February 21, 1920 (she later claimed the year was really 1921), in Wallace, Idaho, a bleak mining town. Her father, Virgil, an itinerant worker from Alabama, had met Mildred Frances Cowan, a hairdresser, in Wallace. They eloped and soon became parents to Julia, whom they nicknamed Judy. By the time the girl was eight, the family was living in San Francisco. In late 1931, Virgil, an inveterate gambler, won a sizable stake in an all-night dice game. The next morning he was found dead. (His murderer was never captured.) Within a few years, Mildred and her daughter moved to Los Angeles. There, Judy enrolled at Hollywood High School. Already the blue-eyed adolescent had a stunning figure.

One day when Judy skipped classes, she stopped for a Coke at the Top Hat Café located not far from her school. The fresh-faced teenager with lengthy auburn hair drew the attention of Billy Wilkerson, publisher of the *Hollywood Reporter*, a trade paper. He referred her to a talent agent who found Turner work as an extra in 1937s *A Star Is Born*. Considering events that occurred years later, it was ironic that her career breakthrough role was in a courtroom drama, *They Won't Forget* (1937). In this assignment she sashayed along a street wearing a form-fitting sweater and a tight skirt. Mervyn LeRoy, that film's producer/director, was so impressed that he signed her to a personal contract at $50 weekly. When he joined Metro-Goldwyn-Mayer in 1938, Judy went along with him. At MGM, she became Lana Turner and sported (at first) bright red hair. Her debut there was in *Love Finds Andy Hardy* (1938). The picture's star, Mickey Rooney, enjoyed a brief fling with the newcomer, which purportedly led to her first abortion.

Lana met renowned bandleader Artie Shaw when they made *Dancing Co-Ed* (1939). Because his ego was even bigger than hers was, she was not interested in this lady-killer. However, one night, to make her current boyfriend jealous, she agreed to have dinner with Shaw. During the evening (February 23, 1940), the couple impetuously flew to Las Vegas and married. Within seven months, the union was over and Turner had had another abortion.

By the early 1940s, Lana was an increasingly important MGM star and one of Tinseltown's leading playgirls. When not partying or marrying, the happy hedonist (at that point usually a blonde) traipsed from slick romantic entries (*Week-End at the Waldorf*, 1945) to glossy costume excursions (*Green Dolphin Street*, 1947) to occasional dramatic showcases (*The Bad and the Beautiful*, 1952).

With her voracious sexual appetite, Lana dated incessantly. Sometimes, she walked down the wedding aisle with the latest man of her dreams. She and Stephen Crane, a restaurateur, wed in 1942; the marriage was annulled when it was discovered his divorce from a prior wife was not final. They re-wed in 1943, and that July their daughter, Cheryl, was born. The couple split in 1944. Her next grand romance of this period was with bisexual movie star Tyrone Power. However, he was still married and didn't wish to commit to Lana. He encouraged her to abort their baby. Her next spouse was Henry J. (Bob) Topping, the heir to a tinplate fortune. Their baby was stillborn in early 1949. With Topping in tow, Lana returned to filmmaking after a two-year absence. Since her husband was suffering a financial downslide, Turner paid for their Beverly Hills mansion. In a moment of depression, the star attempted suicide in 1952; not long afterward, she and Topping divorced.

Although Lana's romance with fellow MGM actor Fernando Lamas fizzled, she took wedding vows with brawny Lex Barker, one of the screen's several Tarzans. The stormy union lasted four years. In her divorce proceedings, Lana cited his "cruel and inhuman conduct." This was spelled out later, when it was disclosed that Barker purportedly had sexually molested Lana's daughter.

In 1956, the much-pampered Lana, now in her mid-thirties, was let go by MGM and found herself professionally adrift. Meanwhile, her tumultuous marriage to Barker was ending. At this vulnerable point swaggering Johnny Steele entered her life.

In retrospect, scrutinizing the chaos that mushroomed from this ill-fated romance, Lana said, "I shake my head, defeated. *What* happened I can never forget, but *why* it happened I'll never really understand. I was weak, I'll admit it. . . . But I never meant anybody any harm—God is my witness to the truth of that."

It all started in the spring of 1957. Lana began receiving phone calls, flowers, and messages from a Mr. John Steele who wanted to meet her. She kept saying no. He persisted. One day he just showed up at her residence. She was incensed that this "tall, husky, and dark-haired" stranger had dared to take such a strong initiative; she usually called the shots with her men. Before long, however, Lana was flattered by his gifts and his knowledge of her favorite foods. His next gambit was to suggest that Turner's teenage daughter, Cheryl, might like to try out the new horse (Rowena) he had purchased. The flirtation continued as Lana filmed *Peyton Place* (1957). Around this time, she discovered that Steele was really Johnny Stompanato and that he worked for mobster Mickey Cohen. For the sake of her career in the morally prim 1950s, she knew she should drop her gangland suitor, but she didn't.

Before long, Lanita (as Stompanato called her) learned more of Johnny's background. Born in Illinois, he was the son of a barbershop owner. He had served in the marines during World War II. After his discharge in China he opened a nightclub there and wed a Turkish woman. After the club venture ended, the couple returned to the Midwest with their baby boy. Leaving his family behind in Illinois, he relocated to southern California, where he met Cohen. The racketeer hired Stompanato as a club bouncer and personal bodyguard. When not functioning as an underworld stooge, Johnny used his good looks on the Tinseltown club circuit. Briefly, he was wed to actress Helen Gilbert; later he married another screen performer, Helene Stanley. That lasted for three years.

Turner finally chose to cool her association with Stompanato. She began dating others, but jealous Johnny persisted. One night he climbed into her apartment by scaling the fire escape and almost smothered her to death with a pillow. She threatened to call the police, but he knew it was an idle warning. She valued appearances above all else.

When a film deal arose to make *Another Time, Another Place* (1958) in England, Turner accepted. Stompanato demanded that he accompany her, but she refused. He reluctantly stayed behind. While coping with on-set problems overseas, Lana recklessly arranged for Johnny to fly to England. He soon arrived at her rented house in Hampstead Heath, outside of London.

Before long, Stompanato became bored with sightseeing and wanted to spend days with Lana on the set. She was fearful that his presence on the soundstages not only would be distracting to her performance but also would alert the ever-prying media to this disreputable member of her entourage. A showdown between the two followed, and he attempted to strangle her when she tried to phone the police. Only the intervention of her maid saved her. Another time, Lana's film costar, Sean Connery, came to her rescue. Finally, Turner called Scotland Yard to arrange for Johnny's deportation. Lana was temporarily at peace to complete the movie.

Incapable of controlling her whims, Turner soon began communicating with Stompanato, who was back in California. She mentioned that she planned to vacation in Acapulco once the film shoot ended. When her plane stopped over in Copenhagen, Johnny was there and already had a ticket on her same flight to Mexico. During their enforced holiday together, Turner bided her time, hoping to shake Johnny when she returned to Los Angeles. Lana was still south of the border on February 18, 1958, when her agent phoned that she had been nominated for a Best Actress Oscar for *Peyton Place*.

Once back in Tinseltown with her career again in high gear, Lana rented a fully furnished house at 730 North Bedford Drive in

Beverly Hills. Her lease was to begin April 1. Meanwhile, she stayed at the Bel-Air Hotel in her favorite bungalow. Despite Johnny's protests, Turner refused to let him accompany her to the Academy Awards on March 26. Instead, she was escorted by her mother and her daughter. Although she lost the prize, Lana was pleased to be a center of attention at the industry event. She invited Cheryl to spend the night with her at her Bel-Air Hotel bungalow, where they chatted for hours. When Turner finally said good night, she discovered that Johnny was waiting in an outer room. They had another vicious argument, which led to her being badly bruised. She got through the traumatic aftermath by resorting to vodka "to blur the edges, even the center of my life."

Forever after, Turner would refer to the April 4, 1958, calamity as "the happening."

As Lana and Cheryl prepared for their April move, Stompanato hovered over Turner's life. He was with her when she stopped at a hardware store to acquire china, silverware, and a cutlery set because hers were still in storage. On April 4, Lana and her unshakable shadow again went out shopping. When they returned late in the afternoon, two of Lana's friends stopped by for drinks. After Johnny left, one of the guests mentioned that he and Stompanato had attended the same military academy. Thus, Lana learned a few more facts about her beau, including that he was seven years younger than his claimed age of 39. She was deeply embarrassed to have been dating a younger man—it just didn't look right.

That evening when Stompanato returned, he was aching for a fight. Frightened by what she imagined was to be a final showdown, she ordered 14-year-old Cheryl to her room. As the argument accelerated, Lana kept insisting the relationship was over. Reportedly, at one point, Johnny threatened to scar her face. By then, a hysterical Cheryl had been shouting for her mother to let her in the bedroom. Turner, thinking the blowup with her lover was over, acquiesced to Cheryl's demand. At that moment, according to the star, Johnny was standing in front of the door. He had just gathered some of his wardrobe from the closet. He had the clothing slung over his shoulder, with his upraised hand grabbing onto the hangers.

While the shouting had been going on, Cheryl had raced downstairs to the kitchen and, in a panic/trance, grabbed a large kitchen knife. Returning upstairs, she stood by her mother's bedroom door with the sharp utensil in her hand. Later, she claimed that her arm involuntarily shot forward when the door opened. The blade plunged into Stompanato's stomach (slicing a kidney, striking a vertebra, and puncturing his aorta). As the teenager backed off in shock, Johnny stepped away from his attacker, gasping, "What have you done?" The victim fell to the floor with his eyes shut.

A hysterical Turner called a physician (whose answering service said he'd call right back), tried to contact her mother (no answer), and attempted to calm her sobbing daughter and minister to the fallen Stompanato. Later, the doctor arrived, as did Lana's mother and Stephen Crane (whom Cheryl had phoned). When the doctor could not revive Johnny, he advised Lana, "Call Jerry Giesler!" The famous Hollywood attorney rushed over to the death scene. It was he who telephoned the Beverly Hills police.

Later that fateful night, Mickey Cohen heard rumors about Stompanato's misadventure at Turner's. He rushed over to 730 North Bedford, where he encountered Giesler. The lawyer told him, "If Lana sees you, she's gonna fall out all together. John's dead; the body's at the morgue." Cohen, who had never liked Lana, insisted later, "I don't believe Cheryl killed him. I don't want to outright accuse anyone, but I don't believe it was Cheryl or Lana who done this thing. Somebody must have come in somehow and stabbed him."

Regardless of Cohen's announced theory, Turner feared hottempered Mickey would seek reprisals against her and Cheryl. He, in turn, became angered at the way Hollywood was closing ranks around one of its own by "protecting" Lana. As such, Mickey released to the press a dozen love notes from Turner to Stompanato hoping to set the record straight about their romance being something both parties wanted. However, his scheme did not win his dead pal any press sympathy, as the media was firmly in favor of seemingly vulnerable Lana. (Meanwhile, Cohen reputedly attempted to blackmail Lana with nude photos that her dead lover had once taken of her when she was sleeping. Because she and Giesler came into possession of the negatives, the gambit failed.)

Within a few days after the killing, Los Angeles County district attorney William B. McKesson held a press conference to emphasize that, despite a celebrity's being involved, this case would be handled like any other. Cheryl, an adjudicated juvenile who had been held in the Beverly Hills jail overnight, was at the county's Juvenile Hall being kept as a material witness. (Meanwhile, Stompanato's body had been flown back to Illinois, where, as a World War II veteran, he was buried with full military honors.)

A hearing on Monday, April 7, determined that Cheryl should be detained so that no one (neither Turner nor Stompanato's friends) could influence the minor's future testimony. At the coroner's inquest held a week later, Cheryl did *not* testify, on the grounds that it would further traumatize her. Instead, it would be Turner who would emotionally relate the details of Cheryl's stabbing Stompanato. On the appointed day, Lana came into the courtroom at the Beverly Hills Hall of Records. Most of the room's 160 seats were reserved for the press, with space allocated for TV cameras and radio microphones. Accompanied by Giesler and Stephen Crane, Lana made her dramatic entrance wearing a decorous gray silk suit. (To some observers, it seemed a replay from a scene in *Peyton Place*—a parallel courtroom scene in which she tearfully took the witness stand on behalf of her teenage daughter.)

For an hour Lana answered questions for the benefit of the 12-person (10 men, 2 women) jury. During the proceedings, she occasionally wiped her perspiring face, and twice she broke down during the questioning. Once she completed her task, the coroner ordered a recess. When the press surrounded the emotionally drained Lana, she swooned in a near faint.

In later testimony, police investigators brought up questions such as why the death weapon—supposedly a new knife—had been scratched and chipped. They wondered aloud why there were no fingerprints on the knife, nor blood splashed in the death room or on Lana. They were also puzzled by unidentified hairs or fibers found on the murder weapon. All these questions remained unresolved.

A high moment of drama occurred when an onlooker at the inquest shouted: "Lies! All lies! . . . This mother and daughter were both in love with [Johnny] Stompanato!" The unidentified man was quickly removed from the courtroom, but it led the media to speculate that he might be a stooge planted by Cohen.

In less than 30 minutes, the jurors reached the unanimous decision that this was a case of justifiable homicide, in which Cheryl Crane had used deadly force because she feared for both her and her mother's lives. The prosecutor chose not to pursue criminal charges in the case. (Later, Stompanato's family filed a civil suit for damages, which was settled out of court.)

District Attorney McKesson did commence legal proceedings to determine Turner's fitness as a parent. Cheryl became a ward of the juvenile court. For the next two years, at her choice, the teenager lived with her maternal grandmother (while Lana made such movies as 1959's *Imitation of Life*). Thereafter, her parents, with the court's permission, had her transferred to the El Retiro Institution in the San Fernando Valley of Los Angeles. Lana explained, "She suffered a severe shock two years ago that isn't easily overcome. This institution is to help girls who need that extra bit of help." During her stay there, Cheryl twice escaped from the facility. Later, the adult Cheryl would work for several years for her father's restaurants and then open her own business.

In the wake of the Turner-Stompanato scandal, Harold Robbins wrote a bestselling fictionalized account of the case, *Where Love Has Gone* (1962). Two years later, in the film adaptation, Susan Hayward played the "Lana Turner" counterpart, with Joey Heatherton as her daughter. In subsequent years, both Lana and Cheryl wrote their life stories, each recounting the disturbing events leading up to Stompanato's death and how the two women coped with one

another in their seesawing emotional relationship (which ended
with Turner's death from cancer in 1995).

To this day there are people who insist that on that long-ago
evening it was actually Lana Turner who ended the life of her combative lover.

Liberace: Playing the Hollywood Game

*"He is the summit of sex—the pinnacle of masculine, feminine, and neuter.
Everything that he, she, and it can ever want. . . . He reeks with emetic
language that can only make grown men long for a quiet corner . . . handkerchief, and the old heave-ho. Without doubt he is the biggest sentimental
vomit of all time. Slobbering over his mother, winking at his brother, and
counting the cash of every second, this superb piece of calculating candy-floss
has an answer for every situation."*
—COLUMNIST CASSANDRA (WILLIAM CONNOR), IN LONDON'S DAILY
MIRROR ON SEPTEMBER 26, 1956

Talented people who are homosexual or bisexual have long been
an integral part of the Tinseltown scene. In the silent era there
were, among many others, J. Warren Kerrigan, Tallulah Bankhead,
Marie Dressler, Janet Gaynor, Alla Nazimova, Ramon Novarro,
Greta Garbo, and William Haines, as well as director Dorothy
Arzner. The careers of some of these personalities carried over into
talkies. During Hollywood's golden age of the 1930s–1950s, among
those fully or partially committed to an alternative lifestyle were Kay
Francis, Claudette Colbert, Charles Laughton, Marlene Dietrich,
Barbara Stanwyck, Cary Grant, Judith Anderson, Cesar Romero,
Tyrone Power, Marjorie Main, Clifton Webb, Farley Granger,
George Nader, Montgomery Clift, Sal Mineo, Raymond Burr, Tab
Hunter, Richard Chamberlain, Anthony Perkins, Rock Hudson,
and James Dean and such film directors as George Cukor, James
Whale, Mitchell Leisen, and Edmund Goulding.

Typically, Tinseltown personalities knew better than to rub the
public's nose in their sexuality. To retain mainstream acceptance,

they usually disguised their sexual orientation through marriages of convenience or such charades as: "I'm too busy with my career to share life with another." In bygone times, with the all-powerful studios controlling both the media and local law enforcers, scandal was generally avoided. Occasionally, a star (such as popular leading man William Haines) got into a predicament that threatened to expose his homosexuality and, in turn, probably destroy the celebrity's career. If the individual refused to cooperate by immediately masking the situation, his studio employers ended the person's contract. It was reasoned that further financial investment in such a person's career was too risky a proposition.

In contrast, there were character actors, such as Franklyn Pangborn and Sterling Holloway, who so clearly fit the image of the overtly gay person (both on and off screen) that the truth of their sexual orientation was obvious to just about everyone. In such instances, no one bothered to further expose these performers' obvious alternative lifestyle. As such, these players continued on their merry way through decades of filmmaking.

On the other hand, in the conservative 1950s, what was Hollywood to do with such a unique personality as Lee Liberace? In the early '50s, this flamboyant pianist had an enormously popular syndicated half-hour TV series in which he played a selection of popular and classical pieces, all adapted to his florid keyboard style. The small-screen outing showcased his offbeat persona: a wide smile that revealed sparkling pearly white teeth, expressive eyes that constantly winked at the camera, bejeweled fingers that tickled the ivories, and a nasal, fey way of chatting between numbers. As an added touch, the minimal set for his show was adorned with an ornate, mock Louis XIV candelabra stationed atop the entertainer's grand piano.

Females, especially middle-aged and beyond, adored Liberace, regarding him a gracious purveyor of wonderful music. They accepted his kitsch and fabulousness as part of the overall package. It probably occurred to only a very small percentage of these adoring fans that this glittery five-foot, eight-inch star with dark, curly hair was, perhaps, not a man's man. For the majority, they were enthralled by this wonderfully family-oriented person who, on air, discussed his beloved parent ("I owe everything to my mother") and featured his violinist brother George.

However, as Liberace's fame grew—he even starred in a major 1955 studio feature—the contemporary scandal magazines published articles about this one-of-a-kind notable that clearly insulted his manhood. The crushing blow occurred when the musician went to England in September 1956 for concert appearances and the London *Daily Mirror* printed a blatant attack on the entertainer's masculinity (as well as his lack of sophisticated musical taste). Liberace's sensitivities were so offended, and his highly lucrative career so threatened, that he took the then audacious offensive by suing this well-established tabloid publication. Liberace knew that if he lost the case, it would end his multimillion dollar career. Like the intrigued public around the world, he waited with bated breath for the outcome of this pivotal courtroom case that focused on such a delicate—and forbidden—subject.

He was born Wladziu Valentino Liberace on May 16, 1919, in West Allis, Wisconsin. His twin brother died at birth. His mother, Frances Zuchowski, was the child of Polish immigrants, and his father, Salvatore Liberace, was from Formia, Italy. (In the household, Wladziu was one of four surviving children. The others were eight-year-older George, five-year-older Angelina, and Rudolph, born in 1931.) The father was a French horn player who had once been a member of John Philip Sousa's renowned band. The Liberaces operated a small grocery shop, with the family living in a cramped apartment behind the store. These years of poverty— and their parents' constant bickering—had a strong impact on the children, especially Wally (as Wladziu was called). In 1926, the Liberaces transferred to nearby West Milwaukee. After a few "prosperous" years, the 1929 Depression put them into financial peril. Frances took a factory job to help support the household.

While all the Liberace offspring were musically inclined, it was Wally—starting at the age of four—who demonstrated a natural affinity for the piano. His controlling mother began him on a regimen of piano lessons and lengthy daily practice sessions. Years later, the future notable complained, "I never had a chance to be a kid." When the boy was seven, he met concert pianist Ignacy Jan Paderewski when the famed musician performed in Milwaukee (where Mr. Liberace played with the city's orchestra). The youngster was tremendously impressed by this great talent who billed himself solely with his surname. Wally determined that one day he would be a one-named star of the concert stage.

As a youngster, Wally spoke with a heavy ethnic accent, which his sixth-grade teacher helped to remedy. Because he was so different from his male classmates (e.g., he loved to cook, sew, and tap dance) this mama's boy spent much time alone. Meanwhile, he continued his piano lessons with an instructor from the Wisconsin College of Music. She arranged a long-term scholarship for the talented youth.

By age 14, Wally was playing piano in Milwaukee saloons, jobs often arranged by George, his violin-playing older brother. Two years later, the teenager, who already was experiencing infatuations with his male schoolteachers, was seduced by a professional football player. Although his Catholic background made Wally guilt-ridden about the sexual experience, the episode introduced Liberace to the clandestine gay world of those times. He embarked on his double life as a closeted homosexual.

During this period, his father abandoned his household to be with a female musician. The mother was so embarrassed by this betrayal that she insisted her offspring never mention the humiliation. This example of secreting the truth impressed Liberace with the "value" of hiding one's private life from others.

In the mid-1930s, Wally often worked at disreputable venues. One of these honky-tonk engagements led to his being seduced by a blues singer, a buxom female. (Later, he often elaborated on this incident to divert public speculation about his homosexuality.) In 1939, he was accepted to join the Chicago Symphony when it performed in Milwaukee. Because they had learned of his unrespectable gigs, a condition of the symphony job required the newcomer to use a different name when appearing at local saloons. Thus, he became Walter Buster Keys at these low-class beer halls, where he often mixed classical and pop numbers into a pleasing amalgam.

When he turned 21 in 1940, Liberace moved to New York, too impatient to slowly develop a classical career. Instead, he focused on the pop field. He also knew that in Manhattan he could indulge his sexual penchant without small-town scrutiny. He now called himself Liberace on stage, adding "Lee" as his new first name in private life. After months of scrounging, he was signed by Music Corporation of America, a prestigious talent agency. He eventually became the lead act at the Plaza Hotel's Persian Room. This led to a tour of swank venues around the United States and Canada.

By the late 40s Lee's career, which by then included successful recordings, had escalated to national prominence. His brother George, who was his manager, helped to concoct a promotional campaign that suggested that his brother was active on the heterosexual dating circuit. No one of consequence bothered to question the ruse. In this period, Liberace read Claude Bristol's *The Magic of Believing* (1948), a bestseller on self-improvement. The book became his creed for life. In 1949, Liberace made his feature film debut, as a waterfront saloon piano player in *South Sea Sinner*.

With his growing income, Lee purchased a new home, this time in Sherman Oaks, California, located in the San Fernando Valley north of Los Angeles. Pampering his flair for the ostentatious, he had a piano-shaped swimming pool installed in the backyard. By then his mother was living with him. Fans thought this gesture touching, but in actuality the entertainer did it largely out of a sense of guilt.

In the early '50s, Liberace started his TV career on the West Coast with a 15-minute local show; this led to a syndicated half-hour series in 1953. His brother George, with whom he was increasingly at odds, played violin on the program. Liberace became a national craze, with more than 45 million home viewers watching his eccentric weekly offering. The one-name performer was earning millions annually, and his fame was spreading to the international scene. When he was featured at the Hollywood Bowl in 1953, he wore a white tuxedo to stand out in the huge outdoor arena. This led the star to try far more outrageous costumes in the coming decades.

In these years, with his effeminate manners, unorthodox costuming, and sensitive ways, Lee had become the butt of jokes from disgruntled male TV viewers. Fearing this growing tide of negativity would permanently damage his major career, Lee's management team constructed a new public image for him. As such, in 1954, *the* woman in Lee's life was no longer his mother. Instead, it was Joanne Rio, a pretty, young club chorine whose family had been his neighbors when he had lived in North Hollywood. He and the fledgling entertainer began keeping company, which was dutifully photographed by fan magazines. That October, Liberace announced that he and Joanne would surely wed. This revelation was followed by a multipart article in the *Los Angeles Mirror* (with Joanne's byline) detailing her "romance" with the famed keyboard artist. Lee claimed to be embarrassed by the pieces, intimating that she had sold the stories to profit from their association. She retorted that the relationship "was just a lot of publicity, and it looks like I got caught right in the middle of it." The couple separated, and that was the end of it for the time being. But it served the purpose of adding a "close" female relationship to his social résumé. (In his 1973 autobiography, Liberace suggested that he and Joanne Rio had been "intimate." An infuriated Rio, by then married, sued Liberace, resulting in an out-of-court settlement. In this messy aftermath it came to light that, back in 1954, Joanne's father had confronted Liberace about the pianist's sexual preferences and insisted that marriage to his daughter would *not* work.)

In 1955 Liberace made headlines when he "dated" middle-aged skating star Sonia Henie. That April, the musician opened the new Riviera Hotel in Las Vegas. His $50,000 weekly salary set a new fee record. He opened his show wearing a white silk lame tuxedo. In the second half of the program, he sported a black tux jacket studded with 1,328,000 sequins. The audience gasped at his audaciousness. Meanwhile, Lee had great hopes for *Sincerely Yours* (1955), in which he played the lead role of a pianist going deaf. However, the movie failed with filmgoers.

On the home front, once he was rich and famous, Liberace risked more open association with young gay men, often inviting them in groups to his home for pool parties. His mother disapproved of these visiting "hillbillies" (as she called them), but he countered that he had earned the right to relax.

Always ambitious and a workaholic, Lee scheduled a European tour in 1956. It included a command performance in London for Queen Elizabeth, as well as prestigious British club and TV engagements. When Liberace disembarked in Southampton on September 25, he was mobbed by hordes of screaming fans. The next day the scurrilous attack on Lee—both as an entertainer and as a man—by Cassandra (columnist William Connor) was published in the *Daily Mirror*. Liberace sued the *Daily Mirror* for libel. However, largely because of the entertainer's busy schedule, it was not until June 1959 that the highly controversial case was heard in Queen's Bench Number Four under the presiding judge, Sir Cyril Salmon. The titillating legal debate captured the world's attention. Dressed impeccably, if a bit flashy, Lee swore in court that he was not homosexual. When asked whether he had "ever indulged in homosexual practices," he responded, "No, sir, never in my life. I am against the practice because it offends convention and it offends society." He informed the court that the Cassandra article had caused him "untold agonies and embarrassment and has made me the subject of ridicule." The landmark case ended in a $22,400 judgment for Liberace from the jury of 10 men and 2 women. Despite the seemingly small sum (actually the highest settlement of any British libel case to that date), Liberace felt vindicated by the result—no matter that he had perjured himself under oath and disappointed his gay contingent who hoped he would "out" himself.

Meanwhile, back in the United States, *Confidential* magazine, a trashy monthly that peeked into celebrities' secrets with just enough facts to usually avoid lawsuits, published in its July 1957 issue an article titled: "Why Liberace's Theme Song Should Be 'Mad About the Boy'!" The piece described in agitated prose that the musician had attempted hanky-panky in an Akron, Ohio, hotel room with a New York publicist in town to promote the pianist's concert. The story claimed that the showman had put sexual moves on the young man and that only with "a combination of wristlock and flying mare" did the publicist flee the room with his virtue intact. The explosive article noted that a similar wrestling match had occurred when the victim had been forced by business necessity to meet again with Liberace in Los Angeles and, still later, in Dallas, Texas.

Brazening it out, Liberace sued *Confidential* magazine and its publisher, Robert Harrison. The baffling case seemed destined for a jury deadlock. However, the plaintiff proved that he was *not* in Dallas on the day cited in the publication and that some other stated facts were untrue. This forced the defendant to make a $40,000 out-of-court settlement. Liberace's victory was not appreciated by the gay minority who wanted more famous people to come out of the closet, making it easier for other gay people.

If, publicly, Liberace had "proved" that he was not homosexual, many in show business and gay circles knew the truth. In 1957, Lee, who had several residences (including one in Hollywood), purchased a Palm Springs home, where, over the years, he entertained a string of gay men.

In subsequent decades, Liberace proved to be a supreme show business survivor. The master showman endured career dips only to rise yet again as the king of Las Vegas entertainment. In his elaborate, glitzy stage productions, his outfits grew more fantastic with the passing years. There seemed to be nothing he wouldn't try, including flying aloft and flapping his mink-lined cape at the astonished audience. Feeling so at ease on stage, he jubilantly camped it up for his audiences, displaying and discussing his elaborate wardrobe, his latest gaudy jewelry, and the other "happy-happies" (i.e., trinkets) he had acquired on recent shopping binges.

Over the years, Lee never officially proclaimed his homosexuality. In fact, in 1973 he repeated publicly, in a press conference, that he was *not* homosexual. He insisted, "The only reason I never got married is because I come from a family of divorce. I'm so tired of people writing stories about me that are cancerous with innuendo."

The private Liberace typically gravitated toward muscular blond young men. A few of them became part of his entourage, sometimes performing in his nightclub show as, say, the chauffeur driving the entertainer on stage in an expensive vintage car. One such blue-eyed man was Scott Thorson, whom Lee met in 1977. At the time, Wisconsin-born Thorson was 18; Liberace was 57. They quickly became lovers. The kept man even underwent plastic surgery to become a Liberace look-alike. In 1980, Lee planned to adopt Thorson as his son. However, he never completed the legal process, concerned that his expanded good life had swelled Scott's ego. The two drifted apart until Liberace, who had found other playmates, had Thorson forcibly ejected from their Beverly Hills apartment in March 1982. That October, Scott filed a $113 million palimony lawsuit trying to embarrass his past keeper into a lucrative arrangement. However, Lee was not to be cowed, no matter how embarrassing this public exposure might be. Eventually, after protracted courtroom preliminaries, the case was settled out of court in 1986 for $95,000.

By then Liberace was suffering from AIDS, an ailment he kept hidden from the world. He completed his third and final highly successful engagement at Radio City Music Hall in October 1986. Already he looked thin and haggard. He retreated to the Cloisters, his Palm Springs home, where he refused to acknowledge his deadly disease, one that had killed his friend Rock Hudson in 1985. On February 4, 1987, Liberace died with his beloved dogs at his side. His physicians stated the primary cause of death was cardiac arrest, but the county coroner's autopsy revealed that he had expired from AIDS. A goodly portion of Lee's extensive estate went to the Liberace Foundation for the Performing and Creative Arts.

Bound by the mores of his era and a paranoia about damaging his "general family audience appeal," the closest Liberace ever came to acknowledging his sexual persuasion was in a statement made months before his death: "With a name like Liberace, which stands for freedom, I'm for anything that has the letters L-I-B in it, and that includes gay lib."

Elizabeth Taylor vs. Debbie Reynolds: Hollywood's Messy Circle of Love

"You know, I don't go around breaking up marriages. Besides, you can't break up a happy marriage. Debbie's and Eddie's marriage has never been a happy one."

— ELIZABETH TAYLOR, IN 1958

"Lemme tell ya, any minute that this little dame [Taylor] spends out of bed is totally wasted."

—MIKE TODD, IN 1957

"Debbie Reynolds was indeed the girl next door. But only if you lived next door to a self-centered, totally driven, insecure, untruthful phony."

— EDDIE FISHER, IN 1999

"I was offended. It's painful to read about your private life in the papers, knowing that strangers are reading about it, too."

— DEBBIE REYNOLDS, IN 1988

Fans' regard for a celebrity is as unstable as quicksand. One day the star is the idol of millions and the next the bane of the globe. Few Hollywood notables have ridden the treacherous roller coaster of public opinion more recklessly than superstar Elizabeth Taylor. The catalyst for her derailment was the March 1958 plane crash in New Mexico that killed her newest husband, producer Mike Todd.

For a spell thereafter, she won everyone's deepest sympathy as the grieving widow and the suddenly single parent of infant Liza Todd. Within weeks after the tragedy, the shattered Taylor abandoned her retreat at the Beverly Hills Hotel for the Todds' Tinseltown home. Soon, Elizabeth bravely returned to filming *Cat on a Hot Tin Roof*. She was cheered as a real trouper who knew that the show must always go on.

By June 1958, however, the tide of public opinion was swiftly turning against regal Taylor. The media snickered that popular singer Eddie Fisher, the protégé of Mike Todd and the husband of actress Debbie Reynolds (by whom he had two children), was spending an inordinate amount of time consoling Liz. By late August, when both Eddie and Elizabeth were in New York—ostensibly on *separate* business matters—he registered at the Essex House while she was booked at the Plaza Hotel. However, they were spotted frequently about town together, and it soon leaked out that he was bunking at Taylor's suite.

Sniffing a major story, syndicated gossip columnist Hedda Hopper phoned Elizabeth: "What's happening with Eddie Fisher? Are the two of you going to marry?" Liz volleyed back, "Last time I looked, Eddie was still married to Debbie Reynolds." The newshound countered, "Well, you can't hurt Debbie like this without hurting yourself more—she's in love with Eddie." The actress snapped, "But he's not in love with her and never has been." An annoyed Hopper needled, "What do you think Mike [Todd] would say to this?" Taylor responded plaintively in her babylike voice: "Well, Mike's dead and I'm alive. . . . What do you expect me to do—sleep alone?"

That did it! Within a flash after that unfortunate statement, Liz was reclassified from a saint to a Jezebel, Debbie Reynolds was elevated into a blessed martyr, and Eddie Fisher sunk to being a scumbag. Not since Hollywood movie star Ingrid Bergman abandoned her husband and daughter in 1949 to cavort with married Italian filmmaker Roberto Rossellini in Rome had the world been so titillated and/or shocked by the reckless actions of a beloved Hollywood notable.

Elizabeth Rosemond Taylor was born in London, England, on February 27, 1932, the second child (brother Howard was born in 1930) of Francis Taylor, an art dealer, and his wife, Sara Warmbrodt, a former actress. The parents, both from Arkansas City, Kansas, had married in 1926 and moved to Europe where they acquired Old Masters paintings to be sold at the Manhattan art gallery of Francis's wealthy uncle. By 1930, they had settled in northern London. As World War II was breaking forth in the late 1930s, the Taylors relocated to the United States. They put down roots in Los Angeles, where Mr. Taylor operated an art gallery at the plush Beverly Hills Hotel.

Young Elizabeth, already a stunning beauty, attracted the attention of the Hollywood film studios, leading to her 1942 screen debut at Universal Pictures. The next year, MGM signed her to a term contract at $100 weekly. She made a strong impression in *National Velvet* (1944). The first adult role for gorgeous five-foot, four-inch Elizabeth was opposite Robert Taylor in *Conspiracy* (1949). The studio gained tremendous publicity when her first marriage— to Nicky Hilton, the playboy son of a hotel magnate—was timed to the release of her latest picture, *Father of the Bride* (1950). However, her turbulent union to abusive Nicky was short lasting. Divorced, she re-wed in 1952, this time to British actor Michael Wilding, who was twice her age. By then she already had a dependency on pain pills. They had two children before separating in 1956 and officially divorcing in 1957. Two days thereafter, Taylor wed producer Mike Todd. Six months later their daughter was born. Thereafter, she began filming *Cat on a Hot Tin Roof* (1958).

Todd was born Avrom Hirsch Goldebogen on June 22, 1907, in Minneapolis, Minnesota, the younger son of a Hasidic rabbi. Childhood jobs included being a shoeshine boy and, later, a carnival pitchman. He quit school after the sixth grade, eager to get on with life. Later, utilizing a new moniker (Mike Todd), he made his place in show business, producing striptease shows and burlesque and then moving on to Broadway productions. He first entered the film business in 1945 and by the mid-1950s was producing such screen spectacles as *Around the World in 80 Days.*

After the 1946 death of his first wife (Bertha Freshman), the mother of Mike Jr., the hustling showman wed screen star Joan Blondell. They divorced in 1950. Go-getter Todd first met Taylor in Hollywood in the early 1950s. Once she separated from Michael Wilding in mid-1956, burly Mike moved in for the kill by pursuing her relentlessly. Later, when he proposed marriage, he presented her with a 25-karat diamond engagement ring, and she accepted. They wed in Acapulco, Mexico, on February 2, 1957, six months before the birth of their love child. Todd was en route to New York to accept a Showman of the Year award when his private plane (*The Lucky Liz*) crashed, killing all on board. Because of a persistent cold, Taylor had not been on that fatal transcontinental flight.

Mary Frances Reynolds was born on April 1, 1932 in El Paso, Texas, the second child (brother Bill was born in 1930) of Ray and Maxene Reynolds. The father was a struggling laborer. In 1940, they relocated to Burbank, California, where Mr. Reynolds worked as a carpenter for the railroad. While at Burbank High, Mary Frances excelled as a baton twirler in the school band. At 16, the pert teenager was selected as Miss Burbank, which led to a Warner Bros. contract and a few brief roles there. When the studio dropped her option, she moved over to MGM.

Moviegoers really took notice of Reynolds's winsome agility in the musical *Singin' in the Rain* (1952). By 1955, five-foot, two-inch Reynolds was dating actor Robert Wagner and was a big favorite of the fan magazines. Because Wagner did not suggest marriage, she fell into a relationship with singer Eddie Fisher. Following a highly touted engagement, she wed him at Grossinger's resort in the Catskills on September 26, 1955. The duo had two children: Carrie Francis (1956) and Todd Emmanuel (1958). Professionally, Reynolds enjoyed a major hit movie with *Tammy and the Bachelor* (1957). To everyone's amazement—including envious husband

Eddie whose singing career was fast tapering off—she had a number one single with the film's theme song, "Tammy."

Edwin Jack Fisher was born in South Philadelphia on August 10, 1928. He was the fourth of seven children in an impoverished Jewish household. His parents were Joseph Fisher, a street peddler, and Russian-born Katherine Monacker. Sonny, as he was nicknamed, began singing professionally in hotels and clubs when he was still a teenager. Fisher soon began a recording career, which spawned such hits as "Anytime" and "Dungaree Doll." In the early 1950s, Eddie spent two years in the army (while cutting records on weekends). Once discharged in 1953, the national sensation starred on TV for several seasons in a musical showcase.

Despite his boyish, innocent look, well-endowed ladies' man Fisher was actually much in demand on the show business social scene and had flings with such legends as Marlene Dietrich and Judy Garland. When jaded Eddie was first introduced to Debbie Reynolds on the MGM lot, he asked the rising starlet to attend his upcoming opening at the Cocoanut Grove. (Before Fisher had asked Debbie to the club event, the game player had invited MGM actress Pier Angeli, a good friend of Reynolds's to the same event. When Angeli realized the situation, she left the nightclub in tears. Fisher was unfazed.)

Initially, Fisher was intrigued that Reynolds was "sweet and unspoiled" and that he "had found a really nice girl—in Hollywood of all places." In public, they made an extremely adorable, seemingly wholesome couple. However, in private the pair wondered whether they were meant for one another. He did not know how to cope with a virgin who always acted like a Girl Scout and who was so health-conscious. Moreover, spendthrift Fisher became increasingly perturbed that she was so thrifty and a workaholic with a penchant for hogging the limelight. In turn, she was bothered by his undisciplined ways and his sycophant entourage. In addition, she was perplexed by his dependency on Dr. Max Jacobsen (Dr. Feelgood) who administered endless amounts of drugs to Fisher that the latter insisted were harmless (!) vitamins and hormones. Yet another issue of contention was that he was Jewish and she was a fundamentalist Christian.

Debbie's *The Tender Trap* (1955) costar, swinging Frank Sinatra—among others—warned Reynolds: "Very difficult life, to be married to a singer. Very hard. . . . You should really think twice about this. . . . You're too young. You'll never be able to make it work. I know." She appreciated the advice, but, like Eddie, felt trapped by the momentum of the pending nuptials that had enthralled all of America.

Despite much trepidation, Debbie and Eddie wed in September of 1955. The newlyweds honeymooned in Atlanta, Georgia, at a bottlers' convention of his TV sponsor, Coca-Cola. At the conference she blithely told attendees that she did not like soft drinks as they were bad for the teeth. Eddie shuddered at her statements. The marriage went sharply downhill from there.

Settling into domesticity, the Fishers found that their conflicting work schedules all too often kept them apart, which was a relief for each of them. When they were together they had little in common. Eddie continued to fawn over his mentor, producer Mike Todd, who was then living with movie star Evelyn Keyes. Said Debbie of her spouse: "He wanted to be Mike Todd. . . . He started walking like Mike, and smoking the big cigars, and salting his language with some of Mike's choice words. . . . Mike was old enough to be Eddie's father and yet he seemed very young, so they really were buddies."

Once Todd began dating Elizabeth Taylor, the Fishers became part of the lovers' inner circle. Although Taylor and Reynolds were MGM coworkers, they had never been fond of one another. Liz regarded Debbie as a professional Miss Goodie Two Shoes. Because the Fishers were so frequently in Mike and Liz's company, they were subjected to the lovebirds' mating ritual, which included Taylor and Todd's embarking on gusty brawls and fierce arguments. Debbie was bewildered by their brand of sexual foreplay (while Eddie was envious). However, Reynolds admitted, "It was fun and exciting to be around Mike and Elizabeth. They were having a great time in their lives, like two kids partying, hugging, loving, touching. With

Eddie, I either felt humiliated or lost." Reynolds also realized that Fisher was constantly comparing her to Liz and that Debbie came up short in Eddie's estimation. Nonetheless, when Todd and Taylor married, the Fishers were part of the small wedding party south of the border.

Debbie enjoyed being a mother to their daughter Carrie. However, her marriage to Eddie had already fallen apart, and they strongly considered divorce. When Reynolds accidentally became pregnant again she thought their new baby, Todd (named in honor of Mike Todd), might help to salvage their tattered domestic life. For a while, it seemed to spark a positive change in the Fishers' household in Pacific Palisades.

Less than a month after the birth of the Fishers' son, Mike Todd died in the March 22, 1958, air crash. Hearing the news, Reynolds rushed to Taylor's home. She found Elizabeth in hysterics. To help out, Debbie took Elizabeth's two boys, ages three and five, back to her house for the time being. When Eddie heard that his idol Todd had perished, he rushed back to Los Angeles from his out-of-town-engagement to be at Elizabeth's side. Together they spent hours reminiscing about Mike. When Todd was buried near Chicago days later, Fisher accompanied the distraught Taylor to the service. Reynolds remained in Beverly Hills with her two children plus Taylor's offspring; she also counseled the bewildered Michael Wilding whose efforts to console his ex-wife had been rudely rebuffed.

Once Eddie and Elizabeth were back in Los Angeles, a routine developed with him spending much of each day at her side. Often, he read to her from the many letters of condolence that continued to pour in. Reynolds thought the two could help one another find closure to their grief over Todd, so she let them be. Unknown to Debbie, Eddie was fast falling in lust with Elizabeth. (Said beguiled Fisher, "Sexually she was every man's dream; she had the face of an angel and the morals of a truck driver.") One day while visiting Taylor, the crooner saw her "dressed in a flesh-colored bathing suit, dangling her feet in the pool. . . . Our eyes met, and that was it. . . .

I was in love with Elizabeth." When they went for a drive the follow-ing day, he told seemingly vulnerable Taylor, "I am going to marry you." Her nonplussed response was, "When?"

After Taylor wrapped *Cat on a Hot Tin Roof,* the Fishers joined her at the picture's premiere. And when Eddie headlined at the Tropicana Hotel in Las Vegas in June 1958, Elizabeth attended the opening accompanied by film industry figure/past boyfriend Arthur Loew Jr. and Mike Todd Jr. Sexy Taylor gained far more audience attention than did wholesome Debbie. In August, Reynolds invited Taylor to join in a celebration of Fisher's 30th birthday. Elizabeth pleaded illness, not wanting to be in Debbie's orbit.

In the coming weeks gossip mounted about Liz and Eddie's special togetherness and the strange love triangle of Taylor, Fisher, and Reynolds. Debbie remained in denial, telling others: "What's wrong with a friend taking a friend out in the evening?" She told herself, "Eddie Fisher wasn't her [Taylor's] type. She had just lost Mike Todd, an exciting, intensely passionate man. . . . Eddie Fisher . . . was only an imitation." Debbie was convinced that man-grabber Elizabeth wouldn't waste her time on Eddie.

When Fisher and Taylor made tongues wag on their late sum-mer Manhattan lark, Reynolds finally confronted the issue. Unable to reach Eddie at his New York hotel, she called Elizabeth's Plaza Hotel suite around 3:00 A.M. A sleepy Fisher answered, and he couldn't bluff his way out of the embarrassing situation. He told Debbie they'd talk when he returned to the West Coast the next day. Coming face-to-face to his wife, he admitted, "I love her and I never loved you." At Debbie's insistence the couple tried a marriage coun-selor, and she kept reassuring the media that their marriage would survive. However, in Eddie's mind, their relationship was over. (One of Fisher's complaints was, "Sex with Debbie was about as exciting as a December afternoon in London.")

Once the public digested the startling news of the Debbie-Eddie-Liz situation, most everyone loudly scorned Taylor and Fisher. However, in actuality, everyone seemed intrigued by this unortho-dox romantic alliance. In contrast, while single-parent Debbie received public sympathy, she was no longer part of America's favorite couple, which diminished her status with the public. A dismayed Reynolds said, "It took a long time to face that."

For whatever reason, Elizabeth became obsessed with converting to Judaism before she wed Fisher (although the idea had not come up when she married Jewish Mike Todd). Reynolds finally agreed to a divorce. She told the court that "another woman"—left unnamed—had destroyed her marriage. She was granted a divorce on February 19, 1959, and was given custody of their children. On May 12, 1959, Elizabeth married Eddie, husband number four, at Temple Beth Sholom in Las Vegas.

Within months of becoming the fourth Mr. Taylor, 34-year-old Fisher, a substance abuser, as was his spouse, was already reeling from his loss of identity and self-esteem (and for being branded a cad for having deserted Debbie and their kids). It led him to observe of Mike, his beloved late mentor, and of Elizabeth, his unmanageable current wife: "Unlike Mike Todd I was never much of a fighter. . . . Elizabeth's tough and I'm a softie. I served as a stabilizing force in her life, but I don't think Mike Todd would have approved of our relationship."

By then, Fisher's singing career had declined. However, he had a new occupation as Taylor's gofer, a job that had glittering perks but gained him little self-respect. Elizabeth made sure that he was given a role in *Butterfield 8* (1960), but it did nothing to earn him future acting assignments.

When Taylor made *Suddenly, Last Summer* (1959) in England, Eddie was in tow. He was again part of her entourage when filming on *Cleopatra* began in the fall of 1960 outside of London. Faithful, demeaned Fisher was present when Elizabeth underwent a health crisis in March 1961 and nearly died. He was among her retinue who accompanied her back to Hollywood to recuperate. (During this period she began an affair in Los Angeles with columnist Max Lerner.) By that fall work on *Cleopatra* reactivated, this time in Rome. In January 1962, Taylor commenced filming her scenes with Richard Burton, cast as her on-camera lover, Marc Antony. So began the momentous love affair heard around the world. In the process, Richard's wife, Sybil, and Elizabeth's equally humiliated spouse, Eddie, were cast aside. Taylor divorced Fisher in Puerto Vallarta, Mexico, on March 5, 1964. (Eddie received a $1 million settlement, while Elizabeth received custody of six-year-old Liza Todd, whom Fisher had earlier adopted.) With Burton now divorced from his mate, he and Taylor wed in Montreal, Canada, on March 15, 1964.

Fisher, Taylor, and Reynolds went on to further marriages and divorces. Eventually, Elizabeth and Debbie, both gutsy survivors of the Hollywood studio system, "mended" their long breach. They even costarred in a TV movie, *These Old Broads* (2001), written by Reynolds's daughter, Carrie Fisher. In Tinseltown no egregious scandalous misdeed is too big to forgive when work and money are involved.

Elizabeth Taylor and Richard Burton: A Love Not for the Ages

"They were the last of their kind, special people who supersede nobility in the minds of Americans and much of the world. They inhabited a make-believe world into which we put them. We encouraged them to do the ridiculous and they didn't let us down. They provided the thrills that made reality disappear for a time, and made our lives a little juicier."

—CIVIL LIBERTIES ATTORNEY AND BURTONS' FRIEND,
MORRIS ERNEST, IN 1976

After Elizabeth Taylor's husband, Mike Todd, died in a 1958 plane crash, she rebounded by taking up with pop crooner Eddie Fisher, who was then wed to popular movie personality Debbie Reynolds, and the public turned against Taylor, labeling her a home wrecker. At the time, Liz told a confidant that she had hooked up with Fisher because, "I thought I could keep Mike's memory alive. But I have only his ghost." A few years later, she would acknowledge, "I didn't love Eddie, and it wasn't I who needed him. I married him because he needed me."

By late summer 1961, Eddie arrived in Rome as part of Elizabeth's retinue for the restart of filming *Cleopatra*. His other half was already in a contentious mood. Since her near-death experience months before while shooting the first attempt at *Cleopatra* at a British studio, she had amazingly regained the world's sympathy. As a result, in April 1961 she won an Academy Award for the mediocre *Butterfield 8*. Becoming restless during her recuperation in Los Angeles, she had indulged in a furtive affair with newspaper columnist Max Lerner. She insisted to bewildered Eddie that it hadn't meant a thing . . . really.

Now Taylor was stuck in Italy to earn her $1 million salary and $3,000 weekly living allowance for starring as the famous Egyptian queen. She was coping with the pressure of knowing that if this overly ambitious screen epic flopped, it would destroy Twentieth Century-Fox Pictures. Self-centered Liz could sometimes shrug off that nagging stress because it was not her prime concern. Instead, she was focused on her empty marriage and a hankering to have a new strong man in her life. To satisfy her primal urge, she did what Taylor did best: she ignited another international scandal. Upping the stakes, this time she was *not* the center of merely a love triangle. She had graduated to being at the core of a scandalous love quartet. It was an unseemly outrage that, once again, shattered the Hollywood facade of conformist respectability.

In a moment of self-reflection, narcissistic Taylor once owned up, "If I believed everything I read about myself in the press I'd have good reason to hate myself." Rather than do that, she turned her venom on others, both on and off the set. Fisher recalled, "Elizabeth fought over anything and everything. I couldn't deal with it, so I tried to appease her, but she would become even more ferocious."

While toiling that fall in Rome with Rex Harrison (cast as Julius Caesar), Taylor had little contact with Richard Burton, who was not yet needed in front of the cameras to perform as Marc Antony. (Elizabeth had first met the stocky, five-foot, nine-inch Welshman in the early 1950s at Hollywood parties. At that time, she had *not* been electrified by the self-impressed, heavy-drinking actor with the pockmarked face who had a reputation for sleeping with his leading ladies.)

Born Richard Walter Jenkins Jr. on November 10, 1925, in Pontrhydyfen, Wales, Burton was the 12th of 13 children born to Richard Jenkins, a coal miner, and his wife, Edith. Aspiring to improve his life culturally and financially, and having a natural flair as an actor, he came under the tutelage of a schoolmaster, Philip Burton, whose surname he later adopted professionally. In 1943, Richard won a scholarship to Oxford University, by which time he had made his professional stage debut. He served with the Royal Air Force from 1944 to 1947 and the next year returned to the stage. Also in 1948, he made his screen debut in *The Last Days of Dolwyn*. While making that film, he met Welsh actress Sybil Williams, whom he wed in 1949. (They had two daughters: Kate in 1957 and Jessica in 1959.) Richard soon rose to prominence on both the London and Broadway stages, and he continued to make features both in England and in Hollywood.

By the end of 1961, Richard was on the *Cleopatra* set preparing for his upcoming scenes. According to Taylor, "He sort of sidled over to me and said, 'Has anybody ever told you that you're a very pretty girl?' And I said to myself, *Oy gevaldt*, here's the great lover, the great wit, the great intellectual of Wales, and he comes out with a line like that."

On January 22, 1962, Taylor and Burton did their first acting together. He had been drinking heavily the night before. She observed that when he attempted to lift a cup of coffee, his hands trembled badly. Said Elizabeth, "My heart just went out to him." Within days, Taylor and Fisher along with Burton and Sybil Williams were often being seen dining out together in Rome. Observers noted that subservient Eddie was being pushed further into the background at these get-togethers. Another indicator that something was in the wind was that Liz had suddenly put away the pictures of Mike Todd that adorned the walls of her villa and had stopped carrying the mangled wedding ring found on her late husband's charred remains.

Movie star Stewart Granger once observed of high-maintenance Taylor: "What I never understood was her incessant need to emasculate the old lover, while making the transition to someone new." Granger was referring not only to how Elizabeth handled her ditching of husband number two, urbane English actor Michael Wilding, but also to her breakup with Fisher.

While Taylor and Burton engaged in their flirtation on and off the film set, a mortified Fisher attempted to maintain his public composure. He had a reprieve from losing Elizabeth altogether because she had recently adopted a German baby girl, Maria. Taylor feared a public split from Eddie would damage her chances of keeping the newest member of her household at the Villa Pappa. Meanwhile, as the steamy Burton-Taylor affair further heated up, Fisher allied with Mrs. Burton, and the two wronged spouses commiserated together.

When news of the indiscretion spread, Burton's friends counseled him that it was a grave error to ditch his family for the much-divorced Elizabeth. In between drinking binges, Richard became remorseful about his infidelity and tried to break it off with Taylor. Her response was to attempt suicide with sleeping pills. Recovering from that episode, she became increasingly possessive and jealous of Burton. In reaction, he imported a shapely playmate to Rome, hoping it would anger Elizabeth into ending the "impossible" situation. It didn't work. It merely strengthened her craving for him. (Husband number two, Michael Wilding, once said wryly of his ex-spouse, "The real tragedy concerning Liz is that there is not a man in the world she cannot have at the snap of her fingers.")

In short order, what had been gossip in Rome became headlines around the world. Liz was again labeled a marriage wrecker, the modern version of the siren she was playing on camera. Every reaction by the rejected spouses (Eddie and Sybil), who had left Rome to save face, was being reported to the enthralled public. Eventually, in reaction to the blatant scandal, newspaper editorials—including one in the Vatican City's *L'Osservatore della Dominica* —castigated the shameless lovers, and Taylor in particular. In public, she put on an indifferent face, but it really upset her when people in the streets of Rome shouted "unfit mother!" at her. Back in Washington, D.C., a congressional bill was introduced to bar the notorious couple from entering the United States. It failed to pass.

By summer 1962, Elizabeth had completed her last scenes in Rome for the spectacle, and the exorbitant production wound to a close. When she eventually saw the completed picture—much cut from its huge original length—she was so upset by the severe edits that she vomited. *Cleopatra* was released in mid-1963, with the $44 million epic grossing $26 million in domestic distribution. It later turned a modest profit from its release abroad.

Having survived the incredible media circus in Rome, Richard and Elizabeth pursued their romance elsewhere, ignoring their individual marital partners and public rebuke. In keeping with the topsy-turvy values of the time, their indulgent behavior made them media darlings and the toast of many levels of society about the globe. To cash in on their notoriety, MGM asked Elizabeth—at her now exorbitant usual salary—to replace Sophia Loren as costar of Burton's new picture, *The V.I.P.s.* The sinful couple arrived in London in December 1962 to start production of the slick soap opera.

By then, Fisher was history for Taylor, but Burton was still undecided whether or not to return to his family. Finally, several weeks into making the glossy *The V.I.P.s*, Richard proposed to Elizabeth, presenting her with a glittery diamond-and-emerald brooch worth $80,000. (She wore a copy of the jewelry in the picture.) If she was pleased with her domestic victory, he remained guilt-ridden for abandoning Sybil and his daughters (one of whom, Jessica, was both schizophrenic and autistic and had to be institutionalized). To cope with his agony, he intensified his alcohol consumption. Not to be outmatched, heavy-drinking Liz proved she could hold her own, even against champion lush Burton. As she had with Mike Todd, Elizabeth reveled in verbal and physical confrontations with her new mate. Their battles on and off the set were legendary.

While Taylor hosted a TV documentary (1963's *Elizabeth Taylor in London*), Burton made 1964's *Becket*. He then flew to Mexico to costar with Deborah Kerr and Ava Gardner in *The Night of the Iguana* (1964). Not intending to let her man out of her sight, Taylor was on hand throughout the production, and she garnered far more media coverage than did the actual cast.

In the meantime, Sybil had divorced Richard in February 1963 in Puerto Vallarta, Mexico. In that same place, 13 months later, Elizabeth shed Eddie Fisher. Ten days later, on March 15, 1964, at the Ritz Carlton Hotel in Montreal, Canada, the extraordinary duo was married by a pastor of a local Unitarian church. At the time, Burton was headlining a pre-Broadway tour of *Hamlet*, a project that garnered him excellent reviews. Because Taylor was in attendance during the Shakespearean trek—usually standing in the wings—audiences thronged to see the Bard performed in modern dress.

For the world, the Burtons were the new international royalty whose every action seemed endlessly fascinating. The paparazzi constantly pursued them. After a while, the notorious couple began playing to this audience, as much intrigued by their incredible fame as was the public. It led the pair to be even more self-indulgent in their material acquisitions, their thoughtless behavior, and their public sparring.

Their lavish lifestyle included owning expensive homes around the globe, a $1 million jet plane (*The Elizabeth*), a $500,000 helicopter, a $1 million yacht (*The Kalizma*), fancy cars (their Rolls Royce Silver Cloud had his and her bars), and much exquisite jewelry. (One of Taylor's most cherished possessions in her prized collection was a $1.05 million diamond. Richard purchased the 69.42-karat gem from Cartier's in 1969. Another of her acquisitions was the 44-karat Krupp diamond, acquired for $305,000.) Their colossal path through life necessitated a large retinue to service the needs of this demanding regal couple, their children, their pets, and so forth. (It was estimated that during their marriage, her wealth reached well over $40 million; his was half that amount. By the standards of the times, it was a tremendous sum.)

The Burtons' splendiferous, gaudy existence quickly ate into their massive fortune. However, because they commanded huge film salaries, they thought tomorrow would take care of itself. (Taylor reasoned, "We get such great pleasure out of spending money. So why not enjoy it?") To spice up their elegantly tasteless existence, they spatted (anything could set one or the other off into a snit or tirade), made up, and repeated the process.

Their tempestuous behavior and extreme mood swings—which the press reported in full detail for agog readers—were fueled by the duo's heavy consumption of alcohol and Taylor's reliance on pills to alleviate real body pains (she was extremely prone to accidents and health misadventures) and imaginary ills.

The couple thrived on their profligate, vulgar, and exhausting ways. Said Burton when asked on a TV talk show how long he would endure being navigated through life by his controlling wife, he smirked, "Oh, I suppose forever."

Despite their constant battles, the duo learned to accommodate one another—at least, to a degree. She knew better than to try to curb his excessive drinking, just as he despaired of restraining her frequent use of expletives or her compulsive need for more costly gems. Having met their match in one another, they reveled in their partnership. Proudly, Richard took Elizabeth to his hometown in Wales, showing her the sights and introducing her to his friends there.

As time passed, Elizabeth, who had never really experienced "normal" domesticity, reveled in the pampered togetherness she shared with Burton. She confided, "Our most precious commodity is being alone—no servants, no anybody—just us. How we cherish it and look forward to it! Sunday is the best day of the week because it often offers that privacy. There are no servants hovering around, or very few." Taylor even indulged an inclination to cook, which led her mate to chide, "You can tell when Elizabeth does the honors [in the kitchen]—not just by the content, but by the aftermath. Invariably, she leaves a mess!" On another occasion, the couple kidded about their excessive closeness. She teased, "Buster, where I goest, thou goest!" He replied, tongue in cheek, "At your side forever, except when I traverse to the men's room!"

To refuel their coffers, the Taylor-Burton tandem made the trashy *The Sandpiper* (1965), followed by the gilt-edged *Who's Afraid of Virginia Woolf?* (1966). For this heavily dramatic assignment as a middle-aged shrew, Elizabeth donned a gray wig and body padding. As the wife of an emasculated associate history professor (Burton) she won her second Academy Award. (Over the years, Burton was nominated for seven Oscars, but he never won one.) *Woolf* was followed by a colorful rendition of Shakespeare's *The Taming of the Shrew* (1967), in which the Burtons invested $1.4 million of their own money. Far less felicitous was the African-set political drama *The Comedians* (1967) and the poorly received adaptation of Christopher Marlowe's *Doctor Faustus* (1968—in which Taylor had a cameo as Helen of Troy). The husband-and-wife love team sunk in Tennessee Williams's *Boom!* (1968). By the time of the atrocious *Hammersmith Is Out* (1972), the couple had nearly exhausted their welcome with filmgoers. This was confirmed the next year, when the couple shifted to the small screen, appearing in the two-part *Divorce His, Divorce Hers.* They were paid astronomical salaries for this tacky venture. It led *Variety* to slam, "Liz and Dick Burton are the corniest act in show business."

By 1973 the globe-trotting Burtons had been together for 12 years, and their marriage had worn as thin as their careers. The couple separated in the spring of 1973 but reconciled after a month. That June, the once lovebirds of the jet set had a more permanent parting. Burton explained, "We both burst apart virtually at the same moment. It got to the state when I was running around like a lunatic, behaving a bit madly, boozing of course." Taylor retreated to California where she was frequently escorted by actor Peter Lawford.

In midyear the couple attempted to patch up their differences. She jetted to New York, but they were together for only hours before they were again battling one another. On July 3, Taylor issued a statement of her official separation, reasoning, "Maybe we have loved each other too much (not that I ever believed such a thing was possible), but we have been in each other's pockets constantly, never being apart except for matters of life and death, and I believe this has caused a temporary breakdown in communications." Twenty days later the couple reunited in Rome, where he was making a movie with Sophia Loren. The truce quickly erupted into fighting, but they patched up each new quarrel. Every change in the status quo received international news coverage, as once again they grabbed the world's attention.

In late April 1974, it was announced that the combative Burtons had split yet again and, this time, sighed their representative, "The breakup is final." Two months later, in Gstaad, Switzerland (where they had a residence), Elizabeth received her divorce. The couple had previously reached an amicable financial settlement.

While Elizabeth was filming *The Bluebird* (1975) in Russia, Richard was often based in New York, where he indulged in assorted flings. Still he wanted to reunite with Taylor, but she had issued an ultimatum: "Booze, no me. No booze, me." A confirmed drinker, he wasn't ready to trade in that crutch. He kept company with Princess Elizabeth of Yugoslavia, then married to a British banker. While Burton considered marrying his new escort, Taylor socialized with Dutch-born Henry Wynberg. She had previously dated the used car salesman, five years her junior, in 1973 when she and Burton were separated. Now that she was divorced from Richard, Taylor and Wynberg lived together in a Beverly Hills home. Henry believed that one day Elizabeth would marry him.

In 1975, Burton was spending time with Jeanie Bell, a young African American model/actress who had appeared in *The Klansman* (1974) with Richard. It was she who helped him (once his physicians had said his alcohol abuse was literally killing him) dry out. By late August, Richard was telling friends that he and Elizabeth would remarry. When he and Taylor flew to Israel—for a pilgrimage to holy sites—they were mobbed by locals. From there they moved on to Africa, where, on October 10, 1975, they wed in a mud hut on a game preserve in Botswana. This time the ceremony was exceedingly simple, with the newlyweds exchanging simple ivory wedding bands. Later, in Johannesburg he gave her a 72-karat diamond wedding band. When asked why they had re-wed, Burton said, "We really cannot keep away from each other."

February 1976 saw Richard back on Broadway in the drama *Equus.* He received glowing reviews. However, he earned a failing mark in his marriage. He had met 27-year-old Susan Hunt, a former model, then in the process of divorcing a British racing car driver. In retaliation, Elizabeth had been sharing bliss with Peter Darmanin, a 37-year-old Maltese businessman. When that relationship fell apart within a month, Taylor retreated to Los Angeles. On July 30, 1976, Burton received a divorce in Haiti. Weeks later he married Hunt in Arlington, Virginia.

Richard and Susan divorced in 1983. That same year, in July, he wed 35-year-old Sally Anne Hay, a film production worker, in Las Vegas. Meanwhile, in December 1976, Elizabeth wed John W. Warner, former secretary of the navy who became a U.S. senator. Five years her junior, he was Episcopalian and a Republican, while she was Jewish and a Democrat. The unlikely union lasted until November 1982.

Single again after seven marriages, Elizabeth tried the Broadway stage in a well-received revival of the drama *The Little Foxes* (1981). In 1983, by then noticeably overweight, she starred in Manhattan in a revival of Noël Coward's comedy *Private Lives.* Her costar was Richard Burton. The lackluster performances were roasted as being caricatures and trading on the costars' past marital notoriety. Nevertheless, playgoers were initially intrigued to see in person these icons of dysfunctional living. On the national tour, which ended in Los Angeles, each lead player suffered from maladies and substance abuse. It was a sad end to the once love team's glory days of 21 years earlier in Rome.

Richard Burton died on August 5, 1984, of a cerebral hemorrhage in Geneva, Switzerland. He was 58. (Taylor fainted when she learned of his passing.) Thereafter, with her acting career on the wane, middle-aged Taylor devoted herself to fund-raising to fight AIDS. In 1988, while undergoing treatment for substance abuse at the Betty Ford Center in southern California, Taylor met divorced former truck driver Larry Fortensky, 38. The oddly matched couple wed in October 1991 and divorced in 1996.

TV talk show host David Frost, who played an unbilled reporter in *The V.I.P.s*, once said, "People today don't realize what a golden couple they were. They were huge! The famous couples of recent memory, such as Tom Cruise and Nicole Kidman—none of them matched the huge fascination of Richard and Elizabeth. At the time, they were the most famous people in the world. And the chemistry between them was real."

Frost might have added that the outrageousness of Taylor and Burton's unseemly behavior when they were in the public eye gave this scandalous relationship almost mythic proportions.

Marilyn Monroe: The Tragic Siren

"You know . . . in a way I'm a very unfortunate woman. All this nonsense about being a legend, all this glamour and publicity. Somehow I'm always a disappointment to people."

—MARILYN MONROE, ON JULY 25, 1962

Marilyn Monroe had one key ambition: "I want to be a big star more than anything. It's something precious." With a 37-23-34 figure and a luminous face, she had all the natural assets to make her wish come true. As she realized her professional goal, she kept hoping that she might be judged more for her acting acumen than for her captivating looks. However, despite ongoing efforts to master her craft, the luscious blonde always remained pessimistic about her thespian abilities: "I knew how third rate I was. I could actually feel my lack of talent, as if it were cheap clothes I was wearing inside. But my God, how I wanted to learn, to change, to improve!"

No matter how smartly Monroe delivered her screen characterizations, she was convinced that she had not succeeded. She always
thought people in the know scoffed at her acting. (Her pitiful—and
unjustified—lack of self-confidence once led her to beg a reporter,
"Please don't make me a joke. End the interview with what I believe....
I want to be an artist, an actress with integrity.")

Over the decades several screen sirens suffered tragic lives (e.g.,
Barbara La Marr, Clara Bow, Jean Harlow, Rita Hayworth, Maria
Montez, Dorothy Dandridge, Lupe Velez, and Linda Darnell).
However, none of them have endured as a popular icon to the same
intense degree as Marilyn has. Monroe possessed that extra dimension of extreme vulnerability that made her so appealing to so
many generations. People find it easy to relate to this tragic figure
who desperately wanted to be respected by her industry peers and,
on a personal level, to be a real woman with a successful marriage
and children. That she felt she failed in all these key areas was the
bane of her emotionally troubled existence. (Ironically, her array
of internal conflicts made her more sympathetic to her legions of
admirers.)

As with another deeply disturbed icon, Elvis Presley, many of
Marilyn's frailties and problems were masked from her adoring
public during her lifetime. In the early 1960s, before tabloid TV
and supermarket publications were revealing celebrities' deepest
secrets and most personal day-to-day activities, many of Monroe's
adherents were unaware of the magnitude of her mounting troubles. Thus, when she died at age 36 in August 1962, her passing
was unexpected to most everyone and a shock to all. Here was a
world-class beauty who seemed to have (or could have had) almost
anything that life could possibly offer, yet it was not enough to satisfy her deep-seated needs or to keep her alive.

What adds elements of scandal to her tragic demise are the
myriad offensive and outrageous conjectures—some presented as
absolute truths—regarding how and why she expired and who, if
anyone beyond Marilyn, was ultimately responsible for her death.

Norma Jeane Mortensen was born in Los Angeles on June 1, 1926. Her mother, Gladys Pearl (Monroe) Mortensen, had previously been married to a businessman, John Baker (by whom she had two children: Jack and Berniece). Gladys was a photo lab technician now wed to a Los Angeles gas company meter man (Martin Edward Mortensen). However, they had separated in early 1925 and he had filed for divorce many months before she became pregnant with Norma Jeane. (There were several other candidates for her biological father, including Charles Stanley Gifford, a foreman at Consolidated Film Industries in Hollywood where young Gladys worked; coworker Harold Rooney; or, perhaps, Raymond Guthrie, a film developer.)

During much of Norma Jeane's youth, the disturbingly erratic Gladys was often institutionalized because of emotional instability. As a result, the girl endured a gloomy childhood in several foster homes and orphanages; she claimed to have been raped when she was only eight years old. One of the consequences of these dismal early years was Norma Jeane's tendency to stutter. Another was her great insecurity, as people of parental authority—including her fragile mother—came into and then vanished from her helter-skelter existence.

In June 1942, to circumvent being dispatched to yet another foster home, 16-year-old Norma Jeane wed 22-year-old James Dougherty, an aircraft factory worker. While he served in the merchant marines during World War II, she worked, for a time, at a defense plant in Burbank, California. The curvaceous teenager began posing—often in form-fitting sweaters—for local photographers. This, in turn, led to modeling for major girlie publications. In July 1946, the would-be actress was screen-tested by Twentieth Century-Fox and signed to a $75-per-week contract. The studio created a new name (Marilyn Monroe) for her. That September the starlet divorced Dougherty.

At Fox, where Betty Grable was the studio's chief blond attraction, Marilyn had a few tiny roles. However, after six months, the newcomer's option was dropped. Thanks to playing the casting-couch game, she was referred to Columbia Pictures where she signed a $125-a-week pact. There she earned a starring part in a quickie musical (1948's *Ladies of the Chorus*). However, she ruined her chances on the lot by refusing to do special favors for studio mogul Harry Cohn. (By this point, Marilyn was involved with vocal coach/music arranger Fred Karger. When he dropped her for another girlfriend, naive Monroe was devastated.)

In late 1948, 22-year-old Monroe met Johnny Hyde, executive vice president of the William Morris Agency. He was married, short, unhandsome, and 31 years her senior. Nevertheless, this high-powered talent representative became her boyfriend and mentor. Thanks to him, she won small but interesting screen assignments in *The Asphalt Jungle* and *All About Eve* (both 1950). Also that year, Johnny, who arranged a new Twentieth Century-Fox agreement for Marilyn, died. (Monroe had frequently ignored her benefactor to pursue other sponsors. After Hyde's death, Monroe was guilt-ridden that she had never been able to reciprocate—beyond sex—Johnny's great feelings for her. Later, she'd say, "I don't know that any man ever loved me so much.")

Ambitious Marilyn finally came into her own at Fox, becoming the lot's new platinum blond bombshell. However, Monroe's rapid rise to fame exacerbated her mounting insecurities, leading her to be late on the soundstage, to be sometimes temperamental, and to be problematic in front of the camera. To steady her course, she allowed herself to come under the control of stern acting coach Natasha Lytess.

Now a bona fide marquee attraction, Marilyn indulged her power by rejecting studio projects, especially those that would further showcase her as a dumb blonde (an image she despised). Meanwhile, Monroe's pleas to be given more dimensional assignments fell on deaf ears, which only increased her frustration and solidified her massive lack of self-assurance.

Off camera, after a two-year courtship, the sex siren married Joe DiMaggio, the famous baseball player, early in 1954. Twelve years her senior, a devout Catholic, and a strong family man, the idolized athlete naively wanted his bride to dump show business to become a homemaker. Unable to abandon her career dream after so long a struggle, she refused. Instead, he became "Mr. Monroe," and his mortification spurred his jealousy and fanned his abusive behavior. The celebrated couple divorced that September.

Fast approaching her thirties and fearful that she must prove that her talents were not just skin deep, Marilyn rebelled even more strongly against the studio. She went to New York where she formed a movie production company and studied at the esteemed Actors Studio. There she came under the influence of Lee Strasberg. His controlling wife, Paula, soon became Marilyn's new acting coach. Like almost everyone in Marilyn's life, the Strasbergs had their personal agendas, and Monroe was a useful vehicle to fulfill their current financial and career needs.

When Monroe finally returned to picturemaking at Twentieth Century-Fox, she earned solid reviews for *Bus Stop* (1956). It prompted her demands for greater control over her pictures, wishes that went unheeded because she was so difficult on the set and so resistant to her employers' career guidance. As the conflicts and pressures intensified, so did her consumption of drugs and alcohol. In an emotional abyss, she sought relief by wedding, in June 1956, famed playwright Arthur Miller. She hoped this much-older, Jewish intellect would protect her against her escalating demons. Months later, Marilyn suffered a miscarriage, as would happen again in 1957 and in 1958. During this emotionally perilous period, she flew to England to star opposite Sir Laurence Olivier in *The Prince and the Showgirl* (1957). It was an unhappy shoot, and the film failed with both the public and the critics. She rebounded with the hit comedy *Some Like It Hot* (1959).

By 1960, complex and bewildered Monroe was visiting psychiatrists regularly, but her problems went so deep that she couldn't respond properly to treatment. Grabbing at straws, Monroe, who was having accelerating problems in her marriage to Miller, embarked on an affair with Yves Montand, her colead in *Let's Make*

Love (1960). However, that liaison fell apart when he returned to Paris and to his actress wife, Simone Signoret.

Years earlier, Arthur Miller had begun writing *The Misfits* (1961) as a tailor-made vehicle for Marilyn (and to provide himself with a new career as a screenwriter). During the difficult location shoot, Monroe was completely out of control and, for a period, had to be hospitalized to detoxify and to regain a degree of emotional stability. By late 1960, she and Arthur began dissolving their marriage, with the divorce occurring in Juarez, Mexico, in January 1961. Because Monroe was by that time displaying severe suicidal behavior, that February, her analyst (Marianne Kris) persuaded Marilyn to enter the psychiatric division of Manhattan's Payne Whitney Clinic. After seven horrendous days of confinement (including being locked in a padded cell—which fulfilled her worst nightmares), the highly distraught star phoned Joe DiMaggio to rescue her. He immediately arranged for her discharge.

In October 1961, Marilyn had met President John F. Kennedy at a dinner party hosted by his sister Pat and his brother-in-law, actor Peter Lawford, at the couple's Santa Monica, California, home. A few months later, Monroe and the chief executive met again at a New York City dinner gathering. The third get-together occurred in late March 1962 at the Palm Springs home of actor/singer Bing Crosby, where she and Kennedy were both houseguests. (Reportedly, on this occasion, Marilyn and JFK shared bedroom intimacies.) Meanwhile, in early 1962, the star, upon the urging of Dr. Ralph Greenson, her current—and very possessive—psychiatrist, purchased a small Spanish-style home (the first abode she owned) on Fifth Helena Drive in Brentwood. Also at the controlling therapist's direction, she hired his acquaintance, middle-aged, stern Eunice Murray, as her housekeeper/companion. (Greenson arranged for Murray to report back to him on all of Monroe's activities.)

Following a long period away from the soundstages, Marilyn returned to the studio in April 1962 to begin a hastily slapped-together romantic comedy, *Something's Got to Give*, which costarred her with Dean Martin. Although Monroe was in luminous physical shape, she was an emotional wreck. On those few days when she appeared on the set, she was often confused and struggling to remember her dialogue.

During Hollywood's golden age, Twentieth Century-Fox would have pampered Marilyn, even at this stage of her greatest stress. However, Fox was currently in desperate financial straits. Having thrown away more than $61 million in pictures the public did not care to see, the studio had banked its future on a colossal epic, *Cleopatra* (1963), starring Elizabeth Taylor and Richard Burton. As the budget on that Rome-filmed saga spiraled out of control, harried executives back in Los Angeles concurred that they must not let *Something's Got to Give* become another financial disaster. Thus, ironically, while strong-willed Taylor's indulgent excesses in Italy were permitted, the Fox management team (then under severe pressure from angry company stockholders) had no tolerance for vulnerable Marilyn's unprofessional behavior, which was causing costly shooting delays.

In mid-May 1962, during one of her many absences from the lot, Monroe went to New York to sing "Happy Birthday" to the president at a Madison Square Garden gala. Because Monroe had so brazenly thumbed her nose at Fox by her well-documented truancy, the studio heads became enraged. Realizing that she had overstepped her bounds, the sex goddess was far more cooperative when she returned to the soundstage in Los Angeles.

On June 1, Marilyn turned 36 and celebrated the occasion with a small party on the set. Six days later, the star was terminated from *Something's Got to Give* due to "unprofessional antics." (The panicking studio long had been looking for an excuse to cancel the expensive film, which they felt, due to its anemic screenplay, would not be a guaranteed box-office success.) Fox filed a $750,000 lawsuit against their former money earner. They attempted to recast Monroe's part, but Dean Martin refused to work on the project with anyone but Monroe. Soon, cooler heads prevailed and the studio suggested a compromise: after Martin completed other film commitments, the vehicle would restart with Marilyn again as leading lady.

Praying that everything would somehow turn out for the best, on August 1, 1962, Fox signed Marilyn to a new pact at $250,000. However, it was all for naught. In the early morning of August 5, 1962, Marilyn was found dead in the bedroom of her Brentwood home. Her passing late the previous night was ascribed to a fatal overdose of Nembutal and chloral hydrate. Three days thereafter, the cinema queen was interred in a crypt at Westwood Memorial Cemetery, only a short distance from her old home lot. It was a bereft Joe DiMaggio who spearheaded the funeral plans.

At the time and right up to the present, there have been an astonishing number of conspiracy theories as to how the wretchedly unhappy movie legend "really" died. (Such creative conjectures have greatly added to Monroe's legend and reflect the depth of fascination the public had, and still has, with the screen star.) Some sources have insisted that her relationship with President Kennedy was far more extensive than their documented few meetings and/ or that she had a romantic tie to Kennedy's brother Robert, the U.S. attorney general. Jumping off from these intriguing assumptions, some observers have suggested that Marilyn was murdered because she knew too many government secrets from her "association" with the Kennedys and, therefore, had to be silenced. Others have claimed that Monroe was a target of the mobs because of her recurring association with movie star/singer Frank Sinatra and his underworld ties. Still other theorists have debated whether Marilyn's passing was suicide or merely an accidental drug overdose or the result of medical malpractice.

None of the police inquiries then, or years later when the matter was reopened, could successfully parse through the case facts due to a variety of factors. The death scene at Fifth Helena Drive had been contaminated by a variety of individuals by the time the police first arrived. There was also the problem of apparent missteps in processing case evidence and the later charting of autopsy results. In addition, there was the misleading—or contradictory or lack of—information supplied by such key people as Eunice Murray, who had been present at the house the night Marilyn died, as well as Monroe's doctors, who were treating her in the days leading up to her passing. All of this has contributed to the scandal and speculation surrounding Marilyn's demise.

About a month before her death, in an interview with *Life* magazine's Richard Meryman, Monroe said of her life in transition: "Nothing's going to sink me, although it might be kind of a relief to be finished with movie-making. That kind of work is like a hundred-yard dash and then you're at the finish line, and you sigh and say you've made it. But you never have. There's another scene and another film, and you have to start all over again."

Judy Garland: The Public Meltdown

"You know how I look on this series? As a secure way of living. I can get up in the morning and go to work and come home at night to things that are familiar to me. I'm so tired of being on the road. . . . I've been living in hotels now for the last three years and I've had it. . . . I want my children to have their own rooms to come home to."

—JUDY GARLAND, IN 1963

In the early '60s, 44-year-old movie star Judy Garland was again on the professional comeback trail. In between singing engagements around the globe, she had earned an Oscar nomination for her dramatic cameo in *Judgment at Nuremberg* (1961), followed by starring roles in such films as *I Could Go On Singing* (1963). In February 1962, she scored with a successful TV variety special, her first in six years. That December she made another sensational small-screen appearance—singing and reminiscing—on *The Jack Paar Show*. This was followed by a command performance at the White House for her pal, President John F. Kennedy. Once again, svelte Garland was juggling several career offers. She seemed to be back on top in her profession.

On the downside, Garland's shaky marriage to her third husband, promoter Sid Luft, was tottering. She and the deal maker, wed since 1952, had two children: Lorna and Joey. Since late 1960, Luft had shunted Judy's talent management to Freddie Fields, who, more recently, had formed Creative Management Associates (CMA) with David Begelman. These days, Garland and Luft were again feuding. An ongoing bone of contention was the control of their offspring (including Liza, Garland's daughter by her second husband, film director Vincente Minnelli).

Inept at money management and constantly fleeced by business associates, Judy, who had earned millions during her lengthy career, was nearly broke. However, with the three major American networks bidding for her services for a weekly TV series, she hoped to stabilize her finances. By early 1963, CBS's president, James T. Aubrey Jr., had signed the veteran singer to an exclusive, multiyear deal potentially worth $24 million. Out of this, the just-under-five-foot songbird would net $25,000 from each weekly show, with the ownership of the videotaped program to be held by her Kingsrow Enterprises (formed with partners Fields and Begelman). An additional lure for Judy was that the future sale of syndication rights to her program were valued at $4 million. The contract allowed Garland to cancel the show after its first 13-week cycle, and it provided options for four additional years of her TV services.

With all this good news Judy should have been jubilant. But mercurial Garland knew herself all too well. Her reputation for unreliability, tardiness, and a strong aversion to rehearsing was the reality, as was her reliance on alcohol and drugs (barbiturates and sedatives). Additionally, she suffered from long-term emotional problems. As a result, her mental and physical condition could spike or crash at a moment's notice. (These factors were known by her management. However, their apparent priorities were to harvest the sizable commissions from Garland's TV coup and to use the deal to lure other big names into their agency.)

The show business community was also well aware of Judy's precarious performance record. *Variety* sharply noted in early 1963:

"Even if Judy Garland survives her initial season of weekly Sunday night hours (and they're placing bets on this one) the chances are indeed remote that she'll want to try again in '64–'65. . . ." *TV Guide* labeled her project the "Great Garland Gamble." Reading such items did nothing to bolster the star's wobbly self-esteem.

As 1963 got under way, Judy did not anticipate the fierce running battle she would soon have with CBS. Already, programming executive Hubbell Robinson, long a Garland champion, was being ousted from his network berth. This left Garland to deal with Hunt Stromberg Jr., a top company vice president. Stromberg would display a vicious disregard for Garland's sensibilities.

In addition, the star would have to contend with hard-edged Mike Dann, the head of CBS network programming. He was a close ally of Jim Aubrey, who ran the network. By this juncture, Aubrey's unrelenting business practices had earned him the nickname of "the Smiling Cobra," and he lived up to his unpleasant reputation in his upcoming dealings with Judy. For some reason, having hired Garland, Aubrey would become disinterested in her. (In contrast, he catered to the welfare of entertainer Danny Kaye, who was also debuting a CBS-TV variety series in the fall of 1963.) Aubrey's apathy toward Judy would quickly turn to enmity when, during the coming TV season, Garland failed to jump through every hoop he crassly ordered.

The ugly tug-of-war between Garland and the corporate "suits" would become a milestone scandal of crude chicanery within the entertainment industry and one that was played out before a shocked viewing public. It led to the "flop" show departing the airwaves on March 29, 1964, after only 26 episodes. Thereafter, a physically and emotionally depleted Garland made new stabs at professional comebacks. However, her botched TV series proved to be her last hurrah, and it was certainly a main contributor to her demise, five years later, at the age of 47 on June 22, 1969.

Born Frances Ethel Gumm on June 10, 1922, in Grand Rapids, Minnesota, she was the third daughter of Frank Avent Gumm, an unsuccessful Irish tenor, and his spouse, Ethel Marion Milne, a vaudeville theater pianist. Before her third birthday, Frances made her singing debut at the local New Grand Theater (which her parents operated). Thereafter, her ambitious mother groomed her youngest girl, as she had her two other daughters, for a show business career.

In 1926, when Frank's homosexuality led to a potential scandal in Grand Rapids, Ethel engineered the family's hasty move to southern California. There, in Lancaster, Gumm operated a movie theater. Meanwhile, the determined mother guided her offspring's careers. In the next few years, the sibling trio toured with their singing act and made movie shorts. Before long, the girls adopted the stage surname of Garland, and Frances changed her first name to Judy.

Judy was signed by MGM in 1935. Her feature film debut was on loanout to Twentieth Century-Fox for the musical *Pigskin Parade* (1936). She returned to MGM where she appeared in, among others, *Thoroughbreds Don't Cry* (1937), the first of 10 vehicles with Mickey Rooney. For playing Dorothy in *The Wizard of Oz* (1939) Garland won a Special Oscar.

Prone to being overweight, Judy was prescribed diet pills by studio physicians. This addiction led to other medications to help the hyperactive talent cope. Her severe insecurities were not helped by her unpromising romantic life. She had been infatuated with bandleader Artie Shaw, but, in February 1940, he eloped with MGM beauty Lana Turner. In reaction, Judy wed another musician, composer David Rose, who was 12 years her senior. When Judy became pregnant she was ecstatic, but both MGM and her mother pressured her to have an abortion. When David acceded to the plan, it doomed their marriage.

Once separated from Rose, Judy lurched into an affair with older, married Joseph L. Mankiewicz, a studio producer/writer. It was he who persuaded Garland to undergo psychiatry. While the sessions helped to a degree, they intensified her rebellious attitude in which she saw herself as life's perpetual victim.

While making *Meet Me in St. Louis* (1944), Judy fell in love with her director, Vincente Minnelli, who was 19 years older and quite effeminate. The couple wed in June 1945 and, the following March, daughter Liza was born. However, their marital idyll was short-lived. Garland suffered from postpartum depression and was angry at being cajoled into signing a new studio deal rather than semiretiring into motherhood. It also bruised her fragile ego that screen star Tyrone Power, with whom she once had a romance, was now dating glamorous Lana Turner. Adding to Judy's troubles, she and Vincente were each far too self-focused to live harmoniously.

During this stressful period, Judy returned to her staggering pill regimen. It left her with terrifying mood swings, paranoia, and the inability to/disinterest in work. Her worsening condition caused her to be replaced in *The Barkleys of Broadway* (1949) and *Annie Get Your Gun* (1950). After being hospitalized for emotional problems, she made *Summer Stock* (1950), but she was again the center of production delays. When she proved too unreliable to make *Royal Wedding* (1951), the studio terminated her contract. Soon thereafter, Judy, who had attempted suicide yet again, divorced Minnelli.

Later, thanks to a new mentor, Michael Sidney Luft, Judy enjoyed fabulous comeback concert engagements at London's Palladium and New York's Palace Theater. Garland married Luft in June 1952, and their daughter, Lorna, was born five months later. Sid engineered Judy's movie return in *A Star Is Born* (1954), which netted her an Oscar nomination. However, her behavior on the soundstages reinforced her reputation as unreliable. Once again, Garland retreated to the concert stage. Her son, Joey, was born in March 1959. Two years later, Judy gave a remarkable Carnegie Hall concert.

When Garland was signed for *The Judy Garland Show*, all that was established was that she would star on a weekly musical variety hour. (It was one of several such genre entries scheduled for the 1963–1964 season.) Judy's camp suggested a concert format, but CBS honchos felt that (1) she would too quickly run out of her repertoire and (2) she required a more conventional show setup that would be consistent, familiar, and viewer-friendly.

Because Jim Aubrey's CBS regime was enjoying big success with its bumpkin comedies (e.g., *The Andy Griffith Show*), it was ordered that Garland's offering must *not* be too sophisticated and must utilize low-brow humor. (As such, hayseed comedian Jerry Van Dyke was hired as a blundering host and foil for Garland.) Then, suddenly, Judy was advised that her showcase would air from CBS Television City in Hollywood rather than from New York, as planned. This meant the star had to relocate to Los Angeles, a city that held too many traumatic memories for her. (The belated location switch led to production delays, leaving little margin for trial and error before the show's debut.) Meanwhile, a depressed Judy took an overdose of sleeping pills. Fortunately, she was rescued. But this incident made the newspapers, stirring up industry fears that Judy was incapable of handling the pressures of a weekly outing.

Upon recovering, Judy gave her all to making her TV project a resounding success. She kowtowed to Aubrey and his underlings. She even performed for network affiliates' executives when they convened in New York City. At the miniconcert, Garland employed her wicked sense of humor by opening her performance with a satirical version of "Call Me Irresponsible."

By June, Garland, Luft (now back in the fold), and the younger children (Liza was then building her show business career in Manhattan) had settled into a newly purchased Brentwood mansion. They soon hosted an impressive housewarming party. Ironically, days later, the Lufts separated for good. (By then, high-strung Judy was ricocheting through a clandestine romance with her manager, David Begelman.)

In mid-June, Judy began actual work on her highly touted series. One of the studios at CBS Television City was adapted to house her show, including the use of a huge carousel to allow sets to sweep in and out of view during the telecast. No one took into consideration that the revolving stage would give Judy motion sickness, would prevent the show's orchestra from being positioned in view of the cast, and would cut down available space for a live studio audience. (Another major problem of Judy's unlucky facility was a faulty sound system, a problem that was not remedied until very late in the show's run.) The studio also did not contain an appropriate dressing room for Garland. Only thanks to congenial producer George Schlatter did a badgered CBS finally provide its star with a 40-foot, $150,000 trailer/dressing room stationed near Stage 43.

On June 24, 1963, the first episode of *The Judy Garland Show* was taped, with Mickey Rooney as the special guest. The *Los Angeles Times* enthusiastically reported: "Judy seemed so assured, so self-possessed, so happy in her work. . . ."

From this high came a crashing low. During a brief hiatus following the first show, Garland learned that David Begelman had allegedly misappropriated $200,000 to $300,000 from her monies. In addition, it seemed he had not paid several expenses that the star had incurred. It was a serious situation that would escalate as more such accounting aberrations came to light. Not wanting to rock the boat with her "boyfriend" and fearing adverse publicity would damage her show's image, Judy let the matter ride. (Eventually, in 1966 and 1967, Garland and Luft sued the agency, Fields, and Begelman, claiming that they had "deliberately and systematically misused their position of trust" in order to "cheat, embezzle, extort, defraud, and withhold" funds. Two years thereafter, Judy dropped her suits and signed a new management contract with the agency!)

During July, episodes two through five of the TV variety show were taped with such guests as Tony Bennett, Lena Horne, and Judy's daughter Liza. Suddenly, when everything seemed to be calming down into a workable routine, an ax fell on August 2. CBS let it be known quite publicly that it was unhappy with the show's format, and much of the staff (including the Judy-friendly Schlatter) was fired. Besides director Bill Hoblin (who exited in a later purge), among the few remaining on "permanent" staff was singer Mel Tormé, the program's musical adviser/guest star. By then, Tormé, distracted with a failing marriage, had ceased being a Garland champion, and she referred to him as "Mel Torment." As the season progressed, he became increasingly passive-aggressive. By the time of the concert-format episodes of *The Judy Garland Show* he was replaced by Bobby Cole. He sued for his unpaid salary balance but later dropped his case. In 1970, Mel authored a mean-spirited history of Judy's chaotic show, *The Other Side of the Rainbow: With Judy Garland on the Dawn Patrol.*

Following the show purge, an edict came down from on high that Judy must be showcased as a more down-to-earth personality. To accomplish this, a discomforted Van Dyke was given even more embarrassing sketch dialogue in which Garland was made the butt of jokes about being an unreliable, out-of-touch, and goofy old dame. (The comedian was so embarrassed at uttering such cruel dialogue that his drinking problem escalated.) Moreover, Judy was warned not to be so touchy-feely with her musical guests because, supposedly, it bothered audiences in the heartland. (Her new posture of reserve made her look uncomfortable and detached from her guests.) It was ordained that she should talk more on the show. (To this command, Garland quipped, "I'm 41 years old, and suddenly they realize I can *talk.*")

The unrelenting barrage of changes was reported in detail by the media. With such massive, constant public tattling, Judy became increasingly insecure. Nevertheless, she remained amenable to authoritarian Aubrey and his underlings as they further distorted the concept for her once-distinctive TV fare. Desperately concerned about how TV viewers would react to her distilled weekly offering when it finally premiered, Judy was even more frightened by the unfavorable time slot that Aubrey had chosen for her offering. He scheduled *The Judy Garland Show* for 9:00 P.M. Sunday, pitting it against the well-established *Bonanza*, the Western series that had been the fourth most popular series aired during the previous season. (Danny Kaye's management had rejected his show being placed in this vulnerable time slot. In contrast, Fields and Begelman cavalierly allowed Garland to be pitted against *Bonanza.* Interestingly, CMA represented David Dortort, the creator and producer of that Western.)

While Judy coped with her newest staff, she further conflicted with Sid Luft over supervision of the children (which led to her obtaining legal custody of the children). By then, when she needed her agent/lover Begelman the most, he was preoccupied with other clients and Garland felt emotionally adrift. She fell back on late-night calls to friends and/or staff, asking them to join her immediately for drinks and talk. This "dawn patrol" soon exhausted her support staff, leading to more dissension on the troubled show. For a time, Judy found a new ally in cabaret singer André Phillipe. Later came movie star Glenn Ford and then show business attorney Greg Bautzer.

The Judy Garland Show premiered on September 29, 1963, to some great reviews (the New York Herald-Tribune called her "sparkling and magnetic") and to some cautionary commentary (the New York Times observed, "The [CBS] busybodies got so in the way that the singer never had a chance to sing out as only she can"). Despite the mixed reaction, that first week the program earned a 35.9 Nielsen rating, compared to Bonanza's 24.7. But the network had insisted on airing one of the weaker shows first, and while many home viewers had tuned in out of curiosity, they were put off by the bland format. Garland's ratings would tumble steadily.

Judy struggled through the next several weeks as the network undermined her with inappropriate guests and slapped-together scripts. When President Kennedy (who had personally encouraged and advised Garland in several telephone conversations during this difficult period) was assassinated on November 22, 1963, Judy was overwhelmed with grief. She suggested a special episode of uplifting patriotic songs, but the network vehemently vetoed her idea. Too angry to care, Judy taped a rousing rendition of "The Battle Hymn of the Republic" as her special tribute to the fallen leader. When aired, the segment received much critical and audience praise. However, her rebellious act cost her points with vindictive Aubrey and his staff.

Before 1963 ended, The Judy Garland Show was working on staff number three, and word had spread that not only would the program *not* return the next year, but also Judy might be replaced in midseason. As the season progressed, the series experienced a few highlights (e.g., the week of "the three belters": Barbra Streisand,

Ethel Merman, and Garland, and the Christmas show featuring Judy's three children). Yet, the public responded best to the few episodes in which Judy sang alone in concert. However, by that time, the series had tumbled to number 66 out of 80 regularly scheduled network shows. In this phase, the distraught and discouraged Garland usually arrived late (if at all) at Stage 43, and she typically was suffering from a drug and/or alcoholic haze.

In early 1964, Garland's fans, aghast at the extremely shabby treatment she was receiving from the network, began a major write-in campaign to save Judy's failing TV offering. In response, CBS announced that, should the series end, the network had other options to showcase the star's talents. But it was all pretense. By mid-January, the cancellation was official. In a rare moment of gallantry, Garland was allowed to announce she was "quitting" the series to spend more time with her children.

With the show's cancellation, critics and fans expressed their strong disgust with such ill treatment of Judy. CBS series star Lucille Ball blasted, "I was furious when one of the biggest stars in America, Judy Garland, was given lines like, 'I'm a little old lady,' and someone started talking about 'the next Judy Garland.' I bet she's glad her series is over. She's the best."

The final segment of *The Judy Garland Show* was taped on Friday, March 13, 1964 (and aired on March 29). By then, the fragile star was overwhelmed by legal difficulties with Luft, a suit initiated by Mel Tormé, and many unpaid bills (including past-due IRS payments). She struggled through the concert-style show, taking a few potshots at network executives in amended lyrics to the song "Here's to Us." Traumatized by the evening's demands, she eventually retreated to her trailer where she found a "gift" from Hunt Stromberg Jr. Accompanying an orchid plant was his card which read, "You were just great. Thanks a lot. You're through." Making the atrocious nightmare even worse was the total absence of her managers. (Callously, they had flown East for the Broadway opening of the musical *Funny Girl*, starring the agency's new lead client, Barbra Streisand.) Because of the poor results taped that night, some of the segments were restaged on March 26. The network replaced Garland's defunct vehicle with two nondescript half-hour game programs.

Thus ended Judy's dream of great financial stability. She spent her remaining years in turmoil, battling substance abuse, insolvency, failed projects, and two more marriages. Ironically, after her untimely death in 1969, the once much-maligned *The Judy Garland Show* took on a new life through the release of soundtrack albums, VHS tapes, and, most recently, DVDs of her television program, now savored as some of her best work.

As Terrence O'Flaherty (*San Francisco Chronicle*) wrote when *The Judy Garland Show* was canceled: "It was the most crisp and stylish musical series of the season. I cannot recall any in television's history where the production was so polished or where the star burned with any brighter intensity. For Garland fans—as well as viewers who seek showmanship and sophistication—the demise is a disaster."

For Garland the TV series debacle was more than just a professional disaster, it was more like a traumatic nightmare. Her treatment by a cruelly disinterested (though initially enthusiastic) network was scandalous. CBS executives seemed oblivious to the particular performance genius of this outstanding star of stage, screen, radio, TV, and recordings. Rarely, if ever, in the history of American TV broadcasting has such a living legend been treated with such total disregard. Because sensitive Judy was so tremendously beloved by the world at large, this brutal and shabby treatment was all the more shocking to her legions of fans who vicariously felt her pain.

Roman Polanski: The Exiled Oscar Winner

"I know the suffering that has gone into his life, especially these last ten years, and I feel that the press has maligned him terribly. He may make for provocative headlines, but with rare exception, the press has never captured the beauty of Roman's soul. . . . If ever a person is deserving of compassion, I think it is Roman. I only hope it is afforded him."

—Producer Robert Evans, in January 1978

The chronicle of Hollywood has been dotted with high-profile trials involving Tinseltown celebrities accused of serious sexual misconduct. These beleaguered luminaries have included Fatty Arbuckle in the 1920s, Errol Flynn and Charles Chaplin in the 1940s, and Tupac Shakur in the 1990s. Among these controversial courtroom cases, few such defendants received the notoriety accorded filmmaker Roman Polanski who, in 1977, was accused of the statutory rape of a 13-year-old Los Angeles girl. (It was this cynical filmmaker who once said, "Normal love isn't interesting. I assure you that it's incredibly boring.") Decades later, the legal proceedings against Polanski remain open due to special circumstances that have only added to the disreputable aura and mystique surrounding this much-discussed case.

Many people's reaction to Oscar-winning Polanski's legal hassle has been governed by how much they treasure the filmmaker's artistic contributions to world cinema. Such an appraisal poses the same philosophical question that long surrounded Frank Sinatra's career. Should artists be judged purely on their creative abilities, or are their private lives and moral values proper ingredients to use in assessing their talents?

In the case of French-born, sybaritic Polanski, the mix of his extraordinary life and artistic accomplishments is complicated by two key biographical factors that have earned him much sympathy: (1) his harrowing experiences as a Jewish youngster in hiding during the Holocaust and (2) the August 1969 murder of his pregnant wife (actress Sharon Tate) by members of Charles Manson's family.

Romek Polanski was born on August 18, 1933, in Paris, France. He was the only child of Polish-born Ryszard Polanski, a failed artist, and his wife, Bula Katz, one of the many White Russians in exile in France. (Bula had been previously married and had a daughter, Annette.) When the boy was three, the Jewish Polanskis (Annette would join them later) returned to the father's homeland in Krakow, the father mistakenly hoping that the anti-Semitic persecution engulfing Europe might be less severe in Poland because of its huge Jewish population.

In 1939, the Germans invaded Poland, and by the end of 1941 the Nazis were busily deporting the Jews to concentration camps. Among those taken from the Krakow ghetto were Bula, Annette, and other relatives of Romek. Not even 10, the diminutive boy went into hiding, joining a band of other youths surviving by their wits. Later, before Mr. Polanski was himself shipped to a Third Reich labor camp, he bribed non-Jewish families to take the youngster into their Roman Catholic households where the newcomer was disguised as one of their children. As such, Romek was shunted from one house to another in different parts of Poland (including stays in rugged farm country). Whenever the boy stayed in urban areas, he often snuck into cinemas. Such moviegoing experiences stirred the youngster's interest in becoming part of the world of cinema.

By the end of World War II, Romek was back in Krakow, where he was reunited with his father and other surviving relatives. Mr. Polanski, who eventually remarried, demanded that his artistic son enroll in a local trade school to become an electrician and gain a secure profession. The artistic teenager quickly became bored with his technical studies, much preferring the entertainment profession. By this point, he'd already begun performing on children's radio programs and, later, would join a local acting troupe. (Because of his short stature—under five feet, five inches—he could easily be cast in the roles of youngsters.) In 1950, the multitalented Romek enrolled in art school while continuing his acting. He made his film debut in a segment of the movie *Three Stories* (1953) and would continue to perform on camera for years.

In 1954, the ambitious Polanski passed the extremely difficult entrance examinations for the directors' program at the Polish National Film Academy at Lodz. During his studies there he directed several short subjects, including 1958's *Two Men and a Wardrobe*, which won several international movie awards. Upon graduating, he was hired as an assistant director with Kamera, one of Poland's film production companies. Meanwhile, in September 1959, Polanski wed teenage Polish cinema actress Barbara Lass (a union that ended in divorce in 1961).

Moving between Poland and France, the filmmaker—now known as Roman Polanski—worked on documentaries and short subjects. In 1962, he directed his debut feature, *Knife in the Water*, which earned him an Oscar nomination. By 1964, Roman was in England, where he wrote and directed two violent English-language features. During the 1960s, elfin-like, sinewy Polanski became a prime participant in London's swinging set, hanging out with the Playboy Club crowd and dating an endless procession of young women.

For the American-based Filmways, Polanski—as director, scripter, and actor—made *The Fearless Vampire Killers or Pardon Me, But Your Teeth Are in My Neck* (1967). Costarring in this satirical feature was statuesque Hollywood actress Sharon Tate, whom the filmmaker wed in January 1968. Several months later, on August 9, 1969, while Polanski was in Europe, Tate was among those murdered at the Polanskis' rented Hollywood Hills home by drugged-out members of Charles Manson's cult.

In 1968, Roman cemented his reputation as a major filmmaker with the release of the Hollywood-made *Rosemary's Baby*. For that box-office bonanza, he received an Academy Award nomination, as he did for the Los Angeles–filmed *Chinatown* (1974). During these years, the restless widower indulged in heavy partying and substance abuse, dividing his time between Hollywood and Europe. When he was not involved with the international jet set on the Continent, his Hollywood inner circle included such persistent Hollywood playboys as Jack Nicholson and Warren Beatty.

In the mid-1970s, the director had become involved romantically with young Teutonic actress Nastassia Kinski, she being 25 years younger than Polanski. By early 1977, Roman was staying at the Beverly Wilshire Hotel planning to make America his permanent home and become a citizen. He had negotiated a development deal for *The First Deadly Sin*, to be the first of several features for Columbia Pictures. Meanwhile, fidgety Polanski was asked by the French-based *Vogue Homme* to shoot a revealing photo showcase of "young girls of the world" for this sophisticated men's magazine.

As he had an attraction for nymphets, Roman was particularly intrigued by this commission in which he planned to focus on nubile 13-year-olds.

There are various accounts of how Polanski found his underage model in L.A. Some versions suggest he had dated the girl's divorced mother the prior year and it was she who recommended her adolescent daughter. Other reports linked director John Huston (who had played a role in Polanski's *Chinatown*) to Roman's finding of his potential model. Still others listed another of Polanski's pals, Henri Sera, as having made the modeling connection for the world-weary director.

In any event, on February 13, 1977, Polanski drove to Woodland Hills in the West San Fernando Valley. There he met with the sexually precocious but unsophisticated girl and her mother to discuss the photo session. (Later, Polanski would describe the husky-voiced young lady as "a good-looking girl, but nothing sensational.") A week later, Roman returned and drove to the end of the street with the girl. There they climbed a hill where she posed for test shots. In the process, the well-developed girl, not wearing a bra, changed her blouse for new poses and was captured on film naked from the waist up. When she returned home, the young model did not give her parent any details of the seminude modeling session.

Roman returned again to Woodland Hills on the afternoon of March 10 to undertake the agreed-upon shoot. Originally, the teenager asked whether a girlfriend might join them, but when Roman arrived, he was in a hurry—to capture the sunlight before it faded—and the two left alone in his car. In his rented Mercedes, they headed to Mulholland Drive in the Hollywood Hills, ostensibly to Jack Nicholson's home. En route, the filmmaker and his model discussed several sexual topics. (He claimed later that she informed him she had already slept with her teenage boyfriend and that she had initially experimented with sex when she was eight.)

At around 4:00 P.M. the duo stopped at actress Jacqueline Bisset's place, which was across the street from Jack Nicholson's place. At the time, Bisset's companion, Victor Drai, was involved in conversation with friends, and Bisset was just returning from a shopping expedition. Roman and the girl went outside by the pool and set to work. While they were there, the girl's mother (to whom Polanski had given a list of checkpoint telephone numbers) phoned to inquire how everything was going and was reassured that the situation was under control. Because the sun was retreating behind trees, Roman and his young charge went over to Nicholson's place, which faced the other side of the hill. Apparently, Nicholson was away (skiing in Colorado), but the star's housekeeper, Helena Kallianiotes, who lived in the smaller of the two homes on the estate, admitted them to Jack's home. Helena agreed to Roman's opening a bottle of champagne found in the refrigerator. Soon thereafter Kallianiotes retreated to her home to complete her cleaning, while Polanski and the teenager sipped champagne.

The ninth-grader later claimed she told Roman that champagne had previously made her ill but that he convinced her to drink some to relax. She also insisted that part of her reason for going to Nicholson's place was to meet the famous actor who she was not aware was away on holiday. Roman took various shots of his young model around the house. Meanwhile, he produced a Quaalude and suggested she try part of one, she having already admitted she had tried the pill previously. She reluctantly swallowed part of a tablet, as did Polanski. Thereafter, he photographed her partially and fully nude in the outside Jacuzzi, and at one point he joined her in the heated water.

In later courtroom testimony, the girl said she was getting nervous about the revealing shoot and that she called her mother for reassurance. She fibbed to Roman that she was having a slight asthma attack, using this as an excuse to conclude the risqué modeling session. He suggested she relax on the couch in the TV room. There he performed oral sex on her before he sexually penetrated her vagina. During this interlude, he inquired when she last had her period (she couldn't remember exactly) and whether she used birth control pills (she didn't). He then had anal intercourse with her. She claimed she had not objected strongly because she was afraid of him. During this encounter, actress Anjelica Huston arrived at the house. (She was then in the process of breaking up with Nicholson and was retrieving some of her possessions.)

Roman chatted briefly with Anjelica through the door, telling her he was getting dressed. Afterward, Polanski returned to his underage partner and, supposedly, climaxed through anal sex. Thereafter, the two dressed. On the way out of the house, the girl said hello to Huston and went to the car, where she started crying. Roman left her for a few minutes to talk with Anjelica. Then he drove the girl home.

Once back in Woodland Hills, the teenager rushed into the house and went upstairs, while Roman chatted briefly with her mother. Later that night the adolescent called her boyfriend and told him what had occurred. The conversation was overheard by the girl's elder sister, who, in turn, told their mother, who phoned the police. Around midnight, the girl was taken to the Parkland Hospital where she was tested for sexual intercourse. During the night she was interviewed by police detectives. Deputy District Attorney James Grodin determined there was sufficient evidence to issue a warrant for Polanski's arrest.

On Friday evening, March 11, as Roman was crossing the lobby of the Beverly Wilshire Hotel with friends, he was detained by police detectives. They escorted him to his room where (via a warrant) they searched his room, gathering up several rolls of undeveloped film and a vial of Quaaludes. Next, they asked the filmmaker to accompany them to Nicholson's house. Using another warrant, they searched the actor's home where they allegedly found cocaine in Huston's possession and a brick of hashish. (Kept apprised of the developing incident by his attorney, Nicholson remained in Aspen, Colorado. Later, the police took his fingerprints in Aspen. The comparison revealed his prints were not those found on the hashish container, and he was cleared of any potential charges in the case.) Later, Polanski was released on $2,500 bail.

As the caper grabbed worldwide attention, Columbia Pictures quickly distanced itself from Polanski by ending the director's association with *The First Deadly Sin*. Soon, Anjelica bowed to pressure and agreed to testify against Roman in exchange for dropping action against her. A grand jury was convened in downtown Los Angeles, and Polanski was indicted on six counts: (1) furnishing a controlled substance to a minor, (2) committing a lewd and lascivious act on a minor, (3) committing unlawful sexual intercourse with a minor, (4) committing an act of rape by use of drugs, (5) committing an act of perversion, oral copulation with the sexual organ of a child, and (6) committing sodomy.

As this nightmare unfolded—with the media constantly raking up the Tate-Manson tragedy—Polanski maintained his innocence. He insisted that the girl had not opposed the sexual intercourse. (The director refused to understand/accept the American theory of statutory rape, which did not hinge on consent.) From his European point of view and his own wild lifestyle, it was hypocritical to charge him with any crime if the girl—no matter what her age— was a willing participant. Meanwhile, *Vogue Homme* announced that Polanski had no actual contract for the freelance photo assignment, a factor that did not help Roman's defense. The filmmaker felt himself a pariah and fretted about his future.

While Polanski and his lawyers prepared for the trial, Nastassia Kinski and her mother arrived in Hollywood. Roman helped finance Kinski's taking an acting course, all of which was noted by the press. To pay for his mounting legal bills, Roman hastily accepted a directorial assignment from Italian movie producer Dino De Laurentiis for the big-budgeted *Hurricane*. By then global interest in the unsavory Polanski caper had grown so intense that an international contingent of reporters had descended on Los Angeles in preparation for the August 9, 1977, trial, which was the eighth anniversary of Sharon Tate's killing. (At this juncture, even though the girl's identity had been kept secret because she was a minor, an industrious photographer had taken a shot of the girl and her mother, which had appeared in a German magazine.)

A day before the case was to start before Judge Laurence J. Rittenband in Santa Monica Superior Court (known as the "celebrity court"), a case compromise was reached. (The prosecution was worried about having the fast-maturing victim, who had a previous—if slight—sexual and drug history, testify in court, while the girl's divorced parents felt the proceedings could be emotionally-damaging to their offspring.) Polanski objected to the notion, but he was persuaded to plead to unlawful sexual intercourse if the other charges were dropped.

Next, Judge Rittenband adjourned the case until September 19. Meanwhile, Polanski worked on preproduction of *Hurricane*. He also met with his probation officer, Irwin Gold, who produced a sympathetic statement of Roman's case history, pointing out how much the defendant had suffered during World War II and reminding the court of the tragic slaying of the defendant's wife, Tate. The details of Gold's report, which somehow circulated in the film colony and elsewhere, also contained glowing letters of praise from such industry figures as film producer Robert Evans, movie notable Mia Farrow (the costar of *Rosemary's Baby*), and producer De Laurentiis. In Gold's summation, he recommended probation for the defendant.

In mid-September, Rittenband surprised everyone when he announced that he was unimpressed by the probation report and that Polanski must undergo go days of psychiatric evaluation at Chino State Prison, east of Los Angeles, near Ontario. The judge, however, allowed a three-month stay for Roman to complete *Hurricane*.

Ten days later, Judge Rittenband happened to see a photo in a Santa Monica newspaper showing Polanski partying at the Munich, Germany, Oktoberfest with several comely women. The adjudicator was furious that Roman was apparently taking his grave situation so lightly (and not being on location in the tropics to make the film). The judge was further infuriated to learn that the young Miss Kinski was in Munich with the filmmaker.

By October 24, Roman was back before the fuming judge explaining that De Laurentiis had sent him to Germany to help raise financing for *Hurricane*, that Nastassia was chaperoned on the trip by her mother, and that the pivotal newspaper photo had cropped out several men seated at the table with Roman and the attractive women at the beer festival. A still dissatisfied Rittenband reluctantly agreed not to rescind the original 90-day stay. However, he insisted (contrary to what he had suggested weeks before to the defense attorney) that he would grant no further such reprieves.

On December 19, 1977, Polanski entered Chino Prison. Because of his celebrity status he agreed to protective custody, which meant, essentially, isolation. (There was concern that in retaliation for his alleged child "molestation" the filmmaker might be gang raped by vengeful convicts or even killed by an inmate seeking to gain celebrity status.) During his 42-day imprisonment, Roman underwent psychological evaluation, volunteered for cleanup duty, and used his spare time to think about his life. (He later said, "I was out of the public eye. I felt secure and at peace.") While Polanski was incarcerated, De Laurentiis reluctantly turned over *Hurricane* to another director.

On January 29, 1978, Polanski was released from Chino. This should have been nearly the end of the legal proceedings. On the contrary, three days later, Roman received another shock. The judge—who had been under public and peer pressure regarding his supposed leniency in this case—said he intended to remand Roman back to prison to complete his 90-day sentence. (This, despite the defendant's prison evaluation, which purportedly suggested Polanski should receive a noncustodial sentence.) Thereafter, the judge threatened that unless the filmmaker voluntarily agreed to leave the United States, Polanski would face the possibility of additional time behind bars, at which time Roman would face forced deportation. (One version of the events had it that the day before this court pronouncement, Polanski was warned that Rittenband intended he should spend years behind bars.)

Realizing he was in a lose-lose situation, Polanski hastily borrowed $1,000 from De Laurentiis and, that evening, flew to England. (During the full course of his legal plight Roman had never been requested to surrender his passport.) Thereafter, he went on to Paris where, as a French citizen, he would be safer from extradition. Understandably, Roman's attorney could not persuade Polanski to return to California for sentencing. Later, the defense counsel filed a complaint with the Los Angeles Superior Court claiming Rittenband displayed strong prejudice in the case and that his deportation order exceeded his judicial scope. Soon thereafter, Rittenband bowed out of the case. The new judge's position was to not pursue the matter unless Roman should return to California.

Over subsequent years, Polanski made a few features (e.g., 1986's *Pirates* and 1994's *Death and the Maiden*), none of which restored his career luster. Meanwhile, in August 1989, he wed French actress Emmanuelle Seigner (35 years his junior), and they had two children. In 2002, the Paris-based Polanski directed *The Pianist*. When the World War II drama was nominated for seven Academy Awards, it was rumored that the long-exiled filmmaker might finally return to Hollywood.

However, at the 75th Annual Oscars on March 23, 2003, Roman was not in attendance as *The Pianist* won three Academy Awards, including one for Polanski in the Best Director category. A few weeks earlier the minor's graphic testimony in the 1977 statutory rape case had been unsealed and published on the Internet on thesmokinggun.com. Amidst all the renewed hullabaloo, the case's victim, Samantha Geimer (now 39, married, and a mother of three residing in Hawaii), said of 69-year-old Polanski, "I would love to see him resolve it, the sooner, the better. . . . If we could just put this to rest, that would be great." While she had forgiven him and thought that "his film should be honored according to the quality of the work," she claimed, "My God, he knew I was just a child. He behaved like a coward and I'll never forget that."

Following his Oscar victory (for which the absent director received a standing ovation at the Oscar broadcast—showing most of Hollywood had finally forgiven him), Polanski said, "I am deeply touched to have received the Oscar for best director for a film which recounts events which are so close to my personal experience, events which helped me to understand that art can transcend pain." He made no mention of his ongoing legal trouble in California, nor the potential of his ever actually working in Tinseltown again.

Bob Crane: The Lustful Photographer

"Crane's final place in history is Hollywood Babylonia. After he was found bludgeoned to death in an Arizona hotel room in 1978, it came out that the Catholic, several-times-married actor had spent much of his last decade compulsively seducing women he'd met on the dinner theater circuit, while a sleazy accomplice named John Carpenter (not the director of Halloween*) joined in and videotaped the reveries."*

—REPORTER BOB STRAUSS, IN THE *LOS ANGELES DAILY NEWS*,
ON OCTOBER 17, 2002

Typically, when a celebrity dies the obituaries and tributes respectfully reconfirm people's existing image of the deceased while reminding them of the departed's professional achievements and personal milestones. However, when the Hollywood notable expires under gory circumstances—especially as a murder victim—then the sudden death remains headline news for days. Should the homicide go unsolved for years, the unexplained demise often becomes legendary. Sadly, sometimes such gruesome, unresolved deaths eventually come to define these tragic entertainers' places in pop culture history. Such has been the result with director William Desmond Taylor, actress Thelma Todd, screen siren Marilyn Monroe, actor Sal Mineo, rapper/actor Tupac Shakur, and many other such notables.

In the instance of glib actor Bob Crane, there was an added twist to the puzzle. Not until his grizzly June 1978 murder did it come to public light that, for many years, the seemingly wholesome radio disc jockey and TV sitcom performer was actually leading a bizarre double life. Apparently, Crane was a sexually compulsive exhibitionist who had turned into a confirmed 1970s' swinger, devoting much of his energies to rendezvousing with women he met while performing on the dinner theater circuit. This serial philanderer blithely documented these ceaseless sexual escapades through photographs and videotaping.

Another facet of Bob's complex personality was his startling naïveté. This trait led him to proudly show his albums of pornographic pictures and tapes to anyone who might drop by his house or even to his own family. He seemed clueless as to how offensive this strange behavior was, just as he had scant sense of the depths or destructive aspects of his compulsive, joyless womanizing.

Robert Edward Crane was born on July 13, 1928, in Waterbury, Connecticut, the younger son of Alfred and Rosemary Crane, and grew up in a middle-class, Catholic household. Mr. Crane was a furniture and floor-covering salesman. As the father's career progressed, he moved his family to nearby, upscale Stamford. As a child, Bob showed an affinity for drumming, and by age 11 he was performing with his own music group. By age 16, Bob had dropped out of high school and, in 1944, had become a percussionist with the Connecticut Symphony Orchestra. However, the irrepressible clown was dismissed two years later for "cutting up" once too often during a performance. Thereafter, he toured the Northeast with several bands. However, by the late '40s the era of the big swing groups had passed, and he was forced to find other work. He needed a dependable income because in May 1949 he wed Anne Terzian, whom he had been dating since he was 14 and she was 12. For a time the couple lived with her family. He was employed in a jewelry store by day and undertook local band gigs at night. (During the course of their two-decade union the couple had three children: Robert David, Deborah Ann, and Karen Leslie.) In 1950, Bob began a career as disc jockey and radio host at East Coast stations.

Congenial Bob soon developed a solid reputation in his field, renowned for his on-air clowning. In 1956, the brash performer was contracted to join KNX radio in Los Angeles. His celebrity interview show quickly developed a strong audience. Before too long, the

"King of the L.A. Airwaves" was earning a healthy $100,000 annual salary. Always restless for the next gig, Crane fantasized about becoming an actor. To gain experience, he performed in local theaters and began winning TV guest spots and occasional movie roles. For a spell, he substituted for Johnny Carson as host on the daytime TV quiz program *Who Do You Trust?*

After guest roles on such TV fare as *Alfred Hitchcock Presents*, Crane won an appearance on the thriving sitcom *The Dick Van Dyke Show*. Donna Reed saw the handsome, five-foot, ten-inch Crane on that outing and thought he would be right to play Dr. Dave Kelsey on her *The Donna Reed Show*. His role as the amiable next-door neighbor on this domestic comedy was supposed to be a one-shot deal, but it led to his becoming a regular on the show in 1963. (He continued with his daytime radio chores during this period.) With his accelerated income, Bob and his family moved to a home in Tarzana, in the San Fernando Valley.

On the surface, the actor was slick, smug, and remarkably unguarded. However, he was actually extremely sensitive. As such, when he overheard remarks that Reed's husband, the show's producer, was unimpressed by his work on the TV series, Crane was sufficiently hurt to leave the program in 1965.

Crane's work on *The Donna Reed Show* led to his being signed to play the imaginative American colonel in *Hogan's Heroes*, an offbeat TV sitcom that premiered in September 1965. Set in a Nazi prisoner-of-war camp (where humor, not work nor horror, was the order of the day), the entry pitted Bob's cagey officer and brash men against the incompetent Colonel Klink (Werner Klemperer) who ran Stalag 13 with his squad of bumbling German troops. The popular program ran for 168 episodes over six seasons. During the show's tenure, workaholic Bob found time to undertake summer stock, talk show appearances, and movies.

Crane's success in the entertainment business dramatically changed him, increasing his urge for extramarital encounters. Such recurrent problems prompted his wife to divorce him in May 1969 (just before their 20th anniversary) and led to a bitter financial

settlement. In October 1970, a few months after the split was finalized, he wed actress Patricia Annette Olsen on the set of *Hogan's
Heroes*. (Under her professional name of Sigrid Valdis, Olsen had
played Hilda, the shapely young German secretary to Klink on several seasons of *Hogan's Heroes*. Valdis had a daughter from a prior
marriage.) The next year, the Cranes had a son, Robert Scott. After
his series left the air, the star was a guest on many TV programs and
made TV movies. He rejected several sitcom pilots, claiming they
were not the right follow-up to his past success.

In 1974, Crane vetoed a $300,000-a-year job as host of an L.A.
radio program that would require him to work on-air just four
hours each workday. Instead, he chose to do *The Bob Crane Show*, an
uninspired TV comedy that sank in 1975. This career failure left the
40-something celebrity embittered. With his options fast declining,
he played a subordinate role in a sappy Walt Disney picture (1976's
Gus) and was soon reduced to a guest stint on TV's *Love Boat*.
(During this troubling period, word spread in the industry about
the actor's penchant for hanging out at topless bars and making
the rounds of clubs and discos. This tacky activity went so against
Crane's established clean-cut show business image that producers
became leery of hiring him.)

By 1978, Crane and his second wife had separated, and she had
filed for divorce. (Their seven-year-old son, Scotty, lived with her.)
To keep active and financially solvent, Bob headlined lightweight
romantic comedies at dinner theaters throughout the United
States. One of his favorite productions was *Beginner's Luck*, a small-
cast sex farce. In June, facile Bob was starring in that play at the
Windmill Dinner Theater in Scottsdale, Arizona, a Phoenix suburb.
During the run, his estranged spouse and their son, Scotty, made
a surprise visit to Scottsdale. Heated arguments resulted, leading
to their hasty retreat to the state of Washington, where they were
vacationing.

At this point in life, Bob had developed the habit of getting
together on his road treks with John Henry Carpenter, a Los
Angeles–based video equipment salesman/repairman. (The pair

initially became pals when Bob wanted to tape his extracurricular sexual escapades and needed recommendations on what video equipment—then still in its infancy—to purchase.) Typically, on their tawdry nights out on the town, Bob and potbellied hanger-on John visited local bars, met compliant young women, and escorted them back to their rooms for bedroom games enhanced with sex toys and such. Reputedly, at some time prior to or during the actor's tragic stay in Scottsdale, Bob had been reconsidering his clueless, compulsive approach to life. He was sincerely thinking of dealing with (or, at least, cutting back on) his sexual addiction. Part of this resolution was to lessen or stop altogether his associating with his seedy sidekick.

On Wednesday, June 28, 1978, after a rather lackluster performance of *Beginner's Luck*, Crane and his slimy shadow, Carpenter, went, with other stopovers in between, to two different Scottsdale bars. Later, witnesses recalled bits of their conversations and remembered that Bob seemed upset about his recent encounter with Patti. Others sensed there was something amiss between Bob and John. (Purportedly, Crane had already informed his friend that they must go their separate ways.) Nevertheless, the pair had drinks with two women. Later, the quartet had gone on to a coffee shop. Subsequently, Carpenter left the others to pack for his return trip to Los Angeles the next morning. Still later, from his Sunburst Motel room, John phoned Bob.

The next afternoon, shortly after 2:00 P.M., Victoria Berry, a cast member of *Beginner's Luck*, came by the star's digs at the Winfield Apartments. Crane had failed to show up for a luncheon appointment to do promotion for the play. Earlier, she had arranged to come by his place to get a newly dubbed copy of a tape of her stage performance to use in getting future acting gigs. When she arrived at apartment 132A, the door of his two-bedroom, ground-floor residence was unlocked. She went inside. As she moved through the place calling for Bob, no one answered. When she reached the bedroom, she spotted someone under a sheet in a fetal position on the bed. Then she observed the pool of blood on a bed pillow and spattered red spots on both the bed and the wall. At first, the upset visitor was unaware who was on the bed. Later Berry said, "I thought it was a girl in his [Crane's] bed with long hair at first. . . ." Upon closer examination, she saw that the person's left temple had been bashed in. She realized now that the body was that of a male, but because of all the damage to the face she wasn't sure whether the victim was Crane or Carpenter.

The police were summoned and arrived on the scene by 2:20 P.M. It was soon determined that the victim was Bob Crane and that his ghastly murder had been accomplished with an unidentified blunt object, such as a car-jack handle. (The murder scene proved there had been no forced entry, nor had there been a struggle.) The coroner later determined that the actor had been struck twice, with the first blow killing him. An electrical cord, snatched from a video camera in Crane's rooms, had been tied in a bow around the deceased's neck after he was dead. As news quickly spread of the performer's death, Bob's former *Hogan's Heroes* teammates registered their great shock. When Werner Klemperer learned of the killing from a TV newscast, he was stunned. "I almost had a heart attack," he recalled.

While the homicide was being investigated, Crane—days shorts of his 50th birthday—was buried on July 5, 1978, at Oakwood Memorial Park in Chatsworth, California. The funeral mass had been held at St. Paul the Apostle Catholic Church in Westwood. More than 200 mourners attended the service, including his first wife and their three offspring, his widow and son, as well as Crane's mother and brother. Among the others there were John Carpenter and Victoria Berry.

Thanks to the high-profile coverage of the killing (especially from the tabloids) and the ongoing police investigation, Bob's dual existence (his extensive number of female sex partners and his massive collection of pornographic photos, tapes, and paraphernalia) quickly became public. Because of the victim's kinky penchants and salacious routines, law enforcers surmised there might well be many potential suspects, including angry boyfriends/husbands of his bedmates, or past female partners who were either jealous or infuriated when they suddenly learned of the secret videotaping of bedroom activity. While several on the case considered John Carpenter a key suspect at one time or another, no formal charges were filed at the time due to insufficient evidence.

Because of the ongoing popularity of *Hogan's Heroes* in constant reruns—and due to the unsolved homicide—Bob Crane's name remained in the news for years to come. In May 1992, after a change-over in prosecutors at the Scottsdale, Arizona, office, the Crane case (number 78-1243) was reopened. This time John Carpenter was named a defendant and arrested the next month. However, because of charges (sexual misconduct with a minor) pending against Carpenter in southern California, it was not until September 1994 that courtroom proceedings in the Crane investigation got under way. Despite the new prosecutor's best efforts (including the use of innovative DNA tests), the evidence from the crime scene and elsewhere had been too compromised over the years. Thus, the case was far stronger on theory than on concrete evidence. Eventually, Carpenter was acquitted of the charges. (Right up to his death in September 1998, John insisted he was innocent.)

Interest in the unresolved Crane killing was heightened with the 2002 release of *Auto Focus*, a feature film directed by Paul Schrader and based on the 1993 book *The Murder of Bob Crane* by Robert Graysmith. Greg Kinnear played sardonic, bewildered, banal Crane, with Willem Dafoe as the sleazy John Carpenter. Made on a $7 million budget, the picture (promoted with the tagline: "A day without sex is a day wasted") earned mixed reviews and failed to find its audience, grossing only $2 million in domestic distribution.

While the big-screen retelling of the murder was found wanting, its production added new facets to the dossier on the intriguing life and wild times of the complicated subject and his extended family. Journalist Robert David, 51, one of Bob's three children from his first marriage, was signed at $20,000 to be a technical adviser for the film. Said the offspring, "What got me interested [in the picture] were the names involved. I knew this wasn't going to be a titillating piece of garbage." (He also had a cameo in the film as an interviewer—employed by a Christian publication—who questions the TV notable on elements of a good marriage.) Scotty, the 31-year-old son of Crane's second marriage, was then a Seattle radio host and also ran a recording studio. Earlier, in 1997, he, along with Patti and another partner, wrote a film script (*Take Off Your Clothes and Smile*) about Bob, but it failed to sell—especially due to the *Auto Focus* project. Understandably he was upset, leading to contention between the opposing sides of the family and the two rival film projects. In spring 2001, he began a website as a tribute to his father. A portion of the unusual site was devoted to XXX-rated photos and videos taken by Crane.

Adding more fuel to the Crane clan dissension and the lore of Bob Crane, his second wife, Patti (who was left his $1.5 to $2 million estate, including his porno collection), in recent years exhumed her husband's body and had it reinterred in an unmarked grave at another cemetery. She never informed the first family of this activity. After much investigation, it was learned that Crane's remains were buried (without a headstone) at Westwood (Village) Memorial Park, the famous Los Angeles cemetery where Marilyn Monroe, Natalie Wood, and other notables had been laid to rest. It was also learned that Patti Crane had purchased the grave site next to Bob's.

Such recent events continue to revive the public's interest in the dishonorable and shocking behavior of the once-popular star whose bizarre murder ended his tawdry hidden life.

4

1980–PRESENT

If anything marked the "new" Hollywood of the 1980s and 1990s, it was the many effects of the technological revolution. Home entertainment had provided a lucrative fresh distribution outlet for movie and TV producers to earn additional revenue on their product. Soon, the DVD player format outranked the use of VCRs. It allowed small-time producers to become influential industry forces, dealing another death blow to the old fiefdom of the studio system.

On a different technology front, the increasingly sophisticated Internet created a remarkable forum for disseminating news and gossip about, among others, show business personalities. Now, when an O. J. Simpson, a Winona Ryder, or a Robert Blake stumbled into a tough legal jam, before their handlers could do damage control, news of the event spread rapidly on the Internet. This often prompted dedicated sites to spring up and monitor such delicate situations. The sites provided the curious with a wealth of unfiltered multimedia information. Unlike the old days, no longer could a celebrity's representatives or a studio put its own spin on an event and bury the situation before it caused career damage.

Natalie Wood: Tragic Goddess

"I'm sure that I will never be able to stop the rumors about Natalie's death. The people who are convinced that there was something more to it than what came out in the investigation will never be satisfied with the truth. Because the truth is, there is nothing more to it. It was an accident."

—ACTOR CHRISTOPHER WALKEN, IN 1984

When a motion picture star dies suddenly in the prime of life, there is always tremendous regret at a famous life's being cut short. Should there be unusual circumstances surrounding the passing, the death often takes on added subtext, with rumors and myths springing up about the screen idol's demise. Such was the case with both James Dean, who died in a 1955 car crash, and Sal Mineo, who was murdered in 1976. Dean and Mineo had costarred in the trend-setting *Rebel Without a Cause* (1955). The leading lady of that landmark youth rebellion feature was Natalie Wood.

Scarcely more than five feet tall, Wood was a giant of churning emotions, bursting with subconscious resentment about her twisted life in which, as a small child, she had been molded into the disciplined breadwinner of her Russian immigrant family. Filled with insecurities about her beauty (which was, in actuality, great), her talent (sizable), and her identity as a person (she masked her "real" self behind the public Natalie Wood image, which she referred to as "the Badge"), the star lurched through life seeking steadying influences. This led to impetuous love affairs (a few sources suggest these may have included lesbian trysts), alcohol and pill dependencies, and destructive emotional shutdowns that often put her screen career on hold.

Wood's chaotic sense of self and overwhelming neediness created an intriguing screen personality. Often in her movie work her vulnerability surfaced in the edgy tone of her voice and the wounded look in her expressive eyes. Her defenselessness registered strongly with moviegoers, many of whom wanted to protect this lovely talent from whatever forces were closing in on her. With such a special rapport with fans, little wonder that her 1981 death by drowning so shocked her caring public.

Since the tragedy, much has been written about Natalie's superstitious mother long having premonitions of Wood's being swept away in deep waters and how her parent's overwhelming fear translated into the star's dreading the water. This state of affairs turned Wood's demise into a sad irony. As with the still unexplained finale of another sex goddess, Marilyn Monroe, Natalie's death led many people to fantasize what they—or anyone—might/should have done to alter Wood's nightmarish end. Adding to the ambiguities surrounding Natalie's death are the conflicting, brief statements from those few individuals who were aboard the yacht cruise that ended with her drowning. The events of Natalie's last days leave us pondering wistfully, "If only . . ."

She was born Natalia Nikolaevna Zakharenko on July 20, 1938, in San Francisco. Several months earlier, her mother, Maria, originally from Siberia, had left her Russian immigrant husband by whom she already had a daughter, Olga, age nine. Maria was now married to Natalia's father, Nikolai (Nick) Zakharenko, a janitor at Standard Oil Company. Maria had great hopes for her newborn and lavished all her love on the child. The volatile Maria was also very superstitious. Once, back in her homeland, a fortune-teller had instructed her to be wary of "dark waters," and she reasoned that this dire warning carried over to her new child. As such, the mother constantly cautioned Natasha (as Natalia was nicknamed) to beware of treacherous "dark waters."

By the time Natasha was four, the family had relocated to Santa Rosa, California. (By then, the family had adopted the father's new surname of Gurdin, which he used when he became a U.S. citizen.) Because Maria was an avid moviegoer, she felt that the picture business might hold the key to Natasha's future success. She became convinced of this when a movie company arrived in Santa Rosa to film location footage for *Happy Land* (1943). Maria made sure that her endearing tyke came to the attention of the picture's director, Irving Pichel. As a result, Natasha won a silent cameo—dropping an ice cream cone—in this Americana drama.

Building on the opportunity, pushy Maria remained in touch with Pichel. The assertive lady had already relocated the family to L.A. by the time the director began preproduction on *Tomorrow Is Forever* (1946). With fierce determination Maria engineered an audition for her gifted child. This time the youngster won a key role—playing a war-traumatized orphan. In the process, Natasha gained a new screen name: Natalie Wood.

With such success, Maria became the ultimate stage mother, one who constantly seized on every acting opportunity for little Natalie. (All this activity was accomplished at the expense of her pliant husband; her "understanding" firstborn, Olga; and Svetlana [Lana], her third and last child.) A career break for Natalie was the pivotal role of Maureen O'Hara's daughter in the classic family fare *Miracle on 34th Street* (1947).

Natalie would say later, "In so many ways I think it's a bore to be sorry you were a child actor—so many people feel sorry for you automatically. At the time I wasn't aware of the things I missed so why should I think of them in retrospect? Everybody misses something or other." In contrast, she told fan publications, "I worked steadily, had a ball, and can't even remember being miserable." In private, she would reflect on her childhood years (when she sometimes earned $1,000 a week and supported her entire household): "I spent practically all of my time in the company of adults. I was very withdrawn, very shy, I did what I was told and I tried not to disappoint anybody."

In RKO's *The Green Promise* (1949), the script required Natalia to cross over a bridge during a nighttime storm. Terrified of undertaking the stunt because of all the phobias built into her by her mother, Wood had to be pressured into doing the sequence. As she walked over the soundstage bridge, a technician accidentally pulled the switch too soon (for the scripted collapse of the bridge), and the structure crashed with Natalie thrown into the "dark waters." The director insisted on completing the scene before the petrified youngster was rescued from the deep. Not only had the traumatized youngster nearly drowned but, in the process, she broke her left wrist.

The Green Promise misadventure left young Natalie with recurring nightmares and a strong distrust of adults who might lie to her (as happened on the set when she was told that this stunt was "safe"). An even more jarring situation occurred while making *The Star* (1952), in which Wood was cast as Bette Davis's offspring. At the last minute, the revised plotline required her to dive into deep water from a sailboat and then swim to a far-off raft. Traumatized at the thought of undertaking such a feat, she panicked when the director forced her to jump into the cold ocean. Davis overheard the girl's hysterics and came rushing out of her dressing room. She ordered the filmmaker to use a double for the scene, which he did. (Ironically, the troublesome sequence was cut from the release print.)

By the early '50s, Wood was an awkward adolescent. No longer winning movie roles so frequently, her education switched from on-set tutors to public classrooms. At Van Nuys High School, she developed new friendships and started dating. As Natalie became more independent, her mother attempted to control her once-compliant child, making her break off a relationship with an older student.

Being cast in *Rebel Without a Cause* (1955) did wonders for Wood's career. She not only won an Academy Award nomination but demonstrated that she had great audience appeal as a shapely young adult. During production she had a whirlwind affair with her director, Nicholas Ray, who was twice her age.

Natalie was under contract to Warner Bros., and the studio promoted a relationship between her and actor Tab Hunter, but their dating was a sham to publicize their joint movies. On the other hand, she was emotionally drawn to bulky Raymond Burr, her colead in *A Cry in the Night* (1956). He was in his late thirties, bisexual, moody, and sensitive. She responded to his intellectual, worldly side, but the studio pushed hard to end that strange relationship.

As Wood reached her late teens, she raced about Tinseltown in her pink Ford Thunderbird, drank, smoked, and gravitated to the likes of Elvis Presley and Frank Sinatra, as well as to such younger actors as Scott Marlowe and Robert Vaughn. Much of her rebellion was in defiance of her strict mother.

Back in the spring of 1950, when gawky, pigtailed Natalie was on the Twentieth Century-Fox lot filming *The Jackpot*, she had noticed 20-year-old Robert Wagner, then working on a World War II movie. She told herself that one day she would like to marry this handsome man. Years later, on her 18th birthday, she joined Wagner for a screening of his new movie *The Mountain* (1956). He had been seeing actress Debbie Reynolds, and she had been dating playboys Nicky Hilton and Lance Reventhow. By the end of that year, Wood and Wagner's romance had progressed to their spending a night of intimacy aboard his boat *My Lady*. (Natalie had not outgrown her fear of dark waters, but she rationalized that being aboard a vessel was different from being in the water itself.)

Natalie and R.J. (as he was known to friends) wed on December 28, 1957. Wagner convinced her to honeymoon on a chartered cruise boat in Florida. However, a violent storm ruined their planned expedition, and they spent their marriage celebration in New York where they were subjected to a media blitz. Returning to the West Coast, they hid out on his latest boat, *My Other Lady*, which they anchored off of Catalina Island.

Distracted by marriage, Wood's career seemed frozen in such disappointing vehicles as *Marjorie Morningstar* (1958) and *All the Fine Young Cannibals* (1960—which teamed her with Wagner). By then Natalie was relying on psychiatric counseling to keep her life on course. Fortunately, her professional status took a giant leap forward with *Splendor in the Grass* (1961), for which she was Oscar-nominated. Much in demand, she snared leads in two major screen musicals: *West Side Story* (1961) and *Gypsy* (1962).

Earning $250,000 a picture—a tidy sum in the early '60s—young, gorgeous, successful Natalie seemed to have everything. The reality was far from the truth. In June 1961, the Wagners had a traumatic confrontation—reputedly over his sexual habits. A hysterical Wood rushed to her parents' Van Nuys home in the East San Fernando Valley. That night she swallowed an overdose of sleeping pills and had to have her stomach pumped. She lost 10 pounds from her petite frame and, on April 17, 1962, filed for divorce from Wagner, charging cruelty.

While making *Splendor in the Grass*, Natalie had not been impressed with her moody costar, screen newcomer, Warren Beatty. Besides, she was married and he was already involved with actress Joan Collins. Things changed by July 1961, as she was separated from Wagner. (He would soon embark for Europe to resurrect his faltering movie career.) By August, Wood and Beatty were a steady item, despite the fact that she was legally still married. Reacting to the end of her dream marriage, she grew increasingly reckless (by the moral standards of the time). When Warren went to Florida to work on *All Fall Down* (1962), she followed him.

In subsequent months, Natalie and Warren happened to be in Italy at the same time that Robert Wagner was there. By then, Wagner was dating actress Marion Marshall. The quartet had drinks together in Rome, with both Wood and Wagner realizing that they still felt a strong attraction for one another. Later that fateful night, R.J. impulsively tried to call his ex-wife's hotel room to suggest they discuss their future. However, the line was constantly busy because Beatty was engaged in one of his marathon business conversations. Deciding that it was not meant to be, Wagner pursued his relationship with Marshall, and they wed in July 1963.

When Wood costarred with Steve McQueen in *Love with the Proper Stranger* (1963—earning her third and final Oscar nomination), her seesawing affair with Beatty had run its course and he had moved on to actress Leslie Caron. Grieving over the difficult breakup, Natalie utilized her emotional pain to enhance her role as the working girl in love with a self-focused musician. Then she began seeing urbane Arthur Loew Jr., a wealthy industry figure. They announced plans to wed, but Wood called it off. A few days later she encountered R.J. at a Beverly Hills restaurant where he was passing out cigars to celebrate the birth of his and Marion's baby girl. The news crushed the emotionally fragile Natalie.

Wood was in no condition to make the costume comedy *The Great Race* (1965) with Tony Curtis and Jack Lemmon. She disliked the project from the start. That November she took another overdose of sleeping pills and had to be hospitalized, the facts being hushed up from the public. In late January 1966, Wood again overdosed on sleeping pills. After recovering, she began dating, among others, Michael Caine, Frank Sinatra, and independent filmmaker Henry Jaglom.

A floundering Natalie accepted the lead in an unpromising romantic comedy, *Penelope* (1966), because it paid a whopping $750,000 fee. Having completed that lackluster entry, she fell into a funk. Warren Beatty popped back into her life hoping to convince her to star opposite him in *Bonnie and Clyde* (1967). However, she was at too low an ebb to accept. Shortly thereafter, she made yet another suicide attempt.

Seeking to find her lost self, Natalie remained off screen for three years. In May 1969, she wed British producer/agent Richard Gregson, and their daughter, Natasha, was born in September 1970. Meanwhile, she enjoyed a career comeback with *Bob & Carol & Ted & Alice* (1969). In August 1971, she and Gregson (whom she caught having an affair) divorced. Around this time, Wagner and Marshall split, and before long Natalie and R.J. were together again. They married for the second time on July 16, 1972, aboard the yacht *Rambling Rose* off the southern California coast. Their daughter, Courtney Brooke, was born in March 1974. Stabilized by her restructured home life, Natalie returned to acting, including two TV movies with R.J.: *The Affair* (1973) and *Cat on a Hot Tin Roof* (1976).

By 1980, Natalie's movie reign had ended. Meanwhile, R.J. was enjoying a career rebirth with his hit TV series *Hart to Hart* (1979–1984). With too much time on her hands, Wood became increasingly jealous of R.J.'s series costar, Stefanie Power (then ending a relationship with veteran film superstar William Holden). Anxious to keep busy, Wood accepted the title role in a forthcoming Los Angeles stage production of *Anastasia*. In the meantime, she took a leading (but thankless) part in MGM's *Brainstorm*, a mad scientist entry that showcased intricate special effects. During six weeks of location shooting in North Carolina, there was gossip that she and married costar Christopher Walken had become chummy (some sources judged it a flirtation; others suggested a more substantial relationship).

The *Brainstorm* cast returned to Los Angeles at the start of November 1981. On Friday, November 27, the day after Thanksgiving, Natalie and R.J., along with Walken (whose wife was back East) went aboard the Wagners' 55-foot cabin cruiser, *The Splendour*. The yacht had a one-man crew (Dennis Davern). They headed to Santa Catalina Island. That evening, Natalie and R.J. reportedly argued over weekend plans. In a huff, she went ashore to Avalon, accompanied by Davern, and stayed overnight at a local hotel. Changing her mind about cutting short the holiday, she and the bearded skipper returned to *The Splendour* on Saturday morning. As the day progressed Wood's mood toward Wagner shifted back and forth. Meanwhile, R.J. ordered their vessel to Isthmus Cove near the town of Two Harbors, around the other side of Catalina. Later in the gloomy day, Walken and Wood went ashore in the dinghy while Wagner was napping. When he awoke, R.J. and Davern took a shore boat to Two Harbors, where they found Natalie and Christopher having drinks at Doug's Harbor Reef Restaurant. Purportedly, Wagner was upset at seeing his wife and Walken being so friendly. Later that evening, after many rounds of drinks, they all returned to *The Splendour*.

Because of seemingly conflicting statements by Wagner and Walken—both of whom would provide only brief remarks to authorities and the press—and Davern (he being the most talkative over the years, giving interviews to publications and TV documentaries), what actually transpired on *The Splendour* that late Saturday night/early Sunday morning of November 28/29 may never be fully revealed. What is known is that for some reason Wood got into the dinghy and disappeared in the dark at a time when the waters were choppy. At 1:30 A.M. on Sunday, an undetermined time after R.J. discovered that Natalie was not aboard *The Splendour*, he used his marine radio to call for help.

The harbor patrol began its search, later joined by the Coast Guard and helicopters. At approximately 7:44 A.M., her body was discovered off Blue Cavern Point. Wearing a red down jacket over her nightgown, she was "hanging, actually, almost in a standing position, with her face down and her eyes open."

On December 2, 1981, the 43-year-old actress was buried at Westwood Memorial Park in L.A. When *Brainstorm* was released in

1983, it was a critical and financial dud. In 1990, Wagner married actress Jill St. John at his ranch in the Santa Monica Mountains not far from L.A.

Speaking about Wood in the late '80s, Wagner said, "When Natalie died, I was embittered. I still get angry about it and I wonder why it had to happen. I have all those feelings of grief and anger that people who've lost someone they love always have. I have lived a charmed life, and then I lost a beautiful woman I loved with all my heart."

Rock Hudson: The Reluctant Good Samaritan

"I am not happy that I have AIDS. But if that is helping others, I can, at least, know that my own misfortune has had some positive worth."
—ROCK HUDSON, IN 1985

Despite decades of medical research, acquired immune deficiency syndrome (AIDS) still remains a devastating plague around the world—affecting victims from all walks of life. Back in the early 1980s, however, AIDS was a disease associated with homosexual activity. Many misguided individuals thought it was God's rightful revenge on those living a socially unacceptable alternative lifestyle.

Given this particular mind-set, it was doubly shocking when veteran columnist Army Archerd wrote on July 23, 1985, in *Daily Variety:* "The whispering campaign of Rock Hudson can—and should—stop. He was flown to Paris for further help. . . . His illness was no secret to close Hollywood friends, but its true nature was divulged to very, very few." Not only was Archerd informing readers about Hudson's then-fatal disease, but he was acknowledging, by implication, that the longtime screen hero was gay.

Within days, Hudson's life-threatening ailment was confirmed to the world in a press release issued in France where the dying man was consulting physicians at the Institute Pasteur. Less than three months later, 59-year-old Hudson, once known as the "Beefcake Baron," was dead.

Actress Morgan Fairchild said at the time: "Rock Hudson's death gave AIDS a face." However, his untimely passing also accomplished something else. It did what decades of Hudson's secret life had avoided: it brought Hudson's homosexuality out of the closet at a time when few celebrities dared to make such a lifestyle revelation. This sudden outing confounded the star's less sophisticated fans who believed that all gays were flamboyant, effeminate, and prissy. For them, it just did not compute that virile, handsome Rock was one of "them." Other fans felt betrayed that this once hunky six-foot, four-inch movie idol had been deceiving his public with a camouflaged personal life.

He was born Roy Harold Scherer Jr. on November 17, 1925, in Winnetka, Illinois. When he was four, his auto mechanic father lost his job and moved to California to find work. The separation from his family led to a divorce. In 1931, Roy's mother, Kay, wed an ex-marine, Wallace Fitzgerald. The latter adopted the boy but always resented him. Moreover, the burly man was abusive to his new family. The troubled marriage ended in the mid-1930s. With the lack of a real father figure, the shy youth and his mother maintained a close bond. Later, while attending New Trier High School, Roy was not a dedicated student. When not busy with part-time jobs, he hung out at the movies and dreamed of becoming a film star.

Seven months after school graduation, Roy was drafted into the navy in World War II. He was stationed in the Philippines. Reportedly, during these years he had his first homosexual experiences. He was discharged from the service in February 1946.

After visiting his mother in Illinois, Roy moved to L.A. where he was reunited with his father, who owned an appliance shop. The ex-navy man hoped to use his G.I. Bill of Rights to study acting at the University of Southern California. Unfortunately, Roy's unremarkable academic record prevented his admission. He took a job driving a truck and began sending photos of himself to studio casting offices.

In September 1947, his photo submission led to a meeting with Henry Willson, then working for film producer David O. Selznick but soon to open his own talent agency. The 36-year-old, pudgy Willson, who made no bones about being gay, took a shine to the young man. The latter became part of Willson's stable of young would-be actors, whose chief credentials were their good looks and catchy professional names. Willson's latest protégé became Rock Hudson. Henry had Rock make studio casting rounds when not taking acting classes. This led to a small role in *Fighter Squadron* (1948).

In 1949, Universal Pictures put Rock under contract at $125 a week. Hudson was thrust into one picture after another, learning on the job. Because the film lot tightly controlled the public's perceptions of its players, Rock was paired with various starlets as his public "dates." However, it was no secret to studio executives that their hunky young talent was gay. The situation was acceptable to Universal only as long as Rock played the heterosexual romantic "game" in public.

In private, Hudson led a quiet social life. His nucleus of friends included Universal contract player George Nader; the latter's lover Mark Miller, who later became Hudson's private assistant; and such others as actress Marilyn Maxwell. Since moving to California, Rock had had several same-sex affairs, but due to his reserve and devotion to his career, the relationships always soured.

Hudson's career break was costarring with Jane Wyman in *Magnificent Obsession* (1954). This successful romantic drama brought Rock public adulation and a salary raise. He purchased his first home in L.A. On the downside, his rising box-office power led to far greater scrutiny of his private life from the fan magazines. They constantly wondered in print (although many of the writers actually knew) why the beefcake stud was still a bachelor in his late twenties.

Rock's industry standing jumped still higher when he was contracted to costar with Elizabeth Taylor and James Dean in *Giant* (1956). It became even more important to hush growing Tinseltown rumors about Hudson's lifestyle, as he could be outed by a publication such as *Confidential* magazine. In the morally conservative '50s, his career could not survive such a bombshell revelation. (At one point, legend has it, to spare Hudson's being outed by *Confidential*, Henry Willson sacrificed another actor client, Rory Calhoun. The agent "allowed" that scandal rag to do an exposé on Calhoun's juvenile delinquency record.)

Meanwhile, Willson took other steps to shield Hudson, the agency's most valuable client. These became clear when, in September 1955, gossip columnist Sheilah Graham reported that "the new 'King' [of Hollywood] has found his queen in the person of pretty and intelligent, brunette Phyllis Gates." This was movie talk that Rock was planning to wed. His bride-to-be, a former flight attendant, just happened to be Henry Willson's secretary. It has never been clear how much Phyllis was aware of, and/or participated in, this contrived romance. In her 1987 autobiography Gates depicted the "romance" as one of fate bringing two parties together in true heterosexual love. Whatever the case, as Rock's "love," Phyllis joined her beau in Texas for some of the location filming of *Giant*. Later, on November 9, 1955, the couple eloped (a scheme orchestrated by Willson to make the event more enticing to the well-alerted media) to Santa Barbara and then honeymooned in Bermuda and New York. The happy bride moved into the groom's home. Close friends of the actor's would later suggest that Hudson, despite his pervading gay lifestyle, initially had strong romantic feelings for Phyllis but that the confinement and responsibilities of marriage quickly ruined the passion.

In 1957, the year that Hudson was Oscar-nominated for *Giant*, Rock costarred with Jennifer Jones in the Italian-shot *A Farewell to Arms*. Upset at the routine of his concocted marriage, Rock became increasingly moody. In August 1958, he and Phyllis divorced. Thereafter, Hudson's gay affairs escalated, but he had the cover of being a recently married man. His screen career reignited when he teamed with Doris Day for *Pillow Talk* (1959). Having established his own production company, Hudson was enjoying great financial success, and he bought a $180,000 estate ("the Castle") high up in

Beverly Hills. In the 1960s Hudson severed his working relationship with Henry Willson, moving on to more aggressive representation. A turning point in Rock's career was starring in *Seconds* (1966), but the heavy drama failed with filmgoers. His lengthy tenure with Universal Pictures ended the next year.

Over the years, Hudson's typical real-life romantic partner was young, blond, muscular, and mustached. He changed form in 1970 when he became involved with Hollywood film publicist Tom Clark (three years Rock's junior), who became central to the star's business and social life. With his movie career sputtering, Hudson starred in a long-running (1971–1977) TV police drama, *McMillan and Wife*.

In 1982, Rock, long a heavy smoker, underwent quintuple-bypass heart surgery. It delayed the filming of his latest TV series, *The Devlin Connection*, which lasted only four months. It was also that year that 57-year-old Hudson met 29-year-old Marc Christian. The bisexual Marc became Rock's new lover and eventually moved into the star's home. This was shortly after Hudson and his longtime friend Tom Clark had had a rift and the latter moved out of the Castle.

At this juncture, Hudson considered taking over a lead role in the Broadway musical *La Cage aux Folles*, which would have given him his first gay acting part. He was also thinking of making the TV miniseries *The Vegas Strip War* and doing an extended guest role on the nighttime TV soap opera *Dynasty*.

Despite the diversion of his relationship with Christian and several new career options, Hudson had been feeling poorly since his return from filming abroad. He had also been noticeably losing weight. He attributed the general malaise to the poor quality of food available on his recent shoot. However, in April 1984 he discovered a small growth on the back of his neck. The next month his doctor took assorted tests. On June 8, 1984, Rock learned that he had contracted the AIDS virus and was suffering from Kaposi's sarcoma, a skin cancer. Shocked by the dreaded news—at the time a death sentence—the star supposedly told only his physician, his personal assistant (Mark Miller), and his business manager (Wallace Sheft) of the damning diagnosis.

In his later lawsuit against Hudson's estate, Marc Christian would claim that he was not told then, or in subsequent months, about Hudson's infectious medical condition and that the couple continued to engage in sex. (In 1986's *Idol: Rock Hudson: The True Story of an American Film Hero* by Jerry Oppenheimer and Jack Vitek, the authors report that an unnamed actor pal of Hudson, in the spirit of helping his beleaguered friend during this difficult time, matched Rock with several sex partners, unthinking—like Hudson—of the fatal consequences it might have on the young men.)

Having spent a lifetime concealing his alternative lifestyle, Hudson was expert in lying to the public and to acquaintances. Now, as an AIDS victim, he disguised his deadly ailment in his dealings with the world. (Some suggest that part of his deception was the result of self-denial about his plight.) As the weeks progressed the celebrity's health further deteriorated. He dropped plans for his Broadway bow but struggled through the making of *The Vegas Strip War* (1984). Twice during the shoot he returned to L.A., casually mentioning to the production staff that he had doctors' appointments. Strange as it seems today, no one not in Hudson's confidence had yet perceived or acknowledged that Hudson's declining health and rapidly disintegrating looks coupled with his homosexuality might mean AIDS.

In August 1984 Hudson signed to make 10 appearances on *Dynasty*, at $100,000 per episode. Meanwhile, he had flown to Paris to seek AIDS treatment at the Institute Pasteur. He pretended that he was taking a vacation and attending a film festival. During his stay in the French capital he received dosages of the HPA-23 antiviral drug. He was encouraged by the French physicians to take a six-month course of treatment, but he insisted he must return to the United States after only six weeks because of his *Dynasty* chores.

Hudson was back in L.A. by October for work on *Dynasty*. By then his relationship with Marc Christian was becoming more tense, a major bone of contention being that they shared so little in common. Rock barely had the energy to make it through his *Dynasty* tasks. His series coworkers were aghast at his debilitated look but attributed it to the aftereffects of his bypass surgery or an eating problem. One small-screen scene with coplayer Linda Evans called for the couple to passionately kiss. When it was learned later that Hudson was suffering from AIDS at the time the sequence was shot, there was an uproar within the film industry—and the public as well—about Rock's dishonorable selfishness in exposing Evans to the deadly AIDS virus. (It was theorized at the time that AIDS could be transmitted by merely touching, let alone from intimate kissing.)

By early 1985, Hollywood's gossipers insisted that Hudson had AIDS. However, the star continued to deny the rumors, including, allegedly, to Marc Christian. In summer 1985, Doris Day was preparing a new cable TV series (*Doris Day's Best Friends*). Unaware of his fatal ailment, she invited Rock to guest on the show's debut episode. Not wishing to disappoint her, he flew to Carmel, California, for the taping. In retrospect, it seemed foolhardy to have accepted the request not only because of his greatly weakened condition but because of his fast-deteriorating physical appearance. At the press conference, the media was shocked by his gaunt look, his disoriented conversation, and his weakened physical condition. (Grim photos of the conference were published around the world.) As he and Day taped their segment, Doris knew her good friend was seriously ill. However, she has always stated she had no idea at the time of his true situation.

A few days thereafter, a much-weakened Hudson went to Paris, telling most of his circle that he was headed to Switzerland to undertake a cure for anorexia (which was his new cover for his AIDS condition). Because Rock had so hotly denied to Marc on several occasions that he had AIDS, Christian would insist later that at this point he still was unaware of his companion's perilous situation. Once in Paris, the AIDS doctors quickly concluded that Rock's disease had progressed too far for any meaningful treatment. Because news had already leaked out about the star's condition, Hudson's camp chose to make its own announcement of his physical status. While the world grieved at the news, Christian later detailed that he was furious at having been so thoughtlessly betrayed by Rock and exposed to the AIDS virus.

Hudson flew back to the United States on a chartered jet and was hospitalized at UCLA. When friends visited, they told Hudson he was now considered a "hero" for having brought the topic of AIDS to the forefront. The star, always such a private person, was puzzled by his newfound public status. Once Rock was transferred back to the Castle to die, Tom Clark returned to care for his long-time friend. In the changing of the guard, Marc was forced to reside in an auxiliary building on the estate. Christian would say later that when he was allowed to converse with Hudson in this period, the latter never apologized for potentially exposing him to AIDS.

By the time of the AIDS benefit in Los Angeles on September 19, 1985—spearheaded by Elizabeth Taylor—Rock's health had deteriorated so much that he could not have composed, had he wanted to, the message delivered on his behalf during the star-studded event. At the fund-raiser, actor Burt Lancaster read the message (composed by Hudson's inner sanctum) in which Rock acknowledged that his "situation" had "brought enormous international attention to the gravity of this disease . . . and is leading to more research, more contribution of funds, and a better understanding of this disease than ever before."

After Hudson's death on October 2, 1985, Marc Christian filed suit against Rock's estate asking $14 million in damages. In 1989, a jury decided that Hudson had partaken in "outrageous conduct" by continuing his sexual relationship with the unsuspecting plaintiff. The $21.75 million verdict in favor of Christian was later reduced to $5.5 million. Thereafter the star's estate appealed, and in 1991 a sealed settlement was reached in the matter.

A few years ago, when the British *Empire* magazine listed the 100 Sexiest Stars in Films, Rock ranked 28th. It seemed that even after Hudson's grueling AIDS death and the highly touted revelations about his hidden homosexuality, the public still preferred to think of Hudson as the screen's manly man.

Saturday Night Live: The Curse

"There have been cast members who drank too much, snorted coke too much, freebased too much. God-knows-what-else'd too much. . . . One brilliant but insecure member of a recent cast slashed himself with razor blades during bouts of severe depression. Talent may itself be a form of neurosis; it usually comes with troubles attached."

—TOM SHALES AND JAMES ANDREW MILLER
IN *LIVE FROM NEW YORK*, 2002

Starting in fall 1975, TV's *Saturday Night* presented a showcase (initially airing every other week) of outrageous humor. The outing—aired live to give it a greater sense of immediacy and spontaneity—mocked popular culture and the worlds of politics and sports. With its seven comedic regulars guided by creator/producer Lorne Michaels, the 90-minute network program, broadcast from NBC's Studio 8H at Manhattan's Rockefeller Center, quickly became a viewing institution and soon changed its title to *Saturday Night Live*. Its initial troupe, The Not Ready for Prime Time Players (Dan Aykroyd, John Belushi, Chevy Chase, Jane Curtin, Garrett Morris, Laraine Newman, and Gilda Radner), set the standards for the unorthodox series' madcap tone. Subsequent cast replacements often sought to outmatch their predecessors—both the creative forces (writing and performing) and, in some cases, the wild, self-destructive lifestyles of some of the original performers.

Accounts of *SNL* alumni constantly refer to the enormous strain the players endured in turning out topical, fun entertainment on a weekly basis. Such chronicles also include how sudden fame gained from the hit show radically affected the comics' professional and personal life. With such a large troupe of laugh makers showcased on the series since its inception, little wonder—per the law of averages—that several of these talents later suffered shocking and/or tragic, life reverses. This recurring situation became known as the curse of *Saturday Night Live.*

Chevy Chase was the first breakout star from *SNL*'s original players. He was born Cornelius Crane Chase on October 8, 1943, in Woodstock, New York, the son of a book writer/editor and his concert pianist wife. His parents divorced when he was four, with his father's new spouse an heir to the Folger coffee fortune.

Despite a privileged background, Chase alluded that his early years were difficult. In reaction to his upbringing, he got into minor scrapes and became clownish (in subtle ways). He was valedictorian of his high school class and an English major at Bard College. Always intrigued with the world of comedy, he gravitated toward show business. He wrote spoofs for *Mad* magazine and was a mime on PBS-TV's *The Great American Dream Machine* (1971). Later, as actor and writer, he contributed to the off-Broadway show *National Lampoon's Lemmings* (1973), followed by the *National Lampoon Radio Hour.* In 1974, he was in the X-rated feature *Groove Tube*, a satire about television, and wrote for the small screen's *The Smothers Brothers Comedy Hour.*

In 1975, while standing in line to see a Monty Python movie at a Los Angeles theater, Chase chatted with Lorne Michaels. The latter was taken by Chevy's sense of humor and auditioned him to come aboard the soon-to-premiere *Saturday Night* show. Originally, Chase was to be head writer, but he convinced Michaels to let him also appear on camera. In short order, the good-looking, smug-acting, five-foot, eleven-inch personality became the hit of the show, especially with his featured segment, "Weekend Update," a satire of TV news. Having the show's only regular solo spot set him markedly apart from others of the troupe. This did not sit well with some of The Not Ready for Prime Time Players (especially John Belushi), who felt they were being shortchanged.

At the end of the highly successful first *SNL* season, Chase moved to Hollywood. Forces at *SNL* felt he was betraying the show's welfare by his abrupt departure. The public assumed he wanted a film career to cash in on his fame and make a great deal more money than his weekly $750 *SNL* salary. According to the comedian, who had been previously wed and divorced, he had fallen in love with a Californian (Jacqueline Carlin). Because she would not move east, he went westward. He soon regretted the tactical error.

In Tinseltown, Chase made a few bad choices in his film projects, and he occasionally returned to host *SNL*. But now he was considered an outsider looking in. (On one return to Studio 8H, in February 1978, he and Bill Murray got into a fight backstage.)

Already, Chevy lamented having left *SNL* so early in its long run. The once cutting-edge Chase settled for being a buffoon in several pictures, and after *Fletch* (1985) his career descended largely into tiresome comedies and anemic sequels of past screen hits. By then married to his third wife, he gained far more currency for his substance abuse treatment at the Betty Ford Center than for such career fiascoes as his 1993 TV talk show. More recently, he cropped up on tributes/retrospectives to *Saturday Night Live*. On such outings, he wistfully (and sardonically) recalled the glory days, which in his case were a springboard to gaining a reputation as an overinflated ego and becoming the sometimes drug-abusing "star" of mostly disappointing pictures.

John Belushi had the sad distinction of being the first *SNL* star to die. His talent was needlessly silenced at age 33, the result of his long-term drug dependency and wildly excessive lifestyle.

In Belushi's tremendous anxiety to reach and then maintain stardom as a comic/actor, he let off steam through an existence governed by reckless substance abuse. A few years before John passed away, he noted of his race to fame: "It comes along with a certain kind of lifestyle. . . . Everything becomes more heightened, takes on more urgency and the tendency to self-destruct heightens too. . . . I get nervous and I am capable of doing something to blow it on purpose."

John Adam Belushi was born on January 24, 1949, in Wheaton, Illinois, where his dad and uncle owned a diner. (One of John's three other siblings, Jim, also became an actor and was an *SNL* player in the mid-1980s.) In high school Belushi, a football player and a drummer in a rock 'n' roll band, became intrigued with act-ing. He studied drama at the University of Wisconsin at Whitewater and, later, at the College of DuPage (in Glen Ellyn, Illinois). During summers, he toiled in stock shows.

While he was working at the Second City Troupe in Chicago, the world of improvisational comedy opened up for burly five-foot, nine-inch John. He found his forte in blending quasi slapstick with satire and drama. By then, the hyperactive talent was relying on an increasing range of drugs (including peyote) and booze to help him come down from on-stage highs or to bolster a performance. In 1973, he joined the off-Broadway show *National Lampoon's Lemmings*, for which, like Chevy Chase, he was both actor and scripter. This was followed by other satirical stage revues.

When *SNL* was casting for its debut comedy troupe, Belushi was initially not interested because he was not fond of the TV medium. However, he was persuaded to join the series, where he proved to be a bundle of joyous on-camera excesses. He brought great physical humor to his characterizations of the samurai warrior, the Greek diner chef, and especially his favorite persona, one of the Blues Brothers (with castmate and great friend Dan Aykroyd). John's blus-ter and crude shenanigans on the show were in great contrast to his teammates—making him stand out all that much more. His off-camera partying made him infamous among his peers. (Physicians cautioned him, to no avail, that his staggering regimen of drugs and liquor could kill him.)

On December 31, 1976, Belushi married his high school sweet-heart, Judith Jacklin, a book illustrator and designer. The couple had been living together since his Second City days. He soon left *SNL* to focus on the more prestigious and lucrative world of films. However, because of his unconventional looks and his fluctuating weight, it was difficult to cast the portly performer in the leading man roles he so desired. While he grappled with conquering Tinseltown, he became more insecure, which led to more frequent food and drug binges. When he was caught up in substance abuse, he didn't want his friends to see him, and he became more reclusive. Then, when sober, he fretted about his growing isolation from those once close to him.

Despite his great comedic potential, Belushi had more misses than hits in Hollywood. Nonetheless, in the early 1980s Belushi was hopeful of carving a new screen image for himself as a dramatic actor fully capable of playing romantic leads. He wrote *Noble Rot*, but Paramount Pictures rejected this potential vehicle, instead wanting him to star in a version of the popular self-help book *The Joy of Sex*. Tremendously upset by this turn of events, John left meetings in New York and returned to Los Angeles alone. There, on March 4, 1982, he embarked on a night of manic partying, hoping to alleviate his dark mood. Instead, his "feast" of drugs led to a fatal reaction to the overdose and he died the next day in his bungalow at the Chateau Marmont Hotel.

In death, the much-missed Belushi became a symbol for scandalous Hollywood excesses and the Me Generation, which refused to acknowledge limits to self-abusive behavior.

At five feet, six inches, Gilda Radner was a bundle of high-voltage energy whom many rated in the same league as physical comedian Lucille Ball. During her highly successful *SNL* tenure (1975–1980), the agile comic displayed boundless energy and a childlike joy. (Because she was supercritical about her looks, she suffered from nagging self-doubts.) Radner rampaged through wacky skits as news reporter Roseanne Roseannadanna, hyperactive six-year-old Judy Miller, or coed Rhonda Weiss, or she spun about the stage in jubilant abandon with such skit partners as Steve Martin or Chevy Chase. Her 1989 death from ovarian cancer, at age 42, left fans bereft and the comedy world without one of its outstanding talents.

She was born on June 28, 1946, the second child of a hotel businessman and his wife, a legal secretary. When the future comedian was 12, her father was diagnosed with a brain tumor. He endured an exceedingly painful two years before dying. The horrific experience traumatized Gilda.

After high school, Gilda attended the University of Michigan where she remained for several years as she dropped in and out. She was too high-energy and iconoclastic to adjust easily to life on the Ann Arbor campus. In 1969, she fell in love with a Canadian sculptor and relocated to Toronto to pursue the relationship. However, the romance ended after 16 months.

Hoping to rebuild her shattered self-esteem, she worked at a Toronto theater, initially in the box office, later in pantomimes performed for elementary school audiences. This footlight experience led to her being cast in the Toronto company of *Godspell* in 1972. From that gig, she moved on to the local edition of Second City, the improvisational comedy troupe. Among her stage coplayers were Dan Aykroyd and Eugene Levy. She came to New York in 1974 to appear in *The National Lampoon Show* with John Belushi, Bill Murray, and Harold Ramis.

When assembling the *SNL* crew, Canadian-born Lorne Michaels recalled Gilda from *Godspell* and other performances in Toronto. She was one of the first hired for the revolutionary ensemble. Her raucous, often bawdy characterizations, bolstered by her trademark agility and a radiating sense of joy, became a show highlight, even in the male-dominated environment. During her stay on the latenight comedy-variety offering, she had a short-lasting romance with fellow cast member Bill Murray.

Michaels announced that he was leaving the mighty *SNL* after its fifth season finale in 1980. Gilda was among those who then decided to depart the hit program, first trying Broadway and then following her peers to Hollywood. However, her showcase entry (1980's *First Family*) was a box-office turkey. During production of *Hanky Panky* (1982) she fell in love with costar Gene Wilder. The two comics wed in the south of Prance in September 1984. While working on the couple's *Haunted Honeymoon* (1984) she had a miscarriage.

In January 1986 Radner suffered from what she thought was chronic fatigue syndrome. A series of physicians attempted to isolate and diagnose her medical problem, which proved to be advanced ovarian cancer. Within days she underwent surgery to remove a huge tumor; this was followed by an enervating course of aggressive chemotherapy. Determined to find humor even in her plight, Gilda and Gene taped home videos of her recovery process. For additional bolstering, she attended meetings of The Wellness Community, a support group for cancer victims.

By June 1987, Radner thought she was on the recovery path. However, "second-look" surgery revealed the presence of cancerous cells, requiring additional chemotherapy. Willing herself to feel better, she eventually made a brief return to TV as a guest on *It's Garry Shandling's Show*. Soon thereafter, her physicians found that her cancer was no longer in remission. She underwent more surgery in October 1988. To keep distracted and to do something constructive, she wrote *It's Always Something* (1989), which focused on her battle against cancer. On Saturday, May 20, 1989, Gilda died in Los Angeles. That evening, on *SNL*, guest host Steve Martin offered a tearful tribute to his late colleague and good friend.

Many seasons of comics had come and gone before rotund, six-foot, three-inch Chris Farley joined the weekly shenanigans at *SNL*. Hearkening back, to some degree, to the physical humor of the late, great John Belushi, Chris's funniness was more juvenile and focused on exploiting his girth. But he did gain an impressive fan base, especially among young viewers.

He was born Christopher Crosby Farley on February 15, 1964, in Madison, Wisconsin. He was the third of five children in the Catholic household of Thomas and Mary Anne Farley. (Chris's younger brother, Kevin, also became a comedian.) As a youngster, Chris suffered from obesity and discovered the trick of making his classmates laugh before they started insulting him.

In high school, Farley employed his bulk on the football field. Craving yet more attention, he became an obsessive party animal, determined always to amuse his peers. At Marquette University in Milwaukee, he majored in theater and communications and explored his religion at this Jesuit school. After graduation, he joined the Improv-Olympics in Chicago. It was a branch of the Second City troupe where his idols (John Belushi and Bill Murray) had trod the boards. By fall 1988, Chris had graduated to the Second City ensemble and had solidified his reputation as a superlative partygoer.

On his debut *SNL* season (1990–1991), Farley shot to prominence with his childlike, crude, perspiring characterizations that delighted in grossed-out situations and exploited his tubbiness. He became infamous for dropping his trousers on camera at the slightest provocation. (Off camera, prankish Farley was renowned for manic moments in which he would go berserk and might turn his staff office topsy-turvy.) With his sudden affluence, Chris indulged his spiraling substance abuse and his attraction to prostitutes. Because his lifestyle was adversely affecting his work, producer Lorne Michaels (who had returned to the helm of *SNL*) intervened, demanding that his out-of-control talent get help or risk being fired. Following three months in recovery, Farley returned to the show. For a time he seemed a reformed individual, devoting his spare time to attending church and working for volunteer programs.

It was not long, however, before Chris found himself back in substance abuse treatment, this time in Los Angeles. When he "graduated," he seemed to have his drug addiction under control but not his excessive gorging on food and dating hookers. Meanwhile he made his big-screen debut in *Wayne's World* (1992). In the scattershot *Tommy Boy* and *Black Sheep* (both 1995, the year he left *Saturday Night Live*), the over-sized comic mugged and did pratfalls in tandem with David Spade, his *SNL* bad-boy pal.

Overwhelmed by his mounting success, Farley was at loose ends in Tinseltown. To bolster his confidence he relied heavily on drugs and booze, as well as food and sex benders. (By then, Chris sometimes weighed 350 pounds.) After further attempts at curbing his excesses, Farley revisited his old stomping grounds when he hosted an October 1997 edition of *SNL*. He was in such bad shape that many there feared he would not get through the evening's fare.

Farley's last weeks were spent in the Windy City, where he splurged uncontrollably on drugs, alcohol, food, and a parade of prostitutes. On December 1, 1997, he died from the cumulative effects of an overdose of cocaine and other drugs. At 33, he had burned out on fame.

For many cast regulars, Phil Hartman was the show's glue throughout his *SNL* years (1986–1994). During his stay, he competed for the limelight with such confreres as Dana Carvey, Mike Myers, Julia Sweeney, Chris Rock, and Adam Sandler. While his younger coplayers gravitated toward more physical humor, clean-cut, five-foot, eleven-inch Hartman focused on wry impersonations (e.g., Frank Sinatra, Phil Donahue, and President Clinton) and more subtle comedy skits. That his successful career would end brutally was the last thing anyone expected for ambitious, well-organized, good-natured Hartman, who had an eye for women.

He was born Philip Edward Hartmann (the performer dropped the final "n" of his surname after entering show business) on September 24, 1948, in Brantford, Ontario, Canada. He was the fourth of eight children of a building supplies salesman and his homemaker wife. Later, the Hartmanns relocated to Connecticut, and, thereafter, to southern California. At Westchester High School in Los Angeles, Phil was elected class clown. After junior college he went to California State University in Northridge, where he majored in graphic arts. After graduating, he earned his livelihood designing album covers for rock groups. In 1970, he wed Gretchen Lewis in what proved to be a short-lasting union.

One evening in 1975, while attending a performance of the Groundlings, a Los Angeles improv group, Phil suddenly popped up on stage to join in the frivolities. It led to his abandoning his staid life and joining the troupe. In late 1982, he wed real estate agent Lisa Strain, but their marriage endured less than three years. Meanwhile, he had met Paul Reubens (aka Pee-wee Herman), who hired him to join his 1980s' TV show. In 1986, Phil appeared in such movies as *Three Amigos!* That same year he joined the *SNL* crew, where he became a reliable ensemble member and sharp writer of skits (later winning an Emmy for his scripting).

By then, Hartman was living with Minnesota-born Vicki Jo Omdahl, a divorcée and would-be actress who had an overwhelming desire to be famous. Phil and Brynn (as she called herself) married in November 1987 and had two children, Sean and Birgen. In the spring of 1994, Phil, then age 46 and the program's oldest cast member, made a career change. The Hartmans returned to southern California. He had supporting roles in such features as 1995's *Stuart Saves His Family* and was a regular on the popular TV sitcom *NewsRadio*, which debuted in 1995.

Off camera, the well-paid personality fed his passion for cars, boats, and marksmanship. Meanwhile, Brynn was becoming more and more unhappy with her subordinate role in the marriage. He suggested she channel her energies into acting, and he tried to maneuver acting assignments for her. The more she pressured him about their disparities, the more he removed himself from the tense domestic situation. By the late 1990s, Brynn was relying increasingly on drugs and drinks. She went into rehab, but the cure did not take, and she promised to undergo new treatment at a Malibu substance abuse facility. During this unsettling period, she grew progressively more jealous of her husband. Such confrontations led to fights in which Brynn became violent and physically abusive.

In the early hours of May 28, 1998, following their latest battle royal, Brynn sneaked into their bedroom and shot Hartman three times. (At the time, the two children were in the house.) Later, after driving to a friend's house to confess the homicide, she returned home where she barricaded herself in the bedroom with her spouse's corpse. There, she shot herself. On June 13, 1998, *Saturday Night Live* broadcast a special tribute to the late star, utilizing clips from Phil's eight seasons on the show.

Months before his life ended so abruptly, Hartman observed, "I'm 49 years old and I'm cautious of the fact that very few people in comedy have careers after age 50. I think there's a notion in our society, and it may be valid, that people aren't as funny when they get older. It's a stigma still attached to the rebelliousness of youth."

Reflecting on John Belushi and his *SNL* peers, John Landis (director of *National Lampoon's Animal House*) said, "They're not simple. Not tragic, not joyous, not silly, but extraordinary in their individual complex and sad and funny ways." One of the show's originals, Chevy Chase discerned of the plight of his profession:

"Entertainers want to be famous and recognized, and there is a long period when that does not happen. . . . So when we are success-ful, we want to go back, want to go home, which is when we were rejected—become a clown, a druggie, a f**kup. . . . Actors search for rejection. If they do not get it, they reject themselves."

In the case of some of the *Saturday Night Live* comedy stars detailed here, the pressures of fame led them down wrong paths in their careers and personal lives. Unable to cope with their pro-fessional and material successes, they stumbled badly in full public view with often disastrous, shocking results.

Rob Lowe: Surviving His Candid Camera Escapade

"Everything was stripped away. The only thing left was who I was. I didn't like who I was. During the last decade I've been trying to find stability, to create the kind of life I always wanted."

— ROB LOWE, ON JUNE 4, 2000

When pre-film fame nude poses of Marilyn Monroe surfaced in the 1950s, their circulation only added to the luscious screen icon's tremendous box-office appeal. The same was true of singer/ actress Madonna 30 years later when two national girlie publica-tions printed revealing modeling shots snapped of her in her starv-ing musician days.

On the other hand, when an explicit home video of hunky movie star Rob Lowe surfaced in late 1988, it was of a far more pru-rient nature. The X-rated material seemed blatantly dirty because it was *not* arty solo still shots made for commercial consumption but rather video footage meant only for private viewing. The home movie featured the young stud enthusiastically romping on his hotel bed with two Southern gals, one of whom was underage.

In the wake of Lowe's 1988 sex tape scandal that outraged and/ or amused many Americans, the actor said, "It was just one of those quirky, sort of naughty, sort of wild, sort of . . . drunken things that people will do from time to time." He further elaborated, "What

238

really angers me is that in Europe no one would have persecuted me like this. They'd have said, 'You were involved in a sex scandal? Really? Great!'" He reasoned, "Show me someone who hasn't done that [i.e., making personal sex videos] and I'll show you someone who's been so sheltered they're gonna be dull." Nevertheless, at the time, extremely handsome, five-foot, eleven-inch Lowe was considered persona non grata in many quarters. Reportedly, after movie star Lowe was sentenced to community service as a result of the sex video scandal, a teacher hissed, "Having Rob Lowe lecturing our children on morals is like inviting Hitler to a Jewish wedding."

Part of the adverse reaction that Lowe faced after his sexually explicit video showcase tape circulated was caused by what he represented to the public. Along with Emilio Estevez, Demi Moore, Judd Nelson, Ally Sheedy, Andrew McCarthy, Molly Ringwald, Charlie Sheen, and a few other young actors, Rob was a charter member of Tinseltown's infamous Brat Pack. These self-involved, highly indulgent Hollywood beautiful people were then in vogue in such shallow features as *St. Elmo's Fire* (1985). At the time, fans envied the Brat Packers' much-hyped privileged lives, while detractors felt these spoiled yuppies were aching for a comeuppance. (Lowe's hecklers referred to him as a "bimboy" and "that Brat Pack's poster boy.")

Looking back on his disgrace and the factors leading up to it, Lowe admitted, "When I was young and crazy, I was young and crazy. It can be hard enough just to *be* in your teens and twenties. Then add fame, money, access, and every single person telling you that you're the greatest person who ever was, and it can be a recipe for disaster."

Robert Hepler Lowe was born on March 17, 1964, in Charlottesville, Virginia, the first child of Charles Lowe, a trial lawyer, and his wife, Barbara, an English teacher. Soon thereafter, the Methodist family moved to Dayton, Ohio, where, in January 1968, their second son, Chad, was born. (He would also become an actor—earning an Emmy—and would marry Oscar-winning actress Hilary Swank.) When Rob was five his mother divorced and remarried.

At age eight, Rob saw a local production of the musical *Oliver!* It changed his life: "When I saw those kids on stage, I wanted to be there. I loved acting, because it was a world outside the world I was living in, a place where I could be someone else." He began acting in summer theater and performing with regional acting groups. Nonetheless, he still found time for other interests. He loved to debate and thought of becoming a lawyer. He already had a strong interest in politics, which led him to operate a lemonade stand to raise funds for Democratic presidential candidate George McGovern.

In 1977, his mother divorced again and moved with her boys to California, settling at Point Dome, a small community north of Malibu. At this time she wed therapist Stephen Wilson, and they had two sons, Micah and Justin.

Not long after becoming a Californian, Rob registered with a Hollywood talent agency and soon was cast in several TV commercials. He attended Santa Monica public school and spent time with such Malibu neighbors as Sean and Chris Penn as well as Emilio Estevez and his brother Charlie Sheen. With his new pals, Lowe and his sibling Chad made home movies using the nearby dunes and surf as backdrops.

Lowe made his professional TV debut in the short-lasting network comedy *A New Kind of Family* (1979). Next came telefeatures such as 1981's *A Matter of Time,* which made him a recognizable small-screen personality. In fact, he became so sufficiently well known that one day as he drove in Los Angeles, a passing car honked at him. The driver asked, "Are you Rob Lowe?" It was actress Melissa Gilbert coming home from her daily shoot on TV's *Little House on the Prairie. A* romance developed that lasted—on and off—for the next six years.

Following graduation from Santa Monica High, Lowe, who was dyslexic and completely deaf in his right ear, was accepted as a film major at both UCLA and USC. However, before classes began in the fall of 1982, he was hired for several acting assignments. These included more TV movies and theatrical features. The feather-weight *Oxford Blues* (1984) made him a sex symbol. While filming *The Hotel New Hampshire* (1984), Lowe had an affair with his five-year-older colead, Nastassia Kinski. He also dated Demi Moore, his costar in such pictures as 1986's *About Last Night. . . .* Along the way, Rob had a much-publicized, quickie romance with Monaco's Princess Stephanie.

By now, Lowe's extracurricular life was making more headlines than his acting (for which he was earning $1 million a picture). Overdoing the liquor, drugs, and sex scene, he began to feel rest-less. "In my late teens and early twenties, I was insulated within the L.A. film world. Your frame of reference is so small, you lose a sense of what's important. I wasn't self-aware. . . . I felt that. . . I was miss-ing out on something better."

As part of his effort to bring stability to his life, Rob proposed to Melissa Gilbert in 1987. It was not until months later that he learned—by tuning into a radio show to which she had called in—that the actress intended to wed actor/playwright Bo Brinkman. Of a more consistent and rewarding nature than his love life was his continued interest in politics.

Earlier in the '80s, Lowe had campaigned for California Democrat Tom Hayden (then married to actress Jane Fonda). Rob enjoyed the experience because, "Campaigning gave me a chance to see what I could bring to the process. It also kept me in touch with my own humanity and gave me a connection to where I came from." Thus, he was receptive when, in July 1988, Hayden invited him to attend the Democratic National Convention in Atlanta to support Michael Dukakis's push for the party's presidential nomination. (The actor's friends soon nicknamed Rob "Senator Lowe.")

On July 17, Rob, a rabid baseball enthusiast, took his camcorder to an afternoon Atlanta Braves game and taped footage there. That evening, he attended a gathering hosted by media mogul Ted Turner. Later, along with Brat Packers Ally Sheedy and Judd

Nelson, Lowe stopped at the local Club Rio. Before being admitted, the doorman insisted on seeing ID. (Baby-faced Rob was 24 at the time.) That episode led him to believe, mistakenly, that everyone within the venue was of legal age.

Inside the nightspot, Rob mingled and conversed with several women. Among those he chatted with was Tara Siebert, a 22-year-old receptionist at a Marietta, Georgia, hair salon. Another he talked with was Jan Parsons, a 16-year-old high school sophomore and an assistant at the same hair establishment. The movie star invited the two back to his hotel room (number 2845 at the Atlanta Hilton). Once there, the chiseled-jawed performer videotaped their bedroom fun and games (on the same cassette that, earlier that month, he had filmed a ménage à trois episode with a woman and a man in France). Later, while Rob was passed out, his guests vanished. When he revived, he noticed that approximately $200 was missing from his wallet and that the videocassette had disappeared as well. Lowe put the matter out of mind as he toured the campaign trail with Dukakis.

Weeks later, Jan's mother came across the revealing tape and discovered the seven-minute footage of her daughter's sexual high jinks. Before long the matter was brought to the attention of Lowe and his lawyer. In response, the Parsons were offered a $35,000 settlement to drop the matter. Instead, Mrs. Parsons filed a civil suit in U.S. district court where she clamed that the film star "used his celebrity status as an inducement to females to engage in sexual intercourse, sodomy, and multiple-party sexual activity for his immediate sexual gratification, and for the purpose of making pornographic films of these activities." Thereafter, the suit was amended to allege "unlawful intercourse." (Once charges had been filed, the FBI and members of the Los Angeles vice squad raided Lowe's home, where they found an elaborate video system installed in the actor's bedroom but no other "pornographic" videos.)

In the meantime, District Attorney Lewis R. Slaton was investigating whether to bring criminal charges (for sexual exploitation of a minor) against Lowe. If found guilty, the reckless actor would face up to 20 years in prison and a $100,000 fine. During this time, copies of Rob's Parisian and Atlanta indiscretions began circulating everywhere. (Reputedly, the hot video netted nearly $1 million in black-market sales.) Some of the spicy footage, in edited format, even appeared on several tabloid television and cable programs.

In July 1989, Judge G. Ernest Tidwell dismissed that part of the parent's lawsuit claiming emotional distress because it "does not allege sufficient facts" under Georgia laws to demonstrate that the defendant intentionally inflicted emotional distress against the minor. (Criminal charges were never pressed by the district attorney.) After meeting with Lowe and his father to "size him up to see if he was OK for the program," the judge utilized Georgia's pretrial intervention plan, an alternative to prosecuting young, nonviolent first offenders. As such, it was decreed that Lowe serve 20 hours of community service (e.g., speaking to students at schools on such topics as drugs and the law) and "stay out of trouble for the next two years of probation." (Payments were also made to the plaintiff in an out-of-court settlement.)

Lowe's judicial punishment was relatively minor compared to the severe professional backlash that he faced. As a result of the lewd tape scandal, he became an outcast in Tinseltown and the political world and a laughingstock to the public at large. He was soon reduced to making such unpromising screen projects as *The Dark Backward* (1991) with Wayne Newton. When Lowe fled Hollywood to make his Broadway debut in *A Little Hotel on the Side* (1992), pundits had a field day.

As he battled his fall from grace, Lowe's drinking and drug usage accelerated. As a result, he entered Arizona's Sierra Tucson rehab center in 1990 and, reportedly, has remained clean ever since. (The actor also underwent treatment for his sexual-addictive behavior.) His most important support came from makeup artist Sheryl Berkoff, whom he'd first met on the set of *The Outsiders* (1983) and then reconnected with while filming *Bad Influence* (1990). They married in July 1991, moved to a six-acre spread in Santa Barbara, and became parents of two sons, Matthew (1993) and John Owen

(1995). Meanwhile, the former party animal began his comeback with an effective cameo in *Wayne's World* (1992). It eventually led to his pivotal role as the White House staffer in the acclaimed TV series *The West Wing* (1999–2003), for which he was Emmy-nominated. After quitting that show, he starred in the short-lasting 2003 TV drama series *The Lyon's Den*, cast as a crusading Washington, D.C., attorney. Meanwhile, he supported Arnold Schwarzenegger in the latter's gubernatorial campaign in California. Finally, with his career and life back on a positive keel, Rob Lowe showed that he was no longer a supermarket-tabloid joke and could begin to hope that his notorious scandal could gradually be forgiven and forgotten.

Woody Allen and Mia Farrow: The Warring Lovebirds

"The inequality of my relationship is a wonderful thing. The fact that I'm with a much younger woman, and much less accomplished woman, works very well. By luck, it's a very happy situation."

—WOODY ALLEN, IN 1997

H ollywood's social history is replete with markedly atypical domestic arrangements, ranging from the 1920s' marriage of convenience between gay actor Edmund Lowe and lesbian Lilyan Tashman to the 1990s' situation in which comedian Andy Dick and his girlfriend lived in the top half of a West Hollywood duplex, while downstairs resided his ex-wife and their son.

No less bizarre was the 1943 joining of comedy giant Charles Chaplin (age 54) and Oona O'Neill (age 17), the actress-daughter of renowned playwright Eugene O'Neill. (That marriage lasted until Chaplin's death in 1977.) Then, there was sultry movie actress Gloria Grahame wed to film director Nicholas Ray (husband number two) from 1948 to 1952. After a third hitching (to writer/director Cy Howard) in the 1950s, she tied the knot in 1960 with her stepson Tony Ray, a relationship that endured 16 years.

Despite the heavy competition, one of the strangest show business unions was that of Woody Allen and Mia Farrow. He was a Jewish, East Coast intellectual, while she was Catholic and a Tinseltown star. Comedic five-foot, five-inch Allen gained show business fame with his endearing schlemiel persona. In contrast, petite Farrow (who weighed 98 pounds), made her mark playing radiant, troubled young gamines (as in TV's *Peyton Place* and the feature film *Rosemary's Baby*). Woody was a self-focused artist, a devotee of Freudian therapy, and a man so engrossed in moviemaking that he cared little for such domestic niceties as children. In contrast, tantalizing Mia, a Hollywood blue blood, envisioned herself a savior of downtrodden youngsters, adopting several along the way.

What Allen and Farrow shared in common was that each had been married twice and both had a penchant for unusual love matches. They also disguised their true personalities beneath their crafted screen images. Woody presented himself as the thinking man's schnook, a befuddled man who insisted, "The two biggest myths about me are that I'm an intellectual, because I wear these glasses, and that I'm an artist because my films lose money." In actuality, he was a shrewd, self-centered, controlling workaholic who lived an elitist existence. While in the public eye Mia was perpetually the vulnerable waif, but this ageless flower child had deeper ambitions. She once admitted, "I want a big career, a big man and a big life. You have to think big—that's the only way to get it. . . . I just couldn't stand being anonymous."

When this unlikely duo came together in 1980—and she began starring in his movies—these two Manhattanites (who lived apart) became the city's favorite celebrity couple. In 1992, the relationship fell apart disastrously when Mia discovered that Woody was having a sexual relationship with her adopted daughter, Soon-Yi Previn, a Vietnamese-born teenager. The extensive media coverage of the vituperative Allen-Farrow battle fully documented each bitter recrimination as Woody sought custody of their three children (two of whom had been adopted by the couple), while Mia charged the filmmaker with allegedly sexually molesting their eight-year-old adopted girl, Dylan. Rarely had domestic strife been uglier or more shocking.

He was born Allan Stewart Konigsberg in the Bronx on December 1, 1935, the first offspring of Martin Konigsberg and Nettie Cherry, second-generation Jewish immigrants. (A second child, Letty, was born in 1943.) The Brooklyn-based family suffered through the Depression, with the bemused father moving from one unpromising job to another while the overly stern mother slaved as a bookkeeper.

Precocious but disaffected (thanks to his unhappy home life), he escaped the domestic skirmishes through going to movies, practicing magic tricks, and following sports. As a teenager, he was bright but disinterested in school. He much preferred to practice his clarinet and his magic tricks. At 17, the budding comedian began sending his self-deprecating jokes—unsolicited—to New York newspaper columnists. To sound more mainstream American, he adopted the professional name of Woody Allen. In 1952, his first jokes were published and he debuted as a stand-up comic. After graduating high school, he entered New York University in the film production program but dropped out, as he subsequently did at City College of New York.

In 1955, Allen was signed by the NBC-TV network and moved to Los Angeles as a scripter for the short-lived *The Colgate Variety Hour*. In March of the next year, Woody wed Harlene Rosen, a Flatbush social club regular who was three years his junior. Back in New York, in 1958, the comedian wrote for TV's *Sid Caesar's Chevy Show*. By 1960 Allen earned $1,700 weekly as a TV comedy writer, regularly visited an analyst, and was a rising stand-up comic. When he and Harlene divorced in 1962, he was already dating actress Louise Lasser, whom he wed in 1966.

Now nationally known as a funster, Allen scripted and acted in *What's New, Pussycat?* (1965). In 1969, Woody had a Broadway hit (*Play It Again, Sam*) with actress Diane Keaton; wrote, directed, and starred in the screen comedy *Take the Money and Run;* and, by 1971, he had divorced Louise Lasser. The screen version of *Play It Again, Sam* (1972) found Allen and Keaton repeating their stage roles and continuing the love affair they had started during the

Broadway production. One of their later collaborations, *Annie Hall* (1977), won several Academy Awards. By the time they coteamed in *Manhattan* (1979), their romance had fizzled.

In November 1979, 40-something, fussy Woody was having a late dinner at one of his favorite establishments, Elaine's on Second Avenue near 86th Street. He was introduced to another diner, Mia Farrow, and was immediately intrigued with this radiant 34-year-old actress.

Maria de Lourdes Villiers Farrow was born on February 9, 1945. She was the second (there was six-year-older Michael) of seven children of Maureen O'Sullivan (the Irish-born movie star famous for playing Jane in the Tarzan series) and John Farrow (the Australian-born screenwriter and director). In the strongly Catholic household, Mia (as she was nicknamed) was the crown princess; her godmother was veteran gossip columnist Louella Parsons, and her godfather was acclaimed director George Cukor.

The Farrows lived grandly. However, there were problems in the household, as the handsome, chauvinistic father played around outside the marriage and was alcoholic and abusive. All of this the mother accepted stoically. Young Mia thought of becoming a nun but later changed her mind. In 1954, she contracted polio and was hospitalized. Later, while recovering at home, she suffered a trauma when her older brother was severely injured when he was hit by a passing car.

Mia and her siblings attended parochial schools in Los Angeles and led a privileged life. By age 11, Mia underwent analysis to deal with her eccentricities and excessive imagination. In the late '50s, John Farrow took his family to Spain where he was directing *John Paul Jones*. Mia had a tiny role in the picture, sparking an interest in show business. This upset Mr. Farrow who insisted, "I never saw a happy actress." Hoping to distract her, he sent her to a convent school in England. While there, 13-year-old Mia was devastated to learn that brother Michael had died in a plane crash in California.

As she neared 16, Mia was back in Los Angeles attending a Catholic preparatory school. She was still enthralled with acting, which prompted her father to ship her to a British finishing school. Later, Mia persuaded her parents to let her return home. In 1962, Maureen O'Sullivan embarked on a summer stock tour of a new play. Late that year, *Never Too Late* played successfully on Broadway. Mia moved to New York City to be near Maureen and to begin her own show business career.

On January 28, 1963, heavy-drinking John Farrow died of a heart attack in Los Angeles. Maureen moved her entire family to Manhattan. Mia got an acting break when she was hired for an off-Broadway production later that year. This led to her making the feature film *Guns of Batasi* (1964). That September, she debuted on the prime-time TV drama *Peyton Place*. Farrow became a huge hit with viewers.

Shy Mia found it difficult to adjust to her popularity. She found distraction, however, with Frank Sinatra, then making a film on the studio lot where *Peyton Place* was shot. The swinging singing/movie superstar, who was 30 years her elder, became enchanted with Farrow. Their relationship accelerated, and the media speculated whether Mia could generate in Frank the same passion that his second wife, movie siren Ava Gardner, had during their stormy marriage in the 1950s. Despite their many differences, Mia and Frank wed in mid-July 1966. Meanwhile, Mia quit *Peyton Place*.

Explosive, dogmatic, chauvinistic Sinatra soon learned that ethereal Farrow was not easily dissuaded from following her whims. One of these was flying to India to study with a trendy guru. Eventually, the couple's many incompatibilities led to their August 1968 divorce.

Mia met German-born composer André Previn in London in late 1967. He was still wed to his second wife, Dory, with whom he sometimes wrote songs. Before long, a romance developed between Previn and the 16-year-younger Farrow. In February 1970, Mia gave birth to his twin sons. In midyear, André and Dory divorced, and that September Previn and Farrow wed in London. In 1973, they adopted a Vietnamese orphan, Lark. The next year, the Previns had a son (Fletcher) and thereafter adopted two more young orphans: Vietnamese Summer Song (Daisy) and Korean Soon-Yi.

The Previns' marriage became strained—with each straying romantically—and they divorced in early 1979. Mia continued making movies and relocated with her brood to New York. She had recently added to the household when she adopted a two-year-old, physically handicapped Korean orphan, Mischa (Moses). That November, she teamed with Tony Perkins for the successful Broadway entry *Romantic Comedy*.

One Wednesday evening in November, a weary Mia was persuaded by movie star Michael Caine and his wife, Shakira, to join them for a late supper at Elaine's. She reluctantly agreed.

When Woody and Mia met at Elaine's they already had subtle personal ties. Allen had earlier cast Farrow's younger sister, Tisa, in a brief role in *Manhattan*. Mia had previously read a *New York Times* Sunday magazine piece on the filmmaker, and she had decided that this bespectacled, balding auteur appealed to her. Following this initial meeting, he invited her to his New Year's Eve party. She came briefly to the crowded function. It was not until the spring— on April 17—that Allen, still immersed in editing his bleak new film (*Stardust Memories*), invited Mia to lunch at fashionable Lutèce. Later, he took her in his chauffeur-driven limousine back to her sprawling eight-room Central Park West rented apartment.

Soon Allen and Farrow were in love. She quickly learned that he enjoyed his privacy and that he was definitely not fond of children interrupting his hectic routine. As such, he never spent the evening at her chaotic, homey West Side place. However, on weekends, she and the children would trek over to his plush Fifth Avenue duplex penthouse, but their time there *always* revolved around Allen's schedule and whims. Whenever Woody and Mia—with or without the kids—traipsed around to one Manhattan spot or another, crowds gaped at the city's most celebrated couple. When she went with her offspring to Frog Hollow, her 60-acre farm near Bridgewater, Connecticut, Woody sometimes accompanied her, but his idiosyncrasies and phobias generally prevented him from staying overnight.

As two past lovers (Louise Lasser and Diane Keaton) had costarred in Woody's features, so did Mia. Her first of 13 was *A Midsummer Night's Sex Comedy* (1982). Although she was the filmmaker's significant other, she was subjected to his parsimonious salary rate, his severe on-set demands, and his total preoccupation with his craft (as well as his hobbies, including his Monday night clarinet playing at Michael's Pub with his New Orleans–style jazz band). Farrow enjoyed a good showcase as a Broadway tootsie in Woody's *Broadway Danny Rose* (1984). She had her choice of female roles in *Hannah and Her Sisters* (1986) but was dismayed, as was her mother, who also performed in the picture, to see how much Allen had drawn on the Farrow clan in creating the distaff characterizations. By now, the bloom was wearing off the Woody-Mia relationship. (There were rumors that Allen had become interested in actress Diane Wiest, a regular in the Allen stock company.)

In mid-1985 Mia, obsessed with expanding her household, adopted yet another child—this time Caucasian and in perfect health. She and a disinterested Woody named the newcomer Dylan. In 1987, Farrow gave birth to Allen's child whom they called Satchel. If Mia thought fatherhood would make Woody more interested in children, she was mistaken, at least initially. Meanwhile, the couple made such films as *Crimes and Misdemeanors* (1989), *Alice* (1990), and *Husbands and Wives* (1992).

In late 1991, Woody coadopted two of Mia's children (Moses and Dylan). Increasingly, he showed a fondness for six-year-old Dylan. As to his biological child, Satchel, he remained remote, perplexed by the boy's complex nature (which led Woody to have the child undergo therapy). By then, sexual relations between Allen and Farrow had almost ceased.

On the afternoon of January 12, 1992, Mia came by Woody's apartment with Satchel in tow. Woody was at his office on Park Avenue. While waiting in the den for her son's therapy appointment to be finished, she came across a stack of Polaroids on the fireplace mantle. She was shocked to discover that the shots of a naked woman were of her 19-year-old, Soon-Yi, a college student who wanted to be in films.

All hell broke loose. After Mia berated Woody on the phone, she and Satchel rushed back to her apartment where, besides telling her children of her appalling discovery, she confronted Soon-Yi. It eventually came out that, since 1990 (according to Soon-Yi; late 1991 in Allen's version), Soon-Yi and Woody had been intimate. (Later, a previously unpublished magazine photo of Woody and Soon-Yi, taken at a New York Knicks game at Madison Square Garden in January 1990, would appear; it showed the couple holding hands.) Bewildered Allen assumed that Farrow's fury—which he had experienced many times over past years—would eventually diminish, especially when he promised to end his affair with the teenager. However, Farrow's wrath increased rather than diminished. Now accustomed to seeing Dylan on a daily basis, Allen was amazed when Mia demanded an end to these visits.

On Valentine's Day, the perplexed comic star brought gifts for the children and gave Mia a box of chocolates. He didn't open her "present" until he was being driven back home. The box contained an old-fashioned card showing Farrow and her nine children. There were cooking skewers piercing each youngster's heart, while a steak knife had been jabbed through Farrow's likeness. The knife was wrapped in a photocopy of one of the Soon-Yi nude shots and contained the notation, "Once my heart was one and it was yours to keep. My child you used and pierced my heart a hundred times and deep." Finally, Allen understood the severity of Mia's anger.

As the two opposing camps formed, Farrow, despite Allen's insistence, refused to return the incriminating Polaroids. However, she agreed to undergo therapy and to take prescription medicine for her mounting depression. Strangely, the couple continued dining together in public with most outsiders still unaware of the domestic brouhaha. During this time, Mia found herself caught between two choices of action: being unforgiving or being sufficiently diplomatic to maintain her bread and butter (i.e., her salary from appearing in the annual Woody Allen movie).

By July, Woody and Mia were entrenched in their enmity, and she lashed out at him when he showed up at Frog Hollow for Dylan's seventh birthday party. (That evening, he insisted on staying over. In the morning he found a note pinned to a nearby wall; it labeled him "Child Molester.") He was now convinced that his relationship with Mia was over, but the two continued to have occasional dinners, even discussing their next film, 1993's *Manhattan Murder Mystery*. In August, a Frog Hollow neighbor told Farrow that her babysitter had been at the Farrow house the previous day and, supposedly, had seen Allen cuddling Dylan in an inappropriate way. (Mia later claimed that Dylan confided that Allen had taken her up to Mia's bedroom where, in the crawl space of the closet, he had allegedly touched her "privates.") After rushing the child to the family pediatrician, who found no apparent evidence of sexual abuse, the matter was reported, by law, to the police. It also came to the attention of the New York City Child Welfare Administration, whose action led nowhere due to an outraged Allen's refusing to cooperate beyond supplying a lengthy confirmation of his emotional stability from his psychiatrist.

Things happened fast and furious in August. Playing the grieving mother to the hilt, Mia hired a high-powered female attorney to protect her interests, while Woody (through his lawyer) filed to gain custody of Moses and Dylan and guard his right with Satchel. Because of the prominence of the two parties, the proceedings ignited a media heyday (one New York paper headlined its article "It's Solo Mia!"). The opposing factions held press conferences and TV interviews to put forth their arguments. To no one's surprise but Mia's, she learned that her part in *Manhattan Murder Mystery* had been recast (with Diane Keaton). The Allen-Farrow contretemps whetted the public's appetite for the couple's latest (and last) movie, *Husbands and Wives*, which was rushed into release in September 1992.

In March 1993, the Child Sexual Abuse Clinic at Yale–New Haven Hospital issued its report, concluding that Dylan had not been abused and that the child, for whatever reason, had not told the truth. It also suggested that Mia should receive counseling to aid her relationship with her young offspring. In contrast, despite his efforts to impress the New York superior court, Woody lost his custody case that June regarding Moses, Dylan, and Satchel. The judge ruled that as a father the show business legend had been "self-absorbed, untrustworthy, and insensitive." Allen was required to pay Farrow's legal fees in the case. As to his biological son, he was allowed brief supervised visits with the boy. Woody spent a small fortune contesting the rulings, but the decisions continued to hold in Mia's favor. By the end of 1995, Farrow stopped allowing Satchel's visits with Allen and the court refused to force the meetings. Later, Mia, who had moved her household permanently to Connecticut, changed her young children's names—all to further sever the connection to Woody.

Mia continued her acting career, wrote her stinging autobiography (1997's *What Falls Away*), and added to her household with more adopted children. Woody continued to turn out his annual pictures and, in June 1997, wed Soon-Yi, with whom he adopted an infant Asian girl, Bechet Dumaine, in spring 1999. To accommodate his growing family, Allen sold his Fifth Avenue penthouse for $14 million and, in turn, purchased a $17 million, five-story townhouse on East 92nd Street.

In the wake of the huge scandal, Allen and Farrow suffered incredibly adverse reaction from the public. This was especially true in the case of Woody, who had seemed such a moral paragon with his lovable, nebbishy, neurotic persona. As had happened with the similarly idolized Ingrid Bergman in the late 1940s when she abandoned her family for her Italian filmmaker lover, Allen proved he was all too human and, for that, moviegoers were slow to forgive—if they ever did.

Heidi Fleiss: Ex-Madam to the Stars

"All those egos, all these actors, all these executives. It'll come out when the time is right."

— HEIDI FLEISS, IN AUGUST 1993

As suggested by the film *L.A. Confidential* (1997), fancy bordellos and high-priced call girls are nothing new within the checkered history of Los Angeles. Going back to the early 20th century, there was the notorious Pearl Morton, a purveyor of girls for hire in the City of Angels. During the Roaring '20s, Lee Francis was the city's premier madam, who boasted an influential clientele of movers and shakers in the film industry and general business. Francis always maintained a fresh supply of chilled imported champagne and Russian caviar at her fancy bordello. Thus, whenever the vice squad made one of their preannounced raids—and there was no one to arrest—she could then graciously serve the "diligent" lawmen appetizing refreshments.

After Lee Francis was jailed for 30 days on a morals charge, Ann Forrester (known as the "Black Widow") stepped into the breech and became L.A.'s top madam in the '30s. Supposedly, Ann's brothel enterprise grossed an impressive $5,000 weekly. By 1940, however, Forrester had been jailed for her unlawful activities. This occurred despite Mayor Fletcher Bowron's request that she be given a light sentence because "her information was of great value in determining the identity of those Police Department members whose honesty was questionable."

The '40s belonged to the Black Widow's protégée, Brenda Allen (a former downtown streetwalker whose real name was Marie Mitchell). Using a series of elaborate party houses located above the Sunset Strip, Brenda catered to the city's wealthy, including movie industry notables. (Allen was reputed to have grossed $9,000 a day from the efforts of her 114 girls. About a third of this income was earmarked for such overhead as bribes, physicians, attorneys, and bail bondsmen.)

Like her predecessors, Brenda maintained secret client files in case she ever got into legal difficulties and needed to call on these decision makers for help. As added insurance, she had an ongoing love affair with LAPD Sergeant Elmer V. Jackson of the vice squad. (He was also a partner in her trade.) Allen's streak of good luck ended in 1948 as a result of law enforcers' tapping her phones and capturing a revealing conversation between her and Jackson. Her arrest caused a scandal, not so much for her black box full of the names of her VIP clientele but because it made clear that her profitable operation involved several corrupt vice cops, even beyond Jackson. When her bordello business tumbled, the stink resulted in the retirement of Police Chief Clemence B. Horrall.

During the '50s, Barrie Benson, Allen's 20-something successor in L.A., operated from an elaborate, gaudy, 13-room Moorish castle on Schuyler Road, north of the Sunset Strip. Among her prized customers were such underworld characters as Sam Farkas, a bodyguard of mob figure Mickey Cohen. Benson's reign ended during the regime of hard-nosed Police Chief William H. Parker.

By the '70s, Tinseltown's elite had turned to Elizabeth Adams (aka Alex Adams and Madam Alex). Originally from the Philippines, Alex was a twice-married woman and the mother of three. Before taking up her bordello activities, she had worked in L.A. as a dance instructor and then as a flower shop employee. She took her elegant call girl service to an international level. Besides servicing the sexual needs of the well-heeled members of Los Angeles commerce, politics, and film, she supplied her "creatures" (her word for her girls) to royalty and big-business men visiting from the Middle East. In addition, Alex dispatched her workers for special lucrative assignments abroad.

Madam Alex charged $1,000 a night for the ministrations of one of her workers and $2,000 if it was an out-of-town job. Thanks to her enterprising ways, she had a $100,000 monthly intake. It allowed her to live luxuriously, first in a Malibu home, then in an eight-room Bel-Air abode. To protect her thriving trade, the Beverly Hills madam became an ongoing police informant. She provided law enforcers with useful data gathered from her staff's bedroom chatter.

All good things, however, come to an end. In 1988, Alex, then in her late fifties, was busted for pandering—allegedly due to a changeover in policy at the vice squad. Because several detectives testified that she had been a most reliable informant, she was able to plea bargain for an 18-month probation. With her downfall, Madam Alex moved to a small white cottage in West Hollywood, ostensibly operating a small catering business. In 1993 she coauthored her memoir, *Madam 90210*.

In the wake of the collapse of Madam Alex's mini-empire came young, enterprising Heidi Fleiss.

Heidi Lynne Fleiss was born on December 30, 1965, the third of six children in her Jewish household based in the Los Feliz district of Los Angeles. Her father, Paul, was a well-regarded pediatrician, while her mother was an occasional elementary teacher. Both parents were confirmed hippies, and their offspring were brought up in an overly permissive atmosphere. As a youngster, rambunctious tomboy Heidi was bursting with energy, restless to try anything new, and determined not to be hemmed in by conventional thinking. She loved the frequent camping trips she and her family took and thrived on playing chess (she became a city champion).

While Heidi had been a relatively well-behaved elementary school student, her attitude changed thereafter. She became increasingly bored with academics and frequently cut classes to go to the beach or to seek out other more daring adventures. (She covered her tracks sufficiently well so that her indulgent parents, who would divorce in 1984, did not find out the truth for some time.) Always enterprising, Heidi organized several friends into a babysitting service. Later, she worked part-time in a flower shop. All this paled when she discovered a new, all-consuming hobby—betting at the racetrack. It so consumed her attention that by 16 she had quit the classroom. Her parents retaliated by enrolling her in a parochial school, but she failed there. Eventually, she earned her GED but never pursued a college degree.

In the summer of 1984, 18-year-old Heidi (drunk and high at the time) was involved in an auto accident in which her sister, Shana, almost lost an arm. Guilt-ridden by the episode, Fleiss spiraled downward. At loose ends, she worked as a waitress. Months later, she attended a party at the Beverly Hills home of Bernie Cornfield. The jet-set financier was 57 years old and was immediately drawn to high-energy Fleiss, who did nothing to disguise her interest in him and his money. They began a four-year affair that saw the couple flying around the world—to his 12th-century castle in Switzerland, to his posh pad in London, to his lush condo in the Bahamas, and for cruises aboard his luxurious yacht. Traveling in such circles gave Heidi a veneer of sophistication and an education into what makes rich people tick. Unfortunately, the high-powered Bernie could not be monogamous, and Fleiss ended the torturous relationship.

Her years with Cornfield had entrenched Heidi's interest in older gentlemen. (Said Fleiss, "After 40, they all look good to me.") While partying at Helena's, a trendy Los Angeles club, she met 50-year-old Hungarian-born Ivan Nagy. He had been a shadowy figure on the Hollywood landscape for years. He had directed a few low-budget features and episodes of TV series and had directed and/or written TV movies. More recently, he had taken offices at Columbia Pictures/Sony Studios but had no real projects in active status. Reportedly, he had turned to bookmaking and was involved in such other activities as drugs and arranging dates for young women for hire.

Five-foot, eight-inch, rail-thin Heidi and the charming Ivan immediately connected. They began a lengthy relationship that was passionate, abusive, and full of love-hate that turned to hate-hate. Besides his circle of hard-partying film industry associates, Nagy had close ties to Madam Alex, the Beverly Hills madam. By 1988, with her growing legal difficulties, Alex was under police surveillance and turned increasingly to Ivan to assist with business and personal matters. Ivan would claim that Heidi already knew Alex when he brought them together, while the procurer—who associated with, but strongly distrusted, Ivan—said, "Ivan brought Heidi here [to

Alex's now modest digs on the fringe of Beverly Hills] and got her to work for me to pay off a $450 gambling debt. He turned her out." In contrast, Fleiss insisted that manipulative Nagy received a $500 referral fee for introducing her to Alex.

In any event, Heidi began associating with calculating, eccentric Alex, helping her with errands. Sometimes Fleiss functioned as one of the madam's call girls, but she found herself ill-suited for that end of the business. After two years of apprenticeship, ambitious Fleiss, supposedly urged on by Nagy, decided to squeeze out her mentor (now that Alex was being forced out of business due to pandering charges and her probation period). Because of Alex's woes, which included diabetes and a heart condition, she was powerless to stop the takeover.

Fleiss had ideas of her own to improve business, claiming smugly that Alex "was not a hard act to follow." She and Nagy discovered that Hollywood was ripe for a new call girl enterprise, and the two quickly learned that there were huge profits to be made by catering to the high-end marketplace. To upgrade the operation, Heidi circulated at several hot L.A. clubs, often in tandem with her good friend Victoria Sellers (daughter of late comedian Peter Sellers and his actress wife Britt Ekland). Heidi made the rounds of the Monkey Bar, On the Rocks, and other such establishments, recruiting workers from the bevy of attractive, fashionable young women interested in earning extra dollars. To satisfy her upscale clientele (who typically paid $1,500 for one night of a girl's service, with Heidi's take being $900), Fleiss made sure her workers were well groomed and well mannered. Like Madam Alex, Heidi not only supplied dates to local VIPs in and out of the film industry (often using Nagy's contacts) but also developed a lucrative operation of supplying call girls both locally and abroad for well-heeled businessmen (especially from the Middle East and Asia). Reputedly, some of Heidi's employees earned up to $20,000 monthly before Fleiss's healthy cut of the gross proceeds. (Nagy would claim later that seemingly sweet Heidi could be a tough cookie in business, allegedly taping her incoming calls so that if a client proved recalcitrant about paying the hefty fee, she could remind the individual that she had documented evidence of their transaction.)

Heidi did so well in business that, in 1992, she purchased the former home of movie star Michael Douglas in the Benedict Canyon area of Beverly Hills. The estate overlooking the city was bought in her father's name. (He later claimed he didn't know of his daughter's actual line of work, thinking she had made a killing as a real estate agent. Paul Fleiss was eventually indicted on three felony counts of conspiring to defraud the IRS, ending up paying a fine, doing community service, and being placed on an extended probation.) Heidi conducted her operations from her plush new headquarters, often hosting parties to drum up new business.

In pursuing success, Fleiss became a celebrity of sorts on the Hollywood scene, known as the "Madam to the Stars." She enjoyed her nearly A-list status, which allowed her to hobnob with film executives (including Robert Evans), name actors (such as Charlie Sheen), and rock stars (like Billy Idol and Mick Jagger). The success, however, overinflated Heidi's ego. She became cocky and careless, bragging too openly about her highly rewarding illicit activities, which increasingly bothered her competitors as well as some of her former call girls and, eventually, local and federal law enforcers.

By 1993, the complex relationship between Heidi and Nagy had become increasingly bitter. There was now a bizarre, vicious triangle as Fleiss, Nagy, and their wily acquaintance, the devious Madam Alex, constantly reshuffled alliances with one another. Ever eager to gain the upper edge over the other two, each held the others in high contempt but, unfathomably, remained drawn to their past cohorts whom they proclaimed meant absolutely nothing to them.

In March of that year, Heidi was fleeced by two West Coast men who, supposedly, came to her attention via Ivan. The individuals claimed to have tapes of Fleiss's conversations with major clients, ostensibly made as part of an FBI surveillance of Fleiss's operation. She paid off the shakedown artists, only to find that these tapes were essentially worthless. From a former vice cop she learned that this wiretap "evidence" was not a product of a government surveillance but was just a scam. Nevertheless, frightened by the experience and fearing that her operation might actually be targeted by law enforcers, she went to the police.

Unlike Madam Alex or her other predecessors, Fleiss had not established herself as an informer for law enforcers. Now, in her discussions with a member of the L.A. County sheriff's department, she babbled on about her knowledge of narcotics activities. When the detective inquired whether she was still a madam, she nervously replied, "Not really. . . . Well, once in a while I still do it." Later, she had another conference with law enforcers, this time an LAPD detective and an FBI member. As before, her mix of brazenness and foolishness led her into thoughtless self-incriminating statements.

Alerted, the Beverly Hills police department put an undercover operative (Sammy Lee) on the case. Going to Jennifer Young (the daughter of late film star Gig Young and a friend of Heidi's), Lee pretended to be a horny Japanese businessman and asked to be introduced to Fleiss. This led to a sting operation in which Heidi allegedly agreed to provide call girls and narcotics for this purportedly affluent Asian customer. On June 9, 1993, when the four Fleiss employees arrived for their assignation at an L.A. hotel, they were arrested. Once in custody, the quartet agreed to cooperate with the police. Two hours later, Heidi was arrested outside her Benedict Canyon home. She put up $100,000 bail but had to face several counts of pandering/pimping and one of narcotics—all felony charges.

When news of Heidi's arrest broke, Hollywood was immediately atwitter. A few of Fleiss's high-profile Hollywood customers (usually through their secretaries) phoned the madam to commiserate over her bad luck. Other industry executives took preemptive action by publicly declaring their innocence and disassociating themselves from their "nonacquaintance" Heidi. One major film studio hired private detectives to determine where the leaks originated that, supposedly, tied some of its executives to Fleiss's service.

The media had a field day with frequently smirking Heidi. (At one point, she hired a public relations consultant to handle the mass of incoming calls from the media, producers, screenwriters, and others offering business proposals.) Initially, she seemed to revel in her burst of notoriety. At times she hinted dramatically to the press that if she took a fall, she would reveal the key names in her little black book. (Hollywood notables quaked at the mere thought of such disclosures.) On other occasions, Fleiss insisted she really had no information to reveal, which baffled those publishers who considered signing her for a tell-all book.

While awaiting trial in state court, fast-living Heidi was remanded to substance abuse treatment at the Impact Rehabilitation Center. To divert her anxiety, she operated a HeidiWear clothing shop in Pasadena, selling her self-designed clothing. Meanwhile, recriminations flew back and forth between Fleiss and her former lover Nagy. While Heidi denounced him as a traitorous informant, she continued to see him. Meanwhile, Ivan thrived on the press attention and gloried in his time in the spotlight. (In August 1993, Nagy and a female associate were arrested on pandering charges but were never brought to trial. This suggested to Fleiss and others that he had, perhaps, provided authorities with information in exchange for his liberty.) As for the ailing Madam Alex—whom Fleiss and Nagy claimed had done them dirt—she sat on the sidelines, amused by the turn of events and especially by her successor's comeuppance. (Alex died of a heart attack in July 1995.)

In an overdose of media blitz it was touted that the Heidi case (often referred to as "Heidigate") could topple top studio executives and might even bring down the regime at one or more major film companies. The press hounded Fleiss about the whereabouts of her infamous black book (actually four red Gucci day planners) that potentially could do so much damage to the film community. Later, it was revealed that the telltale books had been confiscated by the FBI. As for notables outed by her legal skirmishes, actor Charlie Sheen was one of the few to acknowledge publicly his large expenditures—$50,000—for the services of Heidi's girls.

During 1994 Heidi, looking wan and jittery, went on trial in a California courthouse for her state charges. She received a three-year sentence that later was overturned on appeal due to juror misconduct. (Said the relieved Fleiss, "Nothing was worth this kind of punishment, the dragging on.") However, her legal woes were far from over. She was later charged in federal court with money laundering, tax evasion, and attempted pandering. In January 1997, she received a 37-month sentence. After serving more than two years behind bars in Dublin, California, she was granted release in early 1999 and remanded to a halfway house. Hating the new environment, she chose to return to prison for several more months. Finally, in September 1999, Fleiss was freed. (Her federal probation ended in April 2003.)

The former flesh peddler, now yesterday's news and bankrupt, endured a difficult adjustment to her downscaled life. Wanting to enhance her looks, the 30-something personality underwent cosmetic surgery. On an Internet website (laugh.com) she provided sex tips, which were expanded into a 2001 DVD, *Sex Tips with Heidi Fleiss*. More recently, she expanded her HeidiWear line of collegiate-style clothing via a website. In 2003, the enterprising woman published *Pandering*, an unorthodox memoir documenting her rise and fall as a Hollywood madam. She also hosted a San Diego–based radio show, *Sex Advice with Heidi Fleiss*, and opened a boutique (Hollywood Madam) on Hollywood Boulevard. Meanwhile, she had a high-profile abusive relationship with actor Tom Sizemore that saw the battling couple breaking up and reuniting frequently. (Ironically, at one point during their explosive liaison, he reportedly cheated on Heidi with hookers.) Later, after their destructive association ended, Fleiss obtained a protective order against the hot-tempered performer. In August 2003, Sizemore was found guilty of domestic violence, criminal threats, and vandalism against Heidi. He was sentenced to jail time for his criminal activity.

Looking back on her high life, Fleiss has said, "Every day I would think, 'Can life get any better?' And it would." Concerning her contretemps with the law, Heidi admitted, "Sometimes I can't even identify with this outcome." Reflecting on her plush years as Hollywood's favorite madam, she wondered, "Damn! How did I ruin the best job on earth?" What had she learned from her check-ered past? "People will do anything for money. And I don't mean sex. They'll do *anything.*" As for sexual coupling, Fleiss says, "I don't really like sex anymore. I have jewelry now."

O. J. Simpson: The Trial of the Century

"First, everyone understand I had nothing to do with Nicole's murder, I loved her, always have and always will. If we had a problem it's because I loved her so much. . . . I think of my life and feel I've done most of the right things. So why did I end up like this? I can't go on. No matter what the outcome, people will look and point. I can't take that. I can't subject my children to that. This way, they can move on and go on with their lives. . . . Don't feel sorry for me. I've had a great life, great friends. Please think of the real O.J. and not this lost person. Thanks for making my life special. I hope I helped yours."

—O. J. SIMPSON, ON JUNE 15, 1994

As the world looked on in stunned amazement in the mid-1990s, America underwent a traumatic time of truth concerning pow-erful racial issues. It all revolved around the June 12, 1994, murders of Nicole Brown Simpson and her friend Ronald Lyle Goldman out-side her luxurious four-bedroom Spanish-style condo in Brentwood, California. Charged with the brutal double homicide was football legend/movie actor/product spokesman O. J. Simpson. Because the victims were Caucasians and the alleged killer (Nicole's ex-hus-band and the father of their two children) was African American, the racial issue immediately came into full play.

During this "Trial of the Century"—and for a change that descriptor was totally appropriate—spectators around the globe found themselves engaged in heated discussions as to the defen-dant's guilt or innocence of these gruesome killings. What super-charged the intense, ongoing debates (which still continue to this day) was that many people were swayed, to one degree or another, by conscious or subconscious racial bias. This prejudicial factor became even clearer on October 3, 1995, when the jury's verdict was announced. The public's strong reaction to the court's decision proved to be largely divided along ethnic lines.

As the prosecution of Simpson delineated, despite civil rights legislation, bloody riots, and changing times, black-versus-white issues were still a potent force in the United States. These matters gave added levels of complexity to this hugely controversial murder trial, which was televised for all the world to watch, analyze, and debate. Depending on one's viewpoint, the outcome of this high-impact, lengthy three-ring legal circus was disgraceful and downright scandalous or a triumph of the minority over the establishment.

Orenthal James Simpson was born on July 9, 1947, in San Francisco, the third of four children of a couple originally from Louisiana: James Lee Simpson (a sometimes cook, later a Baptist deacon) and his wife, Eunice Durton (an orderly, later a psychiatric technician, at San Francisco General Hospital). As a youngster, Orenthal was stricken with rickets. Because the condition caused him to walk wobbly, he wore homemade leg braces. By the time Simpson was four, his father had left the household, leaving Eunice to bring up her offspring in a rough housing project located in the city's Potrero Hill district. Because Mrs. Simpson worked long hours, the children received little supervision.

Determined not to be a cripple, the boy kept himself mobile, even forcing himself to run, whether participating in baseball or football. As a member of a local street gang, the Persian Warriors, he was constantly on the move—from the police, teachers, and the tough ghetto environment. (Years later, Simpson said, "The cat who grows up in a lower-income environment, he's gonna try a little of everything.")

At Galileo High School, Simpson was an All-City football player. Deciding against joining the army, Orenthal attended City College of San Francisco. As a skillful running back for the campus team, he was named Junior College All-American. With his athletic accomplishments, "Juice" (his sports nickname) was recruited by the prestigious University of Southern California on a sports scholarship.

In his second season with the USC Trojans, his stellar accomplishments earned him the prestigious Heisman Trophy. In the NFL's 1969 draft, Simpson signed with the Buffalo Bills with a $400,000 four-year contract.

In June 1967, O.J. wed his high school sweetheart, statuesque Marguerite Whitley, age 18. Their daughter Arnelle was born in 1968 and son, Jason, in 1970. Over the years, the couple's differences became more apparent; she enjoyed living in their upscale California house with their children and preferred her husband at home more often. When he renegotiated his pact with the Buffalo Bills and was away even more, she grew increasingly frustrated. With his good looks, six-foot, one-inch Simpson had no difficulty in finding romantic distractions elsewhere.

In 1977, 30-year-old Simpson left the Buffalo Bills and played his final two seasons of pro football with the San Francisco 49ers. By then, O.J. had tried his luck in show business. During an off-season break, he made his screen debut in *The Klansman* (1974), which led to more film and TV acting assignments. When not hobnobbing with A-list celebrities, Simpson was a high-priced TV sports commentator and won fat endorsement deals.

During this high-flying period, Simpson, with his carefully crafted image and friendliness, was one of America's favorite personalities. However, his marriage was badly faltering. To help patch up their differences the couple had a third child, Aaren, born in 1977, but by September 1978 the Simpsons had separated, and in March 1978, the star athlete filed for divorce. While the couple's lawyers were negotiating a marital division of O.J.'s impressive net worth, their almost-two-year-old daughter, Aaren, died of respiratory failure, having tumbled into the family's swimming pool a week earlier.

No longer a professional athlete, Simpson focused on his lucrative careers as TV sports commentator, product endorser, and actor. Very much the playboy-about-town, O.J. had a string of quick romances. A more serious encounter was with blond Nicole Brown, a svelte waitress at The Daisy, a chic Beverly Hills club. She was an

18-year-old (born in Frankfurt, Germany, her mother's homeland) who had grown up in affluent surroundings in Orange County, California. The interracial pair began dating in 1978 and within months were living together. As time passed, besides his Tudor-style mansion on Brentwood's North Rockingham Avenue, the couple stayed at his Laguna Beach oceanfront place or, later, at his co-op on New York's fashionable Upper East Side. The attractive pair led an active social life, deflecting any slurs about their interracial relationship. The duo finally married in February 1985, the same year Simpson was inducted into the Football Hall of Fame. The couple had two children: Sydney (1985) and Justin (1988). Meanwhile, whether on the road or back in L.A., O.J. remained an enthusiastic party animal.

Simpson's sagging film career received a big boost when he participated in *The Naked Gun: From the Files of Police Squad!* (1988), cast as a bumbling police detective. The following year, in real life, he was on the opposite side of the law. After coming home from a holiday gathering in the early hours of January 1, 1989, Nicole frantically summoned the L.A. police to the Simpsons' Brentwood compound. In her 3:00 A.M. 911 call, she reported being the victim of verbal and physical abuse from her husband. (This was the ninth such occasion that the law had come to the Simpsons' home because of alleged domestic violence.) This time, the mainstream celebrity (whom Nicole said kept a lot of guns at home) was charged with spousal abuse. He pleaded no contest. As a result, he paid $470 in fines, donated $500 to a battered women's shelter, purportedly did 120 hours of community service, underwent psychiatric counseling, and was given a two-year probation.

Despite the outcome of the much-publicized 1989 spousal abuse episode, matters did not improve between the Simpsons. In March 1992, Nicole finally filed for divorce, which was granted that October. Subsequently, O.J. attempted to revive their relationship, although he was dating actress/model Paula Barbieri and Nicole was seeing other men. During this period, on October 25, 1993, a distraught Nicole called the police to report that her ex-spouse was outside—and then inside—her condo screaming obscenities and threatening her with physical violence.

On Sunday, June 12, 1994, O.J. and Nicole attended—separately—a dance recital in West L.A. for nine-year-old Sydney. Afterward, without O.J., Nicole and her group went out for dinner. When she returned to her condo at 875 South Bundy Drive later that evening, she realized she had left her sunglasses at the restaurant. She called, and Ron Goldman, a waiter there, offered to return them to her. (Chicago-born Goldman, 25, had first met Nicole at a Brentwood gym where they each worked out. The two became friends, and he, reportedly, sometimes visited her home.)

Later that Sunday evening, somewhere between 10:20 and 11:00 P.M., Nicole and Ron were viciously slashed to death. Their corpses were found outside the entranceway to Nicole's split-level condo. O.J. later claimed that he was home at the time of the killings waiting for an airport limousine to take him to LAX for a red-eye flight to the Midwest to attend a prearranged business function involving his chores for Hertz. The plane reached Chicago at 5:30 A.M. CST. An hour or so later, in his room at the O'Hare Plaza Hotel, the LAPD called to advise him of the death of Nicole and Goldman.

After making several calls (including one to his L.A. attorney Howard Weitzman), Simpson left Chicago at 7:41 A.M. CST. By 11:08 A.M. PST he was back in L.A. The police met O.J. at his home at 360 North Rockingham Avenue and escorted him to headquarters for questioning. Later that day, he was released. By this point, the killings had become top priority with the media, who were battling for statements from Simpson and law enforcers.

On June 16, O.J. attended Nicole's funeral, accompanied by their children, along with members of the Simpson and Brown households. The next day, matters heated up when Simpson was charged with first-degree murder and informed that a warrant had been issued for his immediate arrest. (Among the gathered circumstantial evidence were such items as a trail of blood droplets on the south driveway of O.J.'s home, a bloodied glove on the nearby walkway, and unexplained blood spatterings in Simpson's vehicle parked on the street near his house.) While O.J.'s lawyer was upstairs at Simpson's home talking out details of the surrender, the accused, along with A. C. Cowlings (a childhood pal of O.J.'s who was also a former pro football player), fled in Simpson's white Ford Bronco. This led to the much-televised several-hour slow police chase along L.A. freeways. Shortly after 8:00 P.M., the distraught Simpson was back at his Brentwood home where he quietly surrendered to the police. (Meanwhile, the cops had possession of a "farewell" note from O.J., dated June 15, which suggested the suspect might have been contemplating suicide.)

On June 20, Simpson pleaded not guilty to two charges of first-degree murder. Four days later, in the midst of the grand jury investigation, the judge (Cecil Mills) halted the proceeding, insisting that the overblown media coverage had tainted the panel. On July 8, following a preliminary hearing, Judge Kathleen Kennedy-Powell ordered the defendant to stand trial on the murder charges. By then, Simpson had hired his "dream team" of high-priced attorneys, which included Robert Shapiro, F. Lee Bailey, and Alan Dershowitz, with African American Johnnie Cochran coming aboard a few weeks later. Also during this time, the mother of Ron Goldman filed a wrongful death civil suit against O.J., accusing him of murdering her son. (In May 1995, Goldman's father and sister also filed a wrongful death civil lawsuit against Simpson. O.J. lost both civil actions and the plaintiffs were awarded sizable damages.)

Appreciating the extreme sensitivity of this criminal case—involving a celebrity-defendant and the potentially explosive racial issue (in the wake of the 1992 L.A. riots following the Rodney King trial)—the district attorney's office, on September 9, 1994, announced that the prosecution would *not* seek the death penalty but rather a life sentence without parole. The jury panel was chosen out of a pool of 1,000, dropping a great many who indicated preconceived biases in the case. (The selected jury consisted of eight women and four men. Eight members were black, two were Hispanic, and the remaining two were reportedly of mixed race. Thereafter, the selection of twelve alternates took five weeks. During the lengthy trial, ten jurors would be replaced, leaving two alternates. Of the final composition of the jury, ten were female. All told, nine were black, two white, and one Hispanic.)

In early January 1995, with the televised courtroom proceedings preempting regular programming on several TV channels, the defense removed its challenge to the introduction of DNA evidence, while the prosecution withdrew 18 of 62 allegations of spousal abuse. On January 24, Deputy DA Marcia Clark, a Caucasian, began her opening statements before Judge Lance A. Ito.

As the notorious case proceeded, the jury visited the crime scene. In March, LAPD detective Mark Fuhrman, a former marine and veteran lawman, testified about finding two bloody gloves (one at the crime scene, its alleged mate at Simpson's home). During cross-examination, the defense team introduced "proof" of the white witness's racial bias, which countered Fuhrman's denial of such on-the-job prejudice. This point was integral to the defense's theory that Simpson was a victim of a racially motivated police frame-up. (Later in the proceedings, there was a hotly contested battle between the prosecution and defense as to whether Judge Ito was biased because on the tape-recorded evidence, there were alleged slurring remarks made by Fuhrman years back against, among others, Judge Ito's wife, an LAPD captain. Eventually, a few excerpts of the tapes were heard by the panel. Thereafter, Fuhrman invoked his Fifth Amendment rights against self-incrimination and refused to continue to testify.)

The racial issue got further play in April when a dismissed panel member charged publicly that the deputies supervising the sequestered jurors' activities outside the courtroom were, among other claimed wrongdoings, showing partiality to whites over blacks. Several days later, there was a jury "rebellion" in which several panelists appeared at the downtown courthouse wearing black in protest of Judge Ito's removal of a trio of deputies from jury detail in response to the racial bias accusations.

One of the most graphic moments of this headline-grabbing trial occurred on June 15, when Christopher Darden, the African American colead prosecutor, asked Simpson to put on the bloody gloves. Wearing sheer surgical gloves, Simpson stood before the jury and attempted to comply. However, after much pulling and tugging, he announced that his hands were too large to fit into the gloves.

On September 7, it was finally announced that the defendant would *not* testify on his own behalf. Eleven days later, the prosecution conditionally rested its case, followed, days later, by Judge Ito's instructing the jury that they had the option of returning a finding of second-degree murder. On September 22, when the court asked O.J. to confirm that he had waived his right to testify, he made a startling statement: "As much as I would like to address some of the misrepresentations made about myself and Nicole concerning our life together, I'm mindful of the mood and the stamina of this jury. . . . I have confidence . . . that they'll find—as the record stands now—that I did not, would not, and could not have committed this crime. I have four kids—two kids I haven't seen in a year. They asked me every week, 'Dad, how much longer?' . . . I want this trial over."

On October 2, after impassioned closing statements by both sides (which again played on racial bias), the long-sequestered jury began deliberations. Having endured months of courtroom proceedings, the panel reached its verdict in a surprisingly short four hours. Because it was already late in the afternoon, Judge Ito sequestered the panel at their hotel for one final night. At 10:00 the next morning, O. J. Simpson was found not guilty on all counts. The decision was watched by 142 million TV viewers.

Depending on one's interpretation of the presented evidence and one's sympathies, the acquittal of O.J. Simpson was greatly reassuring or, in contrast, horrifying news. Forever encapsulated as part of 20th-century history were the strong reactions of the defendant, prosecution, and defense as the jury foreperson announced the long-awaited verdict. Among the many people interviewed following the conclusion of the trial was Frederic Goldman, the father of one of the victims. He said, "This prosecution team did not lose today. I deeply believe that this country lost today. Justice was not served." (Many observers found it ironic that during his career and personal life, O.J. always presented a homogeneous, nonethnic image, while in this murder case his defense team introduced the race card, allying him strongly with the black community.)

In the wake of the highly controversial trial, the financially beleaguered Simpson, who had lost his lucrative endorsement deals and had huge fees to pay for his legal representation and the lost wrongful death suits, eventually relocated to Florida. There, he had recurring brushes with the law (both as victim and defendant) and pursued various short-lasting romantic relationships. Said the "celebrity" survivor, "I'm a very alive person. I don't like to ever refer to myself as an ex-anything. I try not to look back."

However, the rest of the world would not soon forget the scandalous O. J. Simpson case that had put the American criminal justice system on trial and caused such a tremendous racial backlash.

Tupac Shakur: Dying Too Young

"People need to let him rest in peace, let that rumor rest in peace. Because it's a hard pill to swallow, people don't want to accept it. So they gonna keep that myth or that philosophy goin' on as long as they can because his music lives on and he's a legend. . . . When you make legendary music, people don't want to believe you're gone. . . . "

—RAPPER SNOOP DOGG, IN 1997

For many enthusiasts, rapper/movie star Tupac Shakur not only spoke articulately for his generation but was also a lasting pop culture icon. As with Elvis Presley's untimely death, Tupac's 1996 murder froze the talented gangsta rapper in superstar mode. As such, Shakur's CDs—especially fresh compilations of previously unreleased cuts—continued to sell well years after his passing. For many fans, the myth of this prolific late-20th-century idol is irretrievably intertwined with his still unresolved killing.

With his shaved head, soulful eyes, and resplendent jewelry, Tupac cascaded through his rough-and-tumble life, frequently—and unapologetically—on the wrong side of the law. While several other contemporary African American musicians (including Snoop Dogg, 50 Cent, R. Kelly, Juvenile, and Big Lurch) have had legal brushes, none had the incredible charisma of the highly charged, handsome Shakur. As his fans constantly pointed out, Tupac always knew that his lifestyle doomed him to a short existence, a prophecy fulfilled when he died violently at age 25.

Similar to '50s movie rebel James Dean, Tupac left a relatively small body of movies and filmed interviews. This limited footage, however, confirms Shakur's magnetism. It also reflects his volatile nature and bada** attitude, traits cemented by his difficult ghetto years on the East and West Coasts. As a singer and composer Shakur excelled at gangsta rap, which not only mirrored his explosive lifestyle but inspired the five-foot, seven-inch, muscular artist to expand his reputation as a real-life thug. The much-tattooed Tupac, who bore battle scars from past confrontations, found no shame and little repentance for time spent behind bars.

Other rappers (such as Notorious B.I.G. and Jam Master Jay) met sudden, brutal ends. Like Tupac, their killings remain unsolved by law enforcers. Especially in Shakur's case, speculation and criticism regarding the police's failure to nab his murderers have prompted books, film documentaries, and a steady stream of Internet chat discussions. To this day, many angry Tupac adherents wonder why, with so many potential witnesses to Shakur's slaughter on a crowded Las Vegas street and with the availability of high-tech forensic tools, this homicide still remains a shameful riddle that begs to be answered once and for all.

He was born Lesane Parish Crooks on June 16, 1971, in New York City. His North Carolina–born mother, Alice Faye Williams, had been a founding member of the Black Panthers, an African American activist party to which her husband, Lumumba Abdul Shakur, belonged. She was among the 21 Panthers arrested in April 1969 on conspiracy charges regarding the planned detonation of certain public areas of New York City. While out on bail, she dated Bill Garland, another founder of the Panthers. She became pregnant with his child, which led to Shakur's divorcing her. Following her stay in the Women's House of Detention in Greenwich Village, expectant Alice served as her own lawyer. As a result of her courtroom astuteness, she and 13 other codefendants were acquitted in May 1971.

Soon after Tupac's birth, Garland and Alice split. When the boy was still quite young, she married Mutulu Shakur, another Black Panther. She became Afeni Shakur, and her child was now called Tupac Amaru. (He was named after a long-ago martyred Inca chief, and his new moniker meant "Shining Serpent.") Having moved to the Bronx where she was on welfare, Afeni gave birth to Tupac's half sister, Sekyiwa. Meanwhile, as a result of being accused of participating in a 1971 Brinks truck robbery (in which three victims perished), Mutulu went underground. He was captured in 1986 and sentenced to 60 years behind bars. Another "family" member was Elmer "Geronimo" Pratt. He was a Black Panther deputy minister and the boy's godfather. He earned life imprisonment in the early '70s for the murder of a young Caucasian teacher. (In 1997, his conviction was overturned and he was freed.) All these family figures would be celebrated by Tupac in his rap lyrics.

Afeni and her offspring remained in Harlem, often staying in homeless shelters or with relatives and friends. By 1983, Afeni had a new lover, known as "Legs," a longtime lawbreaker who introduced her to crack. Before long, Legs was jailed for credit card fraud, where he died of a drug-induced heart attack. Tupac was strongly affected by Legs's removal from the family.

Although Tupac thought he wanted to be a revolutionary when he grew up, by age 12 he was writing poetry. Afeni enrolled him in Harlem's 127th Street Ensemble where he appeared in a stage production of *A Raisin in the Sun* at the Apollo Theater.

Afeni and her children moved to Baltimore in 1986, where they scraped by in low-income housing. With his mother's encouragement, Tupac enrolled at the Baltimore High School for the

Arts, where he majored in dance and acting and wrote rap numbers. When a youngster died in a gang-related shooting, a frightened Afeni shipped her children to stay with a family friend in Marin City, California, located across the bay from Oakland. She was unaware that her youngsters were now stuck in the "Jungle," a slum as bad as—or worse than—the one in which they had been living back in Maryland. Tupac was deeply upset about leaving the High School for the Arts, claiming this move was "the point where I got off track."

When Afeni joined her offspring, they found low-income government housing. In this precarious environment, she became severely crack-addicted. Unable to cope with his mother's dangerous habit, Tupac moved in with pals in an abandoned building. By age 17, Shakur, a voracious reader, had dropped out of high school. He survived by working odd jobs, including dealing drugs.

As a great music lover, Tupac became involved in the Bay Area hip-hop scene. He began writing song lyrics, continuing to use his rapper name, MC New York. He and pals formed a rap group (Two from the Crew). A few years later, in 1989, Shakur was hired as a dancer/roadie for Digital Underground. He sang on the group's early 1991 album (*This Is an EP Release*) and, that same year, made his solo debut as a gangsta rapper on his album *2Pacalypse Now*.

During his Digital Underground period, Tupac made his film debut in *Nothing but Trouble* (1991), billed as 2Pac Shakur. He made his cinema mark playing a punk in *Juice* (1992). The rising screen personality took his celluloid role to heart, becoming more thug-like in real life. (Tupac had the words "Thug Life" tattooed across his stomach.)

In the spring of 1992, a Texas state trooper was murdered by a young man who said Shakur's song "Souja's Story" (from *2Pacalypse Now*) had prompted his violent deed. The resultant uproar led to an attempt to ban the sale of Shakur's recording, with Vice President Dan Quayle insisting that Shakur's album "has no place in our society." The hullabaloo only boosted album sales and greatly-enhanced Tupac's "outlaw" status.

In the early '90s, girl-hungry and weed-smoking Shakur was based first in L.A. and then in Atlanta, Georgia. Just as his music and film careers were fast rising, so too were his legal problems. He was a defendant in cases around the country involving a variety of allegations: slapping a woman who had asked for an autograph; attempting to bash another rapper with a baseball bat while at a concert; and inciting a near riot in his nightclub performance (during the skirmish a female patron was paralyzed by a stray bullet). In another high-profile scuffle settled out-of-court by his record label (Interscope), an innocent youngster had been killed in the crossfire between one of Shakur's posse and a rival gang member.

Through legal maneuvers and/or healthy settlement fees—or sometimes pleading to a reduced misdemeanor charge—Shakur maneuvered through his legal entanglements. Then, in Atlanta, on October 31, 1993, 22-year-old Tupac was mixed up in the shooting of two off-duty lawmen. According to witnesses, Shakur and his pals had returned fire on the plainclothes officers when they shot at Tupac's vehicle. The case was dismissed when it was learned that not only had the policemen been drinking and instigated the gunfire but also the weapon used by one of the cops had been confiscated previously in a drug raid and then had disappeared from the police evidence room.

At the same time Shakur had an ongoing feud with filmmakers Albert and Allen Hughes, who had fired him for displaying a vicious temper during rehearsals for the movie *Menace II Society* (1993). Months later, Shakur got into a fight with the brothers at a videotaping. The rapper, originally charged with carrying a loaded, concealed weapon, was eventually convicted of misdemeanor assault and battery. In March 1994, Tupac was sentenced to 15 days in L.A. County jail and to an equal time of community service.

Between court appearances, Shakur composed/recorded numerous songs as well and starred in more films. Meanwhile, in November 1993, the boastful bad-boy star got into fresh difficulties from his encounter with a 19-year-old woman at a downtown Manhattan club. She supposedly gave him oral sex on the dance floor, with the two then adjourning to his classy hotel for more fun and games. A few days later, the female returned to his accommodations, allegedly to retrieve personal items that she'd left behind. She claimed that Tupac and three of his associates sexually assaulted her. Three of the quartet (the fourth had left the scene earlier) were charged with rape and sodomy. After plea-bargaining, one of the trio was released, while Tupac and the other remaining defendant were prosecuted for first-degree sexual abuse.

While out on bail in New York City, Tupac made a late-night visit to the Quad Recording Studios to carry out a last-minute deal to record on another's album. As he and his crew (including pal Randy "Stretch" Walker) entered the lobby of a Times Square building on November 30, 1994, Shakur was shot five times and robbed of $40,000 worth of jewelry by two assailants. Despite his severe wounds, Tupac miraculously survived. (The case remained unsolved, especially after Walker, a witness to the crimes, was murdered in Queens on November 30, 1995.)

The next day, hours after surgery, Tupac checked out of the hospital, determined to hear the court verdict in his case. On December 1, Shakur was acquitted on the sodomy and rape charges but was convicted of sexual abuse. In February 1995, he was sentenced to up to four and a half years behind bars. Once incarcerated, Tupac announced that prison was changing his mind about his thug life. He claimed to be on a more righteous path and had stopped using marijuana. Meanwhile, he theorized that a former rapper associate, Biggie Smalls (Notorious B.I.G.) and Bad Boys Records entrepreneur Sean "Puffy" Combs, among others, were involved in his near-fatality. During his prison time, the musician married college student Keisha Morris, purportedly to have conjugal visits. (Later, the union was annulled.)

While in prison, Tupac's visitors included L.A. attorney David Kenner and his 315-pound client Marion "Suge" Knight Jr. The latter, born and raised in Compton, south of L.A., was a former college football player who had once been a bodyguard for singer Bobby Brown. Thereafter, hulking, six-foot, three-inch Knight, a very confrontational, intimidating personality, had magically raised the funds to cofound and own the L.A.-based Death Row Records. In exchange for Knight's posting of his $1.4 million bail, Shakur agreed to make three albums for the West Coast label. As part of the arrangement, Kenner was appointed Shakur's lawyer in the appeal process. The day Tupac was released from prison he flew to L.A. in a chartered jet to record for his new "family."

Entering into a highly prolific period of writing and recording in which he lived high, wide, and handsome (including acquiring a home for his mother through Knight's funding), Shakur said, "I promised him 'Suge, I'm gonna make Death Row the biggest label in the whole world. . . . I'm gonna take it to the next level." His self-assessment proved accurate when his double CD *All Eyez on Me* became one of 1996's biggest hits.

On other matters, Tupac's inflated boasts were open to debate. He claimed to have been intimate with Biggie Small's wife (urban rock singer Faith Evans), which she hotly disputed. The growing battle of words, rap, and machismo between Tupac and Biggie was paralleled by each individual's record label (i.e., Puffy Combs's Bad Boys Records in New York and Suge Knight's Death Row Records in L.A.). Not forgetting his near-fatality, Shakur, along with Snoop Dogg, made the video "2 of Americaz Most Wanted" (1996), in which representations of Biggie and Puffy are punished for having set up Tupac. In September of that year Shakur was in Manhattan for the MTV Music Video Awards where he got into a scuffle with East Coast rappers.

When not in the recording studios or vacationing in Hawaii or Mexico with Suge, the constantly in motion Shakur made three more films: *Bullet* (1996), *Gridlock'd* (1996), and *Gang Related* (1997). He also moved into a Death Row–leased Calabasas estate (in the West San Fernando Valley) with his steady girlfriend, Kidada Jones, the daughter of musician/entrepreneur Quincy Jones and onetime *Mod Squad* TV star Peggy Lipton.

In the months before his fateful last trip to Las Vegas, Shakur had repeatedly told several people that he did not expect to live to old age. In the meantime, he founded Euphanasia, a firm geared to handle his music and film careers. (It suggested to some observers that Tupac intended to move away from Death Row Records.)

On Saturday evening, September 7, 1996, a heavyweight match between Mike Tyson and Bruce Seldon was held at the MGM Grand Hotel in Las Vegas. Suge Knight was in town for the sporting event. Tupac, a friend of Tyson (with whom he envisioned starting a charity to help disadvantaged youths), was a last-minute attendee. (He had originally planned to go back to Atlanta but had been persuaded by Knight to attend the boxing competition.) He and Knight had front-row seats for the match. That evening, in less than two minutes, Tyson defeated Seldon.

As Tupac, Suge, and their entourage (including bodyguards) left the hotel through the casino, they scuffled with 22-year-old Orlando Anderson, an Orange County gang member who had been involved in a past assault on a Death Row employee. (The melee was captured on hotel video surveillance tapes.) Once security guards broke up the fracas, Shakur, Knight, and the others headed in their fancy cars to the Luxor Hotel where Shakur was staying with Kidada Jones. He changed into something more casual, but he did not wear his usual flak jacket as protection against being shot because he thought things were cool in this party town and, in this arid climate, it was too warm. The group then headed to Paradise Valley Township and to Knight's expensive estate where some of the contingent relaxed while the others changed outfits.

Around 10:00 P.M., following drinks, the group left for Club 662 for a benefit party (at which Tupac would perform) to celebrate the boxing victory and to raise money for charity. Suge had a stake in the nightspot.

Rather than drive with his chief bodyguard, ex-marine and former southern California reserve police officer Frank Alexander, Tupac rode with Suge in a rented black 750 BMW sedan. After heading along Las Vegas Boulevard, they drove along the Strip. In Knight's car, the sound system was blasting, the sunroof pulled back, and the car's dark-tinted windows open. Many along the heavily packed street recognized the rapper and his label employer as they shouted to one another above the din of music. Because of the boxing match, the police were out in force, and several lawmen were already stationed at Club 662.

The fleet was moving east on Flamingo Road shortly after 11:00 P.M. when it stopped for a red light at Koval Lane (not far from the Maxim Hotel). Suge's car was in the middle of the group of cars in their party. While waiting at the intersection, a white, late-model Cadillac with California license plates containing three or four African American men pulled up to the right of Knight's vehicle. An armed assailant in the backseat shoved his pistol out the rear left window and began firing. More than a dozen rounds were discharged, with five bullets penetrating the passenger door and others shattering the windshield. (It was alleged, but later disputed, that some members of Knight's entourage had returned fire.)

Although Knight and Tupac spotted the Cadillac drawing into range, everything happened too fast. Shakur tried to dive into the back of the car, but in the process bullets caught the singer in his middle and lower body. Meanwhile, Knight yanked at his friend, shouting, "Get down!" It was in this mode that a glass (or bullet) fragment hit Suge in the back of his neck. When the bursts of gunfire were over, the rapper had suffered hits in the chest, hip, and left hand.

The driver of the white Cadillac floored his gas pedal, and his car screeched off, taking a right turn into Koval Lane. An old yellow Cadillac (hypothesized to be part of the attack group) followed right behind the Caddy. Meanwhile, although Suge had a cell phone in the car, he didn't call for help. Instead, he made a quick U-turn on Flamingo Boulevard (despite his car having two flat tires and the heavy traffic) and drove erratically eastward, followed by the rest of his group. For some reason, Knight headed back onto the packed Strip, where police vehicles caught up with them after Suge's vehicle rammed into a curb. Thinking this caravan might be the shooting suspects, the cops demanded, at gunpoint, that Suge and the others get out of their cars and lie down on the ground.

Minutes later paramedics arrived, and the profusely bleeding Tupac (sprawled out in the backseat of the BMW) and Suge were rushed to University Medical Center. As the ambulance left the scene, Shakur, having great difficulty breathing, said, "I'm dyin', man."

For the next six days, the hospital did its best (including removing his right lung) to save Tupac's life. However, Shakur had been too badly injured and had lost too much blood. He remained in a coma for several days before expiring at 4:03 P.M. on Friday, September 13.

The police investigation of Shakur's murder posed many questions that remain unresolved, especially since none at the scene of the crime came forward to describe the killer. In the wake of Tupac's death there was a round of gang-related homicides in the Compton–Los Angeles area. This killing spree soon spread to the East Coast, where 19-year-old Yafeu Fula was shot down in Irvington, New Jersey, weeks after Shakur's death. (Fula, who had been in the car behind Tupac's that crucial night, had been the one person who had been somewhat willing to help the police identify the culprit. Somehow, he had been allowed to leave Las Vegas, and he died before providing authorities with an official description or identification.) Next came the also unsolved murder of Biggie Smalls on March 9, 1997, when he was in L.A. for an industry award show. Later, on May 29, 1998, Orlando Anderson, who had been involved in the MGM Grand Hotel scuffle and to many people's thinking was a chief candidate as Tupac's murderer, was killed during a clash at an L.A. car wash. (He had been only briefly interviewed by Las Vegas police, who found no substantial evidence to tie him to Shakur's execution.)

As for Suge Knight, he repeatedly denied recurrent rumors that suggested he was, somehow, involved in Tupac's death. (One theory alleged that Knight owed the late rapper several million dollars of recording revenue; another hypothesis suggested that a deceased recording artist was more valuable as a martyred label employee than as a living defector who, perhaps, planned to work away from Death Row. In contrast, another speculation put Biggie Smalls and

Compton-based Southside Crips gang members as the culprits, with some commentators hypothesizing that Biggie Smalls had paid the death crew to do the job.)

Whatever the actuality behind Tupac's elimination, in late February 1998, Knight was sentenced to a nine-year prison term for his involvement in the Orlando Anderson fracas, which was determined to be a parole violation for him. While Knight served his sentence, he dealt with a suit from Tupac's mother over disputed royalty payments and rights to her late son's music. Suge was released in 2001, at which time he created Tha Row Records as his new recording label. Thereafter, he continued to get into legal jams for parole violations.

Whoever the actual culprit was, Shakur certainly was a celebrity victim of the ongoing gang warfare that crowds the streets of L.A. and also invades the rough-and-tumble rap music industry. To date, Tupac's very public execution remains officially unsolved. Thanks to Shakur's continued record sales and such new films as the documentary *Tupac: Resurrection* (2003), Shakur still remains much in the limelight.

Robert Blake: Baretta on the Loose

"On a scale of 1 to 10, I would say interest will be in the 8-to-10 range. The sex angle of the case will bring in even more viewers. Celebrity combined with the possibility that it might turn into a death-penalty case will really generate interest. Whenever the public learns about the dark side of a high-profile person, whether it's a sports figure or a religious figure or someone in their own community, there's interest."

—MARLENE DANN, COURT TV EXECUTIVE, MAY 2002,
ON TV INTEREST IN THE ROBERT BLAKE TRIAL

Since the mid-1990s' O. J. Simpson double-homicide trial, all murder cases involving celebrities have taken on a whole new media slant. By comparison, they make the press's handling of such earlier celebrity-capers as the 1958 Lana Turner–Johnny Stompanato–Cheryl Crane murder trial seem simplistic.

In assessing how the news media will treat a homicide case involving show business notables, there are definite factors to be considered. The April 2002 arrest of movie star Robert Blake for the 2001 shooting of his wife, Bonny Lee Bakley, led the *New York Times*' Alex Kuczynski to analyze, "Like good theater, public drama requires readily identifiable heroes or villains. They are in limited supply here: the family lawyer . . . described her [Bakley] as a small-time criminal who wanted a famous last name so desperately that she rejected a prenuptial agreement with Mr. Blake that required her to use his birth name. . . . As for Mr. Blake, he embodies all that Hollywood fears and loathes: a once-famous actor now aging into a bad face lift, whose reappearance is an unwanted reminder of what happens after a celebrity is discarded."

On the other hand, there was an 11-month window between Bonny's killing and Robert's arrest that allowed the press to feed the public's interest in the case. Along the way, much was written about the systematic gathering of evidence by the Los Angeles police department and how the district attorney's office was methodically structuring its prosecution against Blake. It was touted this was in reaction to the way matters were mishandled in the circus surrounding the O. J. Simpson trial. As such, the slow buildup in the Bakley investigation helped to create tremendous public curiosity as to Blake's eventual courtroom fate.

Then too, according to Steven Mikulan (*LA Weekly*), in recent years "we've become hooked on the crimestyles of the rich and famous. The media created an appetite for this kind of thing, and now the public needs—demands—that it be fed a celebrity every now and then. TV and the tabloids oblige by building up the suspense and importance surrounding whatever Hollywood miscreants are handy. . . ."

In Blake's case, there was a blurring between his professional and private self. His several convincing tough-guy acting roles caused factions of the public to assume that they revealed aspects of the actual man. In addition, the press played up perceived parallels between plot points of his acting assignments and the real-life murder, seemingly to suggest his guilt.

Michael James Vijencio Gubitosi was born on September 18, 1933, in Nutley, New Jersey, the third child of James and Elizabeth Gubitosi. Because the Depression-weary family was in financial straits, Mrs. Gubitosi had undergone at least two abortions before the unwanted Michael ("Mickey") was born. To make matters worse, the mother reputedly had an affair with her husband's brother, with Michael the product of this illicit relationship. If true, it explained some of the extreme resentment that James displayed toward his younger son.

The father, a blacksmith, had a burning love for show business. To improve their near-poverty existence, Mr. Gubitosi took his offspring to local parks where he'd strum his guitar while the kids sang and danced—and passersby tossed them coins. In later years, a bitter Blake compared his first performing efforts to that of a monkey on a chain working for an organ grinder.

Hoping for increased show business opportunities, the Gubitosi family moved to Hollywood in 1938. While the mother worked as a domestic (later a seamstress), the father labored as a gardener and drove his children to auditions. Before long, Mickey was hired as a regular for MGM's Our Gang comedy short subjects. The father used some of his boy's earnings to open a hardware business.

Now employing the professional name of Bobby Blake, the youngster appeared in feature films such as 1942's *Mokey*. In 1944, he joined the Red Ryder Western movie series. During these busy years, the boy lived a split emotional existence. On the soundstages he felt loved. In contrast, his home life was hellish. His father was a physically abusive alcoholic, and Robert was his chief target. When not being punched, forced to eat from a bowl on the floor, locked in closets, or tied up and left under the porch for long stretches, Blake was ignored at the expense of his less-talented siblings. (Robert also claimed being sexually abused during childhood.) Compounding the situation, Mrs. Gubitosi remained aloof to the boy's plight. In reaction to his dysfunctional upbringing, Robert developed an aggressive tough-guy persona.

Blake endured an awkward adolescence. He was reduced to playing extras and undertaking stunt work. Miserable in his present life and tormented by his past, he experimented with marijuana. Being an undiagnosed dyslexic, Robert early on lost interest in academics. He switched from high school to high school, often expelled because he was a troublemaker. By then he had a strong hatred for the establishment, blaming authority figures for all his problems.

In 1953, Blake entered the army and was eventually stationed at Fort Richardson in Anchorage, Alaska, where he began using heroin and (reputedly) selling drugs. He fell in love with a 16-year-old girl who lived off the base. Her upset parents demanded that Blake be charged with statutory rape. He escaped prosecution by agreeing not to see her again. By 1956, he was discharged from the military. In the same year, his father, now divorced from his mother, died. Robert did not attend his funeral.

Back in Hollywood, the five-foot, four-and-a-half-inch Blake reactivated his acting career. None of his assignments (including many TV parts) earned him major notice, but he found the work more therapeutic than the psychoanalysis he underwent. In November 1962, he wed actress Sondra Kerr. They had two children: Noah (1965) and Delinah (1966). His breakthrough picture was *In Cold Blood* (1967), in which he gave a compelling performance as a savage killer. Having invested so much preparation in the role, he suffered an emotional breakdown when he failed to receive a much-deserved Oscar nomination. It was two years before he worked again. Meanwhile, he developed a self-destructive pattern of rejecting or deliberately losing high-profile big-screen projects.

The '70s saw Blake's career mired in unworthy vehicles, and his reputation as a difficult man on the set increased. The 1975 TV cop show *Baretta* revived his career, earning him an Emmy. However, Robert rebelled against the show's production-line approach. He ended his well-paying *Baretta* chores in 1978. By then, Robert's marriage had soured. The couple divorced in 1983, with Blake gaining custody of the children.

Over his troubled years, Robert kept in the public eye with occasional stellar TV assignments and with frequent confessional appearances on *The Tonight Show Starring Johnny Carson*. There he expounded on his hatred of the Hollywood establishment ("the suits"), his horrific childhood, and other gripes. In 1985, he returned to series TV with *Hell Town*. Despite solid reviews, he quit the program after four months, unable to cope with the show's executives. He fell into a darker funk and almost killed himself.

He made a comeback in the TV movie *Judgment Day: The John List Story* (1993) as a man who murdered his entire family. By *Money Train* (1995), the veteran actor had undergone bad cosmetic surgery that had given him "a lizard face."

By the late '90s, Blake was semiretired and living reclusively at his Studio City compound (the Mata Hari Ranch). Having lived frugally, he had savings of several million dollars. His routine included doing bodybuilding exercises and dance workouts in his home gym as well as tending to his gun collection. Sometimes he drove into the desert or up into the hills on his motorcycle. He occasionally visited local jazz clubs where he'd sometimes meet a woman for anonymous sex. He thought that would be how he would spend his remaining years. Then a new woman entered his life.

Bonny Lee Bakley was born on June 7, 1956, in Morristown, New Jersey, the oldest of three children. Her father, Edward, was a tree surgeon with a heavy drinking problem who sometimes sexually abused and/or beat the young Bonny. The parents fought constantly and ignored their children. Bonny found escape in her fascination with Elvis Presley and envied the wonderful lifestyles of celebrities. In 1963, Mr. Bakley died. His widow married twice again. By then, Bonny was staying with her maternal grandparents. When the grandfather died, the grandmother and Bonny moved into a trailer in a remote part of New Jersey.

As a teenager, Bonny became involved with a nearby nudist colony where her shapely body and outgoing personality made her most welcome. Never liking school, she sought a nontraditional way to get ahead. She discovered that if she placed photo ads in the back of nudist magazines, she could sell poses of herself to willing customers. The money supported her love of traveling around the countryside to attend rock concerts. Along the way, she became obsessed with singer Frankie Valli and pursued him relentlessly but unsuccessfully.

Bakley quit high school in her sophomore year. Renaming herself Leebonny Bakley, she enrolled in modeling school. Thereafter, she modeled for nudist magazines and entered nude beauty contests. When a Greek alien offered to pay her to marry him so he could remain in the United States, she agreed. However, he was an abusive drunk. She reported him to the Naturalization Service, and he was deported.

Bonny was constantly on the go, always scheming to break into show business. To pay for her extended travels, she expanded her photo ads into the back of girlie magazines (and later to swinger publications). She used various aliases and backgrounds for her assorted photos for sale. In the process, she developed a clientele of mostly elderly correspondents who were often easy marks for loans.

In late 1977, she wed Paul Gawron, her first cousin and six years her senior. Ineffectual in the work world, he had a violent nature that appealed to her. The couple had three children, and Gawron became a stay-at-home parent while Bonny trekked around the country fleecing her marks. In the early '80s, Bonny improved her bank accounts by encouraging old men to name her their beneficiary on life insurance policies. In 1982, she divorced Gawron and married, briefly, a record producer/astrologer. Meanwhile, Gawron continued to help with her mail-order scam. She married several more times, not always bothering to get divorced beforehand. One of her victims was an 81-year-old Montana man she wed in 1988. She vanished an hour after they got hitched, and he dissolved their union the next year.

As she grew older and stouter, Bonny concluded that being *with* a celebrity was almost as good as being a star herself. She fastened her hopes on aging rock musician Jerry Lee Lewis and relocated to his home base of Memphis, Tennessee, but her persistence did not lead to a permanent relationship. She began spending more time in L.A., pursuing minor celebrities. In 1989, she was arrested for drug possession in Memphis and fined $550. Meanwhile, her rip-off operation blossomed, and she bought several properties, including one in Thousand Oaks, California. (Later, in the mid-1990s, she was caught on a federal charge of possessing false identification and placed on probation in Little Rock, Arkansas.)

In the summer of 1998, bleached-blond Bonny, age 42, was back in L.A. chasing fame. (Among her ongoing marks was Marlon Brando's son, Christian, who had served five years for killing his sister's boyfriend and now lived in Washington state.) In late August, at a Burbank, California, restaurant/club, she met Robert Blake, at first not quite sure who he was. Later that evening they had sex in the back of his SUV. They developed a casual acquaintanceship. Meanwhile, she continued to sleep with Christian Brando. When she became pregnant in September 1999, Blake didn't believe he was the father and thought she merely wished to trap him into marriage.

On June 2, 2000, Bonny gave birth to a baby girl in Little Rock, where she was still serving out her probation. Not sure who the actual father was, she took her newborn (whom she had named Khristian Shannon Brando) to show Christian, hoping, unsuccessfully, to cement their relationship. In September, she finally agreed to having the infant DNA-tested in L.A., and the test proved the child was Robert's. Thereafter, he grabbed possession of the baby in an elaborate ruse that included actors dressed as cops who ordered Bonny to return to Arkansas because of her parole violation. Next, Blake placed his baby in the care of his daughter, Delinah, in the West San Fernando Valley. When Bonny threatened a lawsuit over the child, Blake reluctantly married her on November 18, 2000, in a quiet ceremony that escaped media detection until Bonny alerted the tabloids. She almost immediately returned to Arkansas to complete her probation sentence.

Once the new Mrs. Blake's probation ended in March 2001, she returned to the West Coast, stopping en route to take care of her mail-order business. By then, she'd renamed the baby Rose Lenore Sophia Blake, hoping that she and Robert could make a fresh start. She met up with Blake and his friend/gofer Earle S. Caldwell in Arizona in mid-April, and they took a sightseeing trip to Sequoia National Park. By the first of May they were back in Studio City where she lived in the split-level guesthouse at his Mata Hari Ranch. They constantly fought over his miserly ways, her mail-order scams, her wanting the baby (still with Delinah) to be in their direct care, and the fact that his sidekick Caldwell was always hanging around. She also complained that she was being followed and was afraid to go out alone. It reassured her that Robert, who had a gun permit, always carried a pistol.

On Friday evening, May 4, 2001, the couple dined at Vitello's, a nearby Italian restaurant that Blake had long frequented. After dinner, they returned to his black Dodge Stealth. It was parked about a block and a half away under a burned-out streetlight, next to a partly constructed home, and only several feet away from a large Dumpster. Robert suddenly recalled he had left his handgun behind at the restaurant. Leaving her in the car with the windows open, but taking the keys, he went back to retrieve the firearm. When he got back to the vehicle, he found a profusely bleeding Bonny slumped over, having been shot twice. By the time paramedics rushed her to the hospital, she was dead.

Blake was questioned the next day by police. They subsequently served him with a warrant to search his house, retrieving various documents and two 9-millimeter handguns (neither one was the murder weapon—that one, unregistered and fingerprint-free, was later found in the Dumpster near the killing site). On May 25, 2001, Robert led a short memorial service for Bonny at Forest Lawn Memorial Park in Hollywood Hills. Her family boycotted the ceremony, insisting that the widower killed his wife. In August, Blake put his Mata Hari Ranch up for sale and moved to Hidden Hills to be with Delinah and little Rose and to have more privacy.

After months of high speculation as to the actor's involvement in Bonny's murder, the LAPD announced in January 2002 that they had made major progress in the Bakley case. Three months later, on April 18, Blake was arrested by the police at his daughter's home and taken—in handcuffs—to be booked at the Parker Center in downtown L.A. (The entire spectacle was captured on live television, interrupting programming.) Simultaneously, Robert's associate Earle Caldwell was arrested in Burbank. Robert was charged with first-degree murder with the special circumstance of lying in wait for the victim, plus two counts of solicitation to commit murder, while Earle was charged with conspiracy to commit murder.

Eventually, Caldwell was allowed $1 million bail, with Blake posting the bond for his friend's release as well as paying for the man's defense attorney. Meanwhile, Robert was repeatedly denied bail. He was housed in a bare eight-by-ten-foot cell in the hospital section of the Men's Central Jail, kept isolated because of his celebrity status. Under the spartan conditions and the strain of the case, Blake lost weight and muscle tone, and his once dyed-black hair was now white. Over the months of confinement, Robert had few visitors except for his legal team. (Rose remained under the care of Delinah, who petitioned for and received permanent custody of the child.)

Over time, one attorney after another dropped out of Blake's costly defense because of the actor's insistence on doing a network televised interview with Barbara Walters from the Men's Central Jail. This high-rated special edition of *20/20* aired on February 26, 2003. *Hollywood Reporter* reviewed the event: "Blake displayed his wide actor's range. He was feisty, at times angry, sometimes sentimental and weepy, and he got in snide shots here and there. . . ." When Walters pressed him about what he'd do if found guilty, he snapped back, "How do you kill a dead man? What are they going to do to me that they haven't done already?"

In one of several asides to Walters, an angry Blake chided those comedians and talk show hosts who made him the butt of jokes and monologues. The outspoken defendant—dressed in his orange prison suit and occasionally chewing on candy bars—admitted he was scared to be released: "If I walk outta here, Barbara, where do I go? Do I walk down the street and watch . . . people cross the street when they see me coming?"

By then the prosecution had, as part of its case, several former stuntmen and others who claimed that Blake had interviewed them about killing Bonny for pay. The actor's lawyer did his best to discredit the witnesses, some of whom had questionable elements in their past and/or were now gravely ill. (Among the defense strategies suggested in the proceedings was that many victims fleeced by grifter Bakley had stronger motives to kill her, including Christian Brando.)

Despite all the defense's theories, on March 13, 2003, Judge Lloyd M. Nash in Van Nuys Superior Court ruled that enough evidence had been presented to show that the defendant had both motive and opportunity to fatally shoot Bakley. As such, he must stand trial for murder (as must Caldwell on his conspiracy charge). However, Nash granted Blake bail, set at $1.5 million. The following day, after nearly a year of confinement, the weak and weary star was released. He told the onslaught of media, "This isn't my day. It's God's day." Robert then was driven to a Malibu retreat where he was placed under house arrest and subjected to electronic monitoring at all times. Later, just before the one-year statute of limitations expired, the four children—including little Rose who was automatically made part of the suit as one of Bonny's heirs—filed a wrongful-death lawsuit against Blake and his bodyguard, seeking unspecified general and punitive damages. Meanwhile, in November 2003, the judge threw out the conspiracy charges against Robert in the Bakley homicide case. (Already charges against Blake's handyman, Earle Caldwell, had been dismissed.) Blake still faced the murder charges in Bonny's death at his early 2004 trial.

In summing up the outlandish spectacle of the Blake murder case, veteran crime reporter Dominick Dunne said in *Vanity Fair* of Robert's 20/20 appearance: "I began to see this case as a theatrical production and a great one at that. . . . This was prime-time television, and, old pro that he is, he didn't waste a second of it. I felt as if I were watching a movie, seeing an actor give a marvelous performance." Dunne ended his piece with: "I have a feeling that Robert Blake is going to create an awesome on-camera drama before this story is over."

Winona Ryder: Shopping Till It Hurts

"The law does not say there is a higher standard of proof for celebrities. The law is the law is the law, no matter who you are. The law doesn't say only poor people steal. It must have occurred to some of you, 'Why would Winona Ryder steal?' Nowhere does it say people steal because they have to. People steal out of greed, envy, spite, because it's there or for the thrill."
—DEPUTY DISTRICT ATTORNEY ANN RUNDLE, ON NOVEMBER 4, 2002

Sometimes people, especially when young, experience a sudden impulse to shoplift. Often it is undertaken as a dare or merely for the thrill of it. Generally such activity remains an isolated episode. For others, the impetus may be financial necessity. Actor Steve Guttenberg admits that when he was a broke college student he once attempted to steal a tube of toothpaste, but he was caught by the store's security guards. The repentant young man was let go after receiving a stern lecture. The irony of the situation was, "At the time, I was studying to be a dentist."

Other people have a psychological need for such activities. The late actor/singer Dean Martin once told a national magazine that he was a "pathological shoplifter" who, whenever he visited a men's clothing store, would "steal a necktie or a pair of gloves or socks." Said Martin, "Everyone has a little larceny in him, a little bit of original sin—only some of it's not too original."

More recently, there was the case of performer Shelley Morrison, who was arrested in April 2003 on suspicion of shoplifting costume jewelry from a Los Angeles department store. Because the retail value of the items was more than $400, the purported theft qualified as a felony. However, the L.A. city attorney's office reduced their charge to a misdemeanor. Eventually, the actress pleaded no contest to the charge, was fined $300, and was placed on a year's probation. Said Morrison, "I've since seen therapists and they explained to me that I left no room for myself and sometimes the mind has a mini earthquake. I did a dumb thing that was so out of character."

Of a more profound nature was the 1966 arrest of Hollywood golden age film beauty Hedy Lamarr in L.A. on shoplifting charges involving an $86 pair of slippers. The notoriety of the headline-making case (settled out of court) caused the performer to lose a comeback film role. In 1991, the 77-year-old former screen siren, who lived modestly but was worth an estimated $3 million, was again arrested, this time for taking $21 of merchandise from a drugstore near her retirement home in suburban Orlando, Florida. After the incident made a media splash, it was quietly resolved between the parties.

Especially in Lamarr's case, her unlawful urge seemed to fit the dictionary definition of kleptomania (i.e., "a compulsion to steal having no relation to need or the monetary value of the object"). Because Hedy had once been such a famous actress, her difficulty seemed more sad than shocking. (In each of her run-ins, the media played up the theme of a once-mighty movie legend becoming a petty thief, suggesting that she was a has-been badly down on her luck.)

The hoopla over Lamarr's arrest was relatively mild, however, in comparison to the tumult generated over a late-2001 incident involving 30-year-old movie star Winona Ryder. The two-time Oscar nominee was arrested at a Beverly Hills department store for allegedly stealing clothing items and hair accessories valued at more than $5,500. After her arrest, it was discovered that she had several different painkilling pills (as well as liquid Demerol) in her purse. As such, she was booked on charges of grand theft *and* possessing pharmaceutical drugs without a prescription.

Depending on one's perspective, Winona's claimed offenses were or were not serious, but certainly they were *not* of major proportion. However, taking its cue from the overzealous prosecution, the media positioned this celebrity misadventure as the biggest criminal case since the O. J. Simpson murder trial in 1995, not so much for the quality of the asserted offenses but because the defendant was a well-known screen personality. On almost a daily basis for months, the public was inundated with news flashes, interviews, and updates on the "earth-shattering" Ryder case, which, somehow, seemingly had captured worldwide attention.

Regarding this feeding frenzy over Winona's "sins," the *Los Angeles Times* reported that, "Whether or not Ryder turns out to be an innocent victim of circumstances, the whole mess has already claimed a victim: the public. . . . Even though cynics scoff at the idea of sympathy for celebrities, most taxpayers should be outraged at the unprecedented expenditure of resources to relentlessly pursue a relatively minor case against someone with no criminal record." Furthermore, according to the *Los Angeles Times*, "The district attorney's office has pursued its case against Ryder with a tenacity typically reserved for murderers. In fact, the prosecution has literally put the Ryder case ahead of murder cases."

Winona Laura Horowitz was born on October 29, 1971. She was the daughter of Michael Horowitz and Cindy Palmer, who were visiting Cindy's relatives in Winona, Minnesota, at the time of the birth. Michael and Cindy had first met in San Francisco a few years earlier. At that time, Cindy's marriage (from which she had two children) was falling apart. Horowitz, like herself, was a highly political hippie intellectual. When Winona was still an infant, the family returned to California, sharing a house in the counterculture section of San Francisco with Cindy's ex-husband and his second wife.

Growing up in an academic atmosphere, Noni (as Winona was called by family and friends) early on developed a strong love of literature. Because Cindy had a great appreciation for old movies, she instilled this enthusiasm in her children, especially Winona. As such, the child became a walking encyclopedia of old Hollywood pictures.

In 1978, Michael and Cindy, now the parents of a baby boy, Yuri, moved their household to a 300-acre site in Elk, California, near Mendocino. The clan joined with a cooperative of seven other families to manage their spread. Because the parents pursued only those endeavors about which they were passionate, they often had no money (let alone electricity or running water). Looking back, the actress occasionally wished that her childhood had been more conventional, but nevertheless, she found it "an amazing way to grow up."

When Winona was 10, her parents finally married and also published a joint book dealing with famous women authors who utilized drugs while writing. In this period, the family relocated to Petaluma, 40 miles north of San Francisco. Suddenly thrust into a more cosmopolitan lifestyle, Winona made a difficult adjustment. Besides an ongoing paranoia about being kidnapped, she developed great concern about the Green River Killer, a serial murderer who roamed the Pacific Northwest. Because she wore unadorned, boyish clothes, had a short hairstyle, and was withdrawn, her peers at school thought she was a geek. When Winona was 12, she had a brief brush with the law: she was placed under citizen's arrest for taking a comic book from a store. According to Winona, when the police brought her home, "My parents tried to beat them up."

One day at school, Winona was pommeled by school bullies who thought she was a gay boy. Thereafter, her parents had Winona schooled at home. Meanwhile, they enrolled her at San Francisco's American Conservatory Theater (ACT), hoping that there she would meet similarly creative youngsters. The shy adolescent reluctantly appeared in school productions and found that she was much more at ease when performing on the stage.

Later, a film-casting agent spotted the teenager at ACT and began sending her on auditions for upcoming movies. Her first role was in the teenage love tale *Lucas* (1986). In making the picture, she dyed her blond hair black (which remained her color on camera) and acquired a new professional surname, Ryder (suggested by her father, who often played Mitch Ryder recordings).

On screen, five-foot, four-inch Winona came into her own as the morbid, weird daughter in *Beetlejuice* (1988). This was followed by a choice assignment in the equally offbeat *Heathers* (1989), a youth-oriented tale full of black humor. By then, Ryder (who boasted large, soulful eyes and an elfin quality) was bothered with the mounting Hollywood hype over her escalating career. She dreamed of retreating from the Tinseltown lifestyle. However, there was always the next intriguing screen part to accept, such as playing the child bride in 1989's *Great Balls of Fire*.

Having had a brief romance with her *Heathers* costar Christian Slater, Winona began a serious relationship with Johnny Depp, the 26-year-old star of TV's *21 Jump Street*. At the time baby-faced Depp was a dedicated hell-raiser, and the tabloids couldn't print enough about the odd couple—shy flower child Winona and wild party-goer Johnny. Meanwhile, having worked on movies nonstop, Ryder caused ripples within show business circles when she dropped out of *Godfather Part III* (1990) because of "exhaustion." She did, however, return to the screen in *Edward Scissorhands* (1990), in which she teamed with Depp. (By then, he was so in love with her that he had "Winona Forever" tattooed on his right bicep.)

The pixyish actress was off the screen for nearly two years waiting for roles that would allow her to play an adult. She returned as the heroine of *Bram Stoker's Dracula* (1992). During production she suffered from an ongoing feeling of being "tired, tense, not very happy," which was diagnosed as anxiousness over separating her professional from her personal identity. She began treatment for anxiety and depression and in the process realized that she and Depp had drifted apart. To start herself on a new path, she relocated to New York City. During this span, Winona, who won a Best Supporting Actress Oscar nomination for 1993's *The Age of Innocence*, combated her addiction to sleeping pills, which she had used to cope with severe insomnia.

Upon ending her romance with Depp in mid-1994, Winona found a replacement—for a time—in David Pirner, lead singer of the rock group Soul Asylum. (Among the other musicians she dated over the years were Beck and Ryan Adams.)

For the 1994 screen remake of *Little Women*, Ryder was again Oscar-nominated. After the unpopular *The Crucible* (1996), Ryder was in the big-budgeted *Alien Resurrection* (1997). During this period, she lived in San Francisco near her family.

Off screen, Ryder became engaged to actor Matt Damon, but that union fell apart. At 30, with her career very much adrift, Winona tackled the romantic comedy *Mr. Deeds* (2002), playing Adam Sandler's leading lady. It was her most mainstream assignment in recent years, perhaps auguring a fresh professional direction. Next, she was scheduled for *Lily and the Secret Planting* in England. However, in August 2001, she dropped out of the low-budget feature due to a sudden, mysterious stomach bug.

Then came Winona's encounter of the bad kind. It started around 4:00 P.M. on Wednesday, December 12, 2001, at the Beverly Hills branch of Saks Fifth Avenue on Wilshire Boulevard. Three hours later she was arrested. It was claimed that she had attempted to leave the store with unpaid merchandise—which ranged from an $80 pair of designer socks to a $1,595 Gucci evening dress—and that she had been taped on the building's security cameras allegedly trying to remove sensor tags from the clothing. (Clerks had supposedly seen her cramming these goods into a bag with items she had purchased earlier.) When she was detained, it was discovered that her purse contained several prescription painkillers. (The prosecutor later stated that Ryder had "more pain medication than would be given to a person with a terminal disease.")

After being detained in the store's basement security office, the movie star was taken to the Beverly Hills police station (only several blocks away), where she was booked. After posting $20,000 bail, she was released at 11:40 P.M. and drove in her black Mercedes back to her $3 million Beverly Hills home. The following day, in response to a press conference held by the Beverly Hills police, the actress's attorney, Mark Geragos, insisted, "It's a misunderstanding on the part of the store." He explained, "There was no theft. I'm telling you right now there was no possession of prescription medications without a prescription. . . . The charges, I'm convinced . . . will be rejected." As to Ryder's reaction to the situation, her attorney responded, "Nobody wants to be on the nightly news with all these rampant rumors." Winona was set to appear on January 11 in Beverly Hills Superior Court. If convicted, she faced up to four years in prison.

The court date was postponed to February 5, when Ryder was charged with felony counts of grand theft, second-degree burglary, vandalism, and unlawful possession of a controlled substance. (She pleaded not guilty to the charges.) Winona's representative said, "We are shocked at what appear to be grossly exaggerated charges." Already the case was becoming popular fodder for the supermarket newspapers.

During this time the department store's surveillance tape of Ryder's bizarre shopping activities was leaked to the media. When screened, it did *not* show Ryder using a scissors, as had been suggested by store workers, to remove antitheft devices from the merchandise. Meanwhile, an apparent cause of Winona's sudden notoriety was the ending of her relationship with 20-something singer/songwriter Pete Yorn. In addition, in advance trailers being shown in theaters and on TV for the upcoming *Mr. Deeds*, Ryder's image was removed by the releasing studio, Twentieth Century-Fox. (When the picture was released to good box office in June 2002, Winona's likeness was not featured on the movie's posters.)

Meanwhile, on TV's *Politically Incorrect* show, actress Shelley Long told host Bill Maher that Ryder's misdeed was "a cry for help." The former *Cheers* star further noted, "Shoplifting is a mental illness. It's addictive and it becomes a habit that has to be broken like any other." On the plus side, there was a healthy sale in L.A. shops of T-shirts emblazoned with "FREE WINONA."

Monday, June 3, 2002, found an extremely demure-looking Winona belatedly showing up in Beverly Hills court for a preliminary hearing. There was testimony from the store's security staff about the defendant's activity at Saks Fifth Avenue on that crucial day. Later, returning from a lunch break, Winona was jostled by overeager media photographers outside the courtroom and, in the crush, injured her right arm. Thereafter, she was taken to a physician for medical attention, and her fractured limb was put in a sling. When she returned to court three days later she was ordered to stand trial on the charges. By that time, the prosecution had filed a motion to show the court a pattern of behavior by having alleged similar prior acts of Ryder's claimed shoplifting admitted into the proceedings. (Later, this motion—involving purported incidents of the defendant's shoplifting at Barneys New York in May 2000 and October 2001, as well as at Neiman Marcus in Beverly Hills in November 2001—was not allowed by the judge to be made known to the jury. However, the court transcripts with this information became known to the press after the trial ended and were immediately detailed to the public.) Meanwhile, on June 15, the defendant pleaded not guilty to the charges.

With the coverage of the Winona situation in massive overdrive, Ryder's attorney again requested that the L.A. County district attorney's office be removed from the case for their "efforts to humiliate my client and stop her from having the right to a fair trial." However, Beverly Hills superior court judge Eldon S. Fox denied the request, suggesting that attorney Geragos's unhappiness was with a spokesman of the DA's office and not the office itself. The August 13 pretrial hearing remained on the calendar. Meanwhile, at a West Hollywood theater, Rex Lee starred in drag in the satirical play *My Name Is Winona and I'm a Shoplifter.*

After several further delays in the legal process, Winona finally had a bit of good news when prosecutors stated they planned to ask the judge to dismiss the charge of illegal possession of prescription painkillers because the defense had provided a sworn statement that Ryder had reason to possess such medication. Many observers still assumed that this media circus would somehow end with an out-of-court settlement and/or a plea bargain. (Reportedly, the prosecution offered a deal in which if Winona pled guilty to one count of felony grand theft, she would receive a sentence of community service, up to three years of probation, and likely no jail time. Ryder rejected the proposal.)

In the protracted "case of the century," jury selection began on October 24, 2002, leading to six men and six women being chosen, including the former head of a major studio who had produced three of Winona's features. By October 29, the second day of the trial (and Ryder's 31st birthday) the much-discussed full 90-minute security tape was shown. The next day, jurors were told by witnesses that, after she was apprehended for the alleged acts, Ryder told a security guard, "Didn't my assistant pay for it?" and had later explained to the guards that she was preparing for upcoming film roles involving shoplifters.

By November 4, 2002, Winona's shoplifting case went to the jury, with Ryder having chosen not to testify during the seven-day trial. (A dramatic point in the case occurred when a defense witness, a former Saks employee, claimed that, shortly after the incident in question, the store's security head had told him, "I will nail that Beverly Hills b***h for shoplifting charges.") After two days of deliberation, the jury unanimously convicted this first-time offender of felony grand theft and felony vandalism, while clearing her of the burglary charge (because there was no evidence of premeditation). Prosecutors announced they did *not* plan to demand jail time at her sentencing hearing December 6 but, rather, would ask to have Ryder placed on probation. Said Deputy DA Ann Rundle, "We were simply asking for Ms. Ryder to take responsibility for her conduct, and that's what this trial has been about." (The results of this case were deemed sufficiently momentous for TV stations to break into their regularly scheduled programming to air the update.)

On December 6, at her sentencing, Winona was ordered to complete 480 hours of community service, undergo drug and psychiatric counseling, and pay approximately $10,000 in fines and restitution. Judge Fox also warned the defendant, "If you steal again, you will go to jail." Although Ryder did not address the court at her sentencing, she jumped up in anger when the prosecution belittled the defense's mention of the defendant's past charitable efforts on behalf of a foundation for missing/kidnapped children. Later, through her publicist, Ryder released a statement about her reaction to the judgment: "Winona accepts responsibility for what happened. . . . She will fulfill her sentence as laid out by the judge."

Even then, the much-hyped case did not die. In December 2002, the Medical Board of California revoked the license of a local area physician who had been prescribing an overload of addictive drugs to wealthy patients such as Ryder. Later that month, a probation report on Ryder was made public that revealed that, according to the Drug Enforcement Administration, between 1996 and 1998, Winona had 20 doctors write 37 prescriptions, often using an alias. (This and other factors had led the DA to request drug counseling for the defendant.)

On April 7, 2003, Ryder received a good report card from Judge Fox for completing the community service part of her three-year probation, which included working with groups that helped people with cancer, the blind, and children with AIDS. At the hearing, Winona's lawyer asked whether, because Ryder had paid all the fines and was now owner of the merchandise in litigation from Saks Fifth Avenue, she might hold an auction and donate the proceeds to charity. The request was declined. In mid-2003, with this episode now somewhat behind her, Ryder, who had been reclusive and lost weight during her time in the legal spotlight, signed to film *The Heart Is Deceitful Above All Things* (2004) in which she played a psychologist.

Proving that this "scandalous" shoplifting case had entered the realm of pop culture, in June 2003, a San Diego high school put on a musical play titled *Sticky Fingers: A Tale of Saks, Lies and Videotape*. Reportedly, the department store donated shopping bags for the satirical production.

BIBLIOGRAPHY

Adams, Alex, and William Stadiem. *Madam 90210: My Life as Madam to the Rich and Famous.* New York: Villard, 1993.

Agan, Patrick. *The Decline and Fall of the Love Goddesses.* Los Angeles: Pinnacle, 1979.

Alexander, Frank, with Heidi Siegmund Cuda. *Got Your Back: Protecting Tupac in the World of Gangsta Rap.* New York: St. Martin's, 2000.

Amburn, Ellis. *Warren Beatty: The Sexiest Man Alive.* New York: HarperEntertainment, 2002.

Anderson, Joan Wester. *Forever Young: The Life, Loves and Enduring Faith of a Hollywood Legend.* Allen, Tex.: Thomas More, 2000.

Basinger, Jeanine. *Silent Stars.* Hanover, N.H.: Wesleyan University/ University Press of New England, 1990.

Bastfield, Darrin Keith. *Back in the Day: My Life and Times with Tupac Shakur.* New York: One World/Ballantine, 2002.

Baxter, John. *Woody Allen.* New York: Carroll & Graf, 1998.

Bego, Mark. *Rock Hudson: Public and Private.* New York: Signet, 1986.

Belushi, Judith Jacklin. *Samurai Widow*. New York: Carroll & Graf, 1990.

Bentley, Eric, ed. *Thirty Years of Treason*. New York: Thunder's Mouth/Nation, 2002.

Bergman, Ingrid, and Alan Burgess. *My Story*. New York: Delacorte, 1980.

Bernhard, Sandra. *Confessions of a Pretty Lady*. New York: Perennial/Harper & Row, 1989.

Billingsley, Kenneth Lloyd. *Hollywood Party: How Communism Seduced the American Film Industry in the 1930s and 1940s*. Rocklin, Calif.: Forum, 1998.

Blanche, Tony, and Brad Schreiber. *Death in Paradise*. New York: Four Walls, 2001.

Bodeen, DeWitt. *From Hollywood: The Careers of 15 Great American Stars*. South Brunswick, N.J.: A. S. Barnes, 1976.

Botham, Noel. *Valentino: The First Superstar*. London: Metro, 2002.

Bret, David. *Errol Flynn: Satan's Angel*. London: Robson, 2000.

———. *Valentino: A Dream of Desire*. London: Robson, 1998.

Brooks, Tim, and Earle Marsh. *The Complete Directory to Prime Time Network and Cable TV Shows: 1946-Present*. 20th anniversary ed. New York: Ballantine, 1991.

Brownlow, Kevin. *Hollywood: The Pioneers*. New York: Alfred A. Knopf, 1979.

Bugliosi, Vincent. *Outrage: The Five Reasons Why O. J. Simpson Got Away with Murder.* New York: W. W. Norton, 1996.

Buhle, Paul, and Dave Wagner. *Radical Hollywood.* New York: The New Press, 2002.

Cader, Michael, ed. *"Saturday Night Live": The First Twenty Years.* Boston: Houghton Mifflin, 1994.

Cerasini, Marc. *O. J. Simpson: American Hero, American Tragedy.* New York: Pinnacle, 1994.

Clark, Tom, with Dick Kleiner. *Rock Hudson: Friend of Mine.* New York: Pharos/Scripps Howard, 1989.

Clarke, Gerald. *Get Happy: The Life of Judy Garland.* New York: Random House, 2000.

Considine, Shaun. *Bette & Joan: The Divine Feud.* New York: Dell, 1989.

Craddock, Jim, ed. *VideoHound's Golden Movie Retriever,* 2003. Detroit, Mich.: Visible Ink, 2002.

Crafton, Donald. *The Talkies: American Cinema's Transition to Sound: 1926–1931.* Berkeley: University of California Press, 1999.

Crane, Cheryl, with Cliff Jahr. *Detour: A Hollywood Story.* New York: Avon, 1988.

Crawford, Christina. *Mommie Dearest.* 20th anniversary ed. Moscow, Idaho: Seven Springs, 1997.

Crawford, Joan. *My Way of Life.* New York: Simon & Schuster, 1971.

Crawford, Joan, with Jane Kesner Ardmore. *A Portrait of Joan.* New York: Paperback Library, 1964.

Cunningham, Ernest W. *The Ultimate Marilyn.* Los Angeles: Renaissance, 1998.

Datcher, Michael, and Kwame Alexander, eds. *Tough Love: The Life and Death of Tupac Shakur.* Alexandria, Va.: BlackWords, 1997.

David, Lester, and Jhan Robbins. *Richard & Elizabeth.* New York: Ballantine, 1977.

Davis, Don. *Fallen Hero.* New York: St. Martin's, 1994.

DiOrio, Al, Jr. *Little Girl Lost: The Life and Hard Times of Judy Garland.* New York: Manor, 1975.

Drop, Mark. *Dateline: Hollywood: Sins and Scandals of Yesterday and Today.* New York: Friedman/Fairfax, 1994.

Drosnin, Michael. *Citizen Hughes.* New York: Holt, Rinehart and Winston, 1985.

Dyson, Michael Eric. *Holler If You Hear Me: Searching for Tupac Shakur.* New York: Basic Civitas, 2001.

Edmonds, Andy. *Bugsy's Baby: The Secret Life of Mob Queen Virginia Hill.* New York: Birch Lane, 1993.

——. *Frame-Up!* New York: Avon, 1991.

——. *Hot Toddy: The True Story of Hollywood's Most Shocking Crime— The Murder of Thelma Todd.* New York: Avon, 1989.

Eels, George. *Robert Mitchum.* New York: Jove, 1985.

Epstein, Edward Z., and Joe Morella. *Mia: The Life of Mia Farrow.* New York: Dell, 1991.

Farrow, Mia. *What Falls Away.* New York: Bantam, 1998.

Feder, Sid, and Joachim Joesten. *The Luciano Story.* New York: Awards, 1972.

Finch, Christopher. *Rainbow: The Stormy Life of Judy Garland.* New York: Grossett & Dunlap, 1975.

Finstad, Suzanne. *Natasha: The Biography of Natalie Wood.* New York: Harmony/Crown, 2001.

Fisher, Eddie. *Eddie: My Life, My Loves.* New York: Berkley, 1982.

Fisher, Eddie, with David Fisher. *Been There, Done That.* New York: St. Martin's, 1999.

Fleiss, Heidi. *Panderings.* Los Angeles: Hour Entertainment, 2003.

Fleming, E. J. *Hollywood Death and Scandal Sites.* Jefferson, N.C.: McFarland, 2000.

Fox, Julian. *Woody: Movies from Manhattan.* Woodstock, N.Y.: Overlook, 1996.

Frank, Gerold. *Judy.* New York: Dell, 1975.

Freeland, Michael. *The Two Lives of Errol Flynn.* New York: William Morrow, 1979.

Fried, Richard M. *Nightmare in Red.* New York: Oxford University Press, 1990.

Gallick, Sarah, with Nicholas Maier. *Liza Minnelli: Divinely Decadent.* Boca Raton, Fla.: AMI, 2003.

Gates, Phyllis, and Bob Thomas. *My Husband, Rock Hudson.* New York: Doubleday, 1987.

Giroux, Robert. *A Deed of Death: The Story Behind the Unsolved Murder of Hollywood Director William Desmond Taylor.* New York: Knopf, 1990.

Godfrey, Lionel. *The Life and Crimes of Errol Flynn.* New York: St. Martin's, 1977.

Golden, Eve. *Golden Images.* Jefferson, N.C.: McFarland, 2001.

———. *Platinum Girl: The Life and Legends of Jean Harlow.* New York: Abbeville, 1991.

Goodall, Nigel. *Winona Ryder.* London: Blake, 1998.

Grant, Robert, and Joseph Katz. *The Great Trials of the Twenties.* Rockville Centre, N.Y.: Sarpendon, 1998.

Graysmith, Robert. *The Murder of Bob Crane.* New York: Berkley, 1994.

Greene, Myra. *The Eddie Fisher Story.* Middlebury, Vt.: Paul S. Eriksson, 1978.

Groteke, Kristi, with Marjorie Rosen. *Mia & Woody: Love and Betrayal.* New York: Carrol & Graf, 1994.

Hamann, G. D. (ed.). *Errol Flynn in the* 30's. Los Angeles: Filming Today, 2003.

———. *Hollywood Divorces in the 30's.* Los Angeles: Filming Today, 2003.

——. *Hollywood Scandals in the 40's*. Los Angeles: Filming Today, 2003.

——. *Hollywood Scandals in the 30's*. Los Angeles: Filming Today, 2003.

——. *Ingrid Bergman in the 30's & 40's* Los Angeles: Filming Today, 2003.

——. *Thelma Todd in the* 30's. Los Angeles: Filming Today, 2000.

Harris, Warren G. *Clark Gable*. New York: Harmony/Random House, 2002.

——. *Natalie & R.J.: Hollywood's Star-Crossed Lovers*. New York: Dolphin/Doubleday, 1988.

Heymann, C. David. *Liz: An Intimate Biography of Elizabeth Taylor*. Secaucus, N.J.: Citadel/Carol, 1995.

Horne, Gerald. *Class Struggle in Hollywood: 1930—1950*. Austin: University of Texas Press, 2001.

Hudson, Rock, and Sara Davidson. *Rock Hudson: His Story*. New York: William Morrow, 1986.

Jacobson, Laurie. *Hollywood Heartbreak*. New York: Fireside/Simon & Schuster, 1984.

Johnes, Carl. *Crawford: The Last Years*. New York: Dell, 1979.

Kelley, Kitty. *Elizabeth Taylor: The Last Star*. New York: Dell, 1982.

Kiernan, Thomas. *The Roman Polanski Story*. New York: Delilah/Grove, 1980.

King, Greg. *Sharon Tate and the Manson Murders.* New York: Barricade, 2000.

Kirkpatrick, Sidney D. *Cast of Killers.* New York: Penguin, 1986.

Knappman, Edward W., ed. *American Trials of the 20th Century.* Detroit, Mich.: Visible Ink, 1995.

Kobler, John. *Capone: The Life and World of Al Capone.* New York: Putnam, 1971.

Koszarski, Richard. *An Evening's Entertainment: The Age of the Silent Feature Picture,* 1915–1928. Berkeley: University of California Press, 1994.

Lambert, Gavin. *Nazimova.* New York: Knopf, 1997.

Lardner, Ring, Jr. *I'd Hate Myself in the Morning.* New York: Thunder's Mouth, 2000.

LaSalle, Mick. *Dangerous Men.* New York: St. Martin's, 2002.

Lasky, Betty. *RKO: The Biggest Little Major of Them All.* Santa Monica, Calif.: Roundtable, 1989.

Latham, Caroline, and Jeannie Sakol. *All About Elizabeth: Elizabeth Taylor, Public and Private.* New York: Onyx/Penguin, 1991.

Leaming, Barbara. *Marilyn Monroe.* New York: Crown, 1998.

———. *Polanski: The Filmmaker as Voyeur.* New York: Simon & Schuster, 1981.

Leider, Emily W. *Dark Lover: The Life and Death of Rudolph Valentino.* New York: Farrar, Straus and Giroux, 2003.

Lewis, Judy. *Uncommon Knowledge.* New York: Pocket Books, 1994.

Liberace, with Tony Palmer, ed. *The Things I Love.* New York: Grossett & Dunlap, 1976.

Linedecker, Clifford L. *OJ: A to Z: The Complete Handbook to the Trial of the Century.* New York: St. Martin's, 1995.

Love, Andrea. *The Ultimate Celebrity Love Secrets & Scandals Book.* Bristol, UK: Carlton, 1998.

Luft, Lorna. *Me and My Shadows: A Family Memoir.* New York: Pocket, 1998.

Martin, Mart. *Did He or Didn't He?* New York: Citadel/Kensington, 2000.

——. *Did She or Didn't She?* New York: Citadel, 1996.

Marx, Samuel, and Joyce Vanderveen. *Deadly Illusions: Jean Harlow and the Murder of Paul Bern.* New York: Random House, 1990.

McCann, Graham. *Woody Allen.* Cambridge: Polity, 1992.

McDouglas, Dennis, and Mary Murphy. *Blood Cold: Fame, Sex, and Murder in Hollywood.* New York: Onyx/New American Library, 2002.

McGilligan, Patrick, and Paul Buhle. *Tender Comrades.* New York: St. Martin's, 1999.

Meade, Marion. *The Unruly Life of Woody Allen.* London: Weidenfeld & Nicholson, 2000.

Messick, Hank. *The Beauties & the Beasts: The Mob in Show Business.* New York: David McKay, 1973.

Metz, Allan, and Carol Benson. *The Madonna Companion: Two Decades of Commentary.* New York: Schirmer, 1999.

Meyers, Jeffrey. *Inherited Risk: Errol Flynn and Sean Flynn in Hollywood and Vietnam.* New York: Simon & Schuster, 2002.

Mitchell, Corey. *Hollywood Death Scenes.* Chicago: Olmstead, 2001.

Morella, Joe, and Edward Z. Epstein. *Gable & Lombard & Powell & Harlow.* New York: Dell, 1976.

Morris, Michael. *Madame Valentino: The Many Lives of Natacha Rambova.* New York: Abbeville, 1991.

Morrison, Toni, and Claudia Brodsky Lacour, eds. *Birth of a Nation'hood: Gaze, Script, and Spectacle in the O. J. Simpson Case.* New York: Pantheon, 1997.

Mungo, Ray. *Liberace.* New York: Chelsea House, 1995.

Munn, Michael. *The Hollywood Connection: The True Story of Organized Crime in Hollywood.* London: Robson, 1993.

———. *The Hollywood Murder Case Book.* New York: St. Martin's, 1987.

Navasky, Victor S. *Naming Names.* New York: Penguin, 1981.

Oppenheimer, Jerry, and Jack Vitek. *Idol: Rock Hudson: The True Story of an American Film Hero.* New York: Villard, 1986.

Parish, James Robert. *The Fox Girls.* New Rochelle, N.Y.: Arlington House, 1971.

———. *Hollywood Bad Boys.* New York: Contemporary, 2002.

———. *The Hollywood Book of Death.* New York: Contemporary, 2001.

———. *Hollywood Divas.* New York: Contemporary, 2002.

———. *Hollywood's Great Love Teams.* New Rochelle, N.Y.: Arlington House, 1974.

———. *The Paramount Pretties.* New Rochelle N.Y.: Arlington House, 1972.

———. *The RKO Gals.* New Rochelle, N.Y.: Arlington House, 1973.

———. *Today's Black Hollywood.* New York: Kensington, 1995.

Parish, James Robert, and Don E. Stanke. *Hollywood Baby Boomers.* New York: Garland, 1992.

———. *The Leading Ladies.* New Rochelle, N.Y.: Arlington House, 1977.

Parish, James Robert, and Gregory Mank. *The Best of MGM: The Golden Years:* 1928–1959. New York: Arlington House/Crown, 1981.

Parish, James Robert, and Lennard DeCarl. *Hollywood Players: The Forties.* New Rochelle, N.Y.: Arlington House, 1976.

Parish, James Robert, and Michael R. Pitts. *The Great Hollywood Musical Pictures.* Metuchen, N.J.: Scarecrow, 1992.

———. *Hollywood Songsters.* 2nd ed. New York: Routledge, 2002.

Parish, James Robert, and Ronald L. Bowers. *The MGM Stock Company: The Golden Years.* New Rochelle, N.Y.: Arlington House, 1973.

Parish, James Robert, with Steven Whitney. *The George Raft File*. New York: Drake, 1974.

Parish, James Robert, and William T. Leonard. *The Funsters*. New Rochelle, N.Y.: Arlington House, 1979.

———. *Hollywood Players: The Thirties*. New Rochelle, N.Y.: Arlington House, 1976.

Parker, John. *Polanski*. London: Victor Gollancz, 1993.

Pero, Taylor, and Jeff Rovin. *Always Lana*. New York: Bantam, 1982.

Pogel, Nancy. *Woody Allen*. Boston: Twayne, 1987.

Polanski, Roman. *Roman*. New York: William Morrow, 1984.

Prideaux, James. *Knowing Hepburn and Other Curious Experiences*. Boston: Faber and Faber, 1996.

Pyron, Darden Asbury. *Liberace: An American Boy*. Chicago: University of Chicago Press, 2000.

Quirk, Lawrence J., and William Schoell. *Joan Crawford: The Essential Biography*. Lexington: University Press of Kentucky, 2002.

Radner, Gilda. *Gilda Radner: It's Always Something*. New York: Avon, 1990.

Reynolds, Debbie, and David Patrick Columbia. *Debbie*. New York: William Morrow, 1982.

Roberts, Jerry. *Robert Mitchum: A Bio-Bibliography*. Westport, Conn.: Greenwood, 1992.

Roberts, Jerry, ed. *Mitchum: In His Own Words.* New York: Limelight, 2000.

Rossellini, Isabella. *Some of Me.* New York: Random House, 1997.

Royce, Brenda Scott. *Hogan's Heroes.* Los Angeles: Renaissance, 1998.

——. *Rock Hudson: A Bio-Bibliography.* Westport, Conn.: Greenwood, 1995.

Rubin, Sam, and Richard Taylor. *Mia Farrow: Flower Child, Madonna, Muse.* New York: 2M Communications/St. Martin's, 1989.

Saltman, David. *Gilda: An Intimate Portrait.* Chicago: Contemporary, 1990.

Sanders, Coyne Steven. *Rainbow's End: "The Judy Garland Show."* New York: Zebra/Kensington, 1990.

Schatz, Thomas. *Boom and Bust: American Cinema in the* 1940s. Berkeley: University of California Press, 1999.

Schechter, Scott. *Judy Garland; The Day-by-Day Chronicle of a Legend.* New York: Cooper Square, 2002.

Schmallegcr, Frank. *Trial of the Century: People of the State of California* vs. *Orenthal James Simpson.* Upper Saddle River, N.J.: Prentice Hall, 1996.

Schulman, J. Neil. *The Frame of the Century? Was O. J. Simpson Framed by His Biggest Fan?* East Mills Valley, Calif.: Pulpless.com, 1999.

Scott, Cathy. *The Killing of Tupac Shakur.* Las Vegas, Nev.: Huntington, 1997.

Sealey, Shirley. *The Celebrity Sex Register.* New York: Fireside/Simon & Schuster, 1982.

Server, Lee. *Robert Mitchum: "Baby, I Don't Care."* New York: St. Martin's, 2001.

Shales, Tom, and James Andrew Miller. *Live from New York: An Uncensored History of "Saturday Night Live."* Boston: Little Brown, 2002.

Shipman, David. *Judy Garland: The Secret Life of an American Legend.* New York: Hyperion, 1992.

Shulman, Irving. *Valentino.* New York: Trident, 1967.

Sifakis, Carl. *The Mafia Encyclopedia.* 2nd ed. New York: Checkmark/Facts on File, 1999.

Slide, Anthony. *The New Historical Dictionary of the American Film Industry.* Landham, Md.: Scarecrow, 1998.

———. *Silent Players.* Lexington: University Press of Kentucky, 2002.

Smith, Ronald. L. *Who's Who in Comedy.* New York: Facts on File, 1992.

Spada, James, with Kare Swenden. *Judy & Liza.* Garden City, N.Y.: Dolphin/Doubleday, 1983.

Spignesi, Stephen J. *The Woody Allen Companion.* Kansas City, Mo.: Andrews and McMeel, 1992.

Spoto, Donald. *Marilyn Monroe.* New York: HarperCollins, 1993.

——. *Notorious: The Life of Ingrid Bergman.* New York: Da Capo, 1997.

——. *A Passion for Life: The Biography of Elizabeth Taylor.* New York: HarperCollins, 1995.

Stenn, David. *Bombshell: The Life and Death of Jean Harlow.* Raleigh, N.C.: Lightning Bug, 2000.

——. *Clara Bow: Runnin' Wild.* New York: Cooper Square, 2000.

Summers, Anthony. *Goddess: The Secret Lives of Marilyn Monroe.* New York: Onyx/New American, 1986.

Sumner, Robert L. *Hollywood Cesspool.* Murfreesboro, Tenn.: Sword of the Lord, 1955.

Thomas, Bob. *Joan Crawford.* New York: Bantam, 1978.

——. *Liberace.* New York: St. Martin's, 1987.

Thompson, Dave. *Winona Ryder.* Dallas, Tex.: Taylor, 1996.

Thorson, Scott, with Alex Thorleifson. *Behind the Candelabra: My Life with Liberace.* New York: E. P. Dutton, 1988.

Toobin, Jeffrey. *The Run of His Life: The People v. O. J. Simpson.* New York: Touchstone/Simon & Schuster, 1997.

Tormé, Mel. *It Wasn't All Velvet.* New York: Zebra/Kensington, 1988.

——. *The Other Side of the Rainbow with Judy Garland on the Dawn Patrol.* New York: Galahad, 1970.

Tornabene, Lyn. *Long Live the King: A Biography of Clark Gable.* New York: Pocket Books, 1976.

Turner, Lana. *Lana: The Lady, the Legend, the Truth.* New York: E. P. Dutton, 1982.

Us magazine, eds. *Winona.* Boston: Little, Brown, 1997.

Valentino, Lou. *The Films of Lana Turner.* Secaucus, N.J.: Citadel, 1979.

Vaughn, Robert. *Only Victims: A Study of Show Business Blacklisting.* New York: Limelight, 1996.

Vibe magazine, eds. *Tupak Shakur.* New York: Three Rivers, 1997.

Walker, Alexander. *Rudolph Valentino.* London: Penguin, 1977.

Wayne, Jane Ellen. *Crawford's Men.* New York: St. Martin's, 1988.

——. *Gable's Women.* New York: St. Martin's, 1987.

——. *The Golden Girls of MGM.* New York: Carroll & Graf, 2002.

——. *Lana: The Life and Loves of Lana Turner.* New York: St. Martin's, 1995.

——. *Marilyn's Men.* New York: St. Martin's, 1992.

Wiles, Buster, with William Donati. *My Days with Errol Flynn.* Santa Monica, Calif.: Roundtable, 1988.

Wood, Lana. *Natalie: A Memoir by Her Sister.* New York: Putnam, 1984.

Woodward, Bob. *Wired: The Short Life & Fast Times of John Belushi.* New York: Pocket, 1984.

Young, Paul. *L.A. Exposed.* New York: St. Martin's, 2002.

Young, Robert, Jr. *Roscoe "Fatty" Arbuckle: A Bio-Bibliography.* Westport, Conn.: Greenwood, 1994.

Publications

Biography
Classic Film Collector
Classic Image
Current Biography
Daily Variety
Ebony
Empire
Entertainment Weekly
Film Threat
Filmfax
Films in Review
Films of the Golden Age
Globe
Hollywood Reporter
In Style
Jet
L.A. Weekly
Los Angeles Daily News
Los Angeles Times
Movie Collectors World
Movieline
National Enquirer
New Times—Los Angeles

New York Daily News
New York Observer
New York Post
New York Times
Newsweek
Parade
People
Playboy
Premiere
Sight & Sound
Star
Time
Total Film
Us Weekly
Vanity Fair

Internet Websites

All Movie Guide: allmovie.com
All Music Guide: allmusic.com
Court TV's Crime Library: crimelibrary.com
E! Entertainment TV Online: eonline.com
Internet Movie Database: pro.imdb.com
The Smoking Gun: thesmokinggun.com

Television

ABC: *Primetime*
A&E: *Biography*
E! TV: *Mysteries & Scandals*
E! TV: *True Hollywood Stories*
Syndicated: *Access Hollywood*
Syndicated: *Entertainment Tonight*
Syndicated: *Extra: The Entertainment Magazine*

ABOUT THE AUTHOR

Photo by Levon

James Robert Parish, a former entertainment reporter, publicist, and book series editor, is the author of many major biographies and reference books of the entertainment industry including *Whitney Houston, The Hollywood Book of Love, Hollywood Divas, Hollywood Bad Boys, The Encyclopedia of Ethnic Groups in Hollywood, Jet Li, The Hollywood Book of Death, Gus Van Sant, Jason Biggs, Whoopi Goldberg, Rosie O'Donnell's Story, The Unofficial "Murder, She Wrote" Casebook, Let's Talk! America's Favorite TV Talk Show Hosts, The Great Cop Pictures, Ghosts and Angels in Hollywood Films, Prison Pictures from Hollywood, Hollywood's Great Love Teams,* and *The RKO Gals.* Mr. Parish is a frequent on-camera interviewee on cable and network TV for documentaries on the performing arts in both the United States and the United Kingdom. He resides in Studio City, California. His website is at www.jamesrobertparish.com.

Made in the USA
Lexington, KY
25 September 2017